Bureaucracy in a Democratic State

Bureaucracy in a Democratic State

A Governance Perspective

KENNETH J. MEIER
LAURENCE J. O'TOOLE JR.

The Johns Hopkins University Press
Baltimore

2 4 6 8 9 7 5 3 1

The Johns Hopkins University Press
2715 North Charles Street
Baltimore, Maryland 21218–4363
www.press.jhu.edu

Library of Congress Cataloging-in-Publication Data

Meier, Kenneth J., 1950–
Bureaucracy in a democratic state : a governance perspective / Kenneth J. Meier
and Laurence J. O'Toole, Jr.
p. cm.
Includes bibliographical references and index.
ISBN 0-8018-8356-3 (hardcover : alk. paper) — ISBN 0-8018-8357-1 (pbk. : alk. paper)
1. Bureaucracy.   2. Democracy.   3. Public administration.
I. O'Toole, Laurence J., 1948–   II. Title.
JF1501.M435 2006
302.3′5 — dc22   2005029019

A catalog record for this book is available from the British Library.

To the memory of Dwight Waldo, in whose circle of students we first met.

With his knowledge of political theory, he taught us much about the normative standards of democratic governance.

With his erudition about bureaucracy, as it is found around the planet and through the ages, he taught us well about the need to treat the real world with respect.

With his senses of both humor and perspective, he taught us to appreciate and enjoy the foibles, ironies, and exhilarations of this calling.

Contents

Preface

Can the imperatives of an administrative system be reconciled with the norms of democratic governance? Or is bureaucracy, with its expertise, insulation, and byzantine procedures, the enemy of popular control? These questions have been raised wherever administrative institutions have been a key element in a broader pattern of purportedly democratic rule. Deep suspicions have typically been aroused in situations in which anonymous bureaucrats and their managers make decisions that affect the outputs and outcomes of public policy. Bureaucrats themselves, on the other hand, have been known to treat political overseers with some suspicion, if not outright disdain and evasion.

These tensions have not dissipated with the rise of more complex patterns of "governance" that encompass multiple organizations and stakeholders in networks to co-produce policy results—a set of developments receiving particular attention recently in Western Europe and North America. Indeed, the challenges posed by such broadened notions of "bureaucracy," loosely speaking, for democratic governance are even greater.

In this book, we address these central questions by examining the results of bureaucratic and political interactions in some governance settings, to test for several of the most frequently mentioned, or feared, patterns of influence and to see whether bureaucratic systems weaken or strengthen the connections between public preferences and policy results. We make use of two sets of conceptual lenses: the mainstream perspective of political science on the bureaucracy-democracy nexus and the standard treatment of the subject in the research literature on public administration.

Political science typically sees the democratic impulse as shaping bureaucracy, if at all, from above. The literature in this field assumes the necessity for "political control" of administrative systems by political overseers, and it tests for the health of democratic systems by seeking evidence that those at the top direct those at the bottom. Although relevant for considering the question of bureaucracy and democracy, we argue that this approach suffers from many serious limitations and does not effectively get at the nub of the issue.

Public administration researchers, along with related specialists in public management and public policy, have generally ignored the political science literature on political control of the bureaucracy. This group of scholars has dismissed the political science work as quantitatively advanced but substantively trivial. Public administrationists have offered a more sophisticated perspective on how bureaucracy operates in putatively democratic systems, but they have also held to a rather sanguine view of bureaucracy in such settings. Serious students of public administration see the values held within administrative systems as a—even the—key element. We agree with this last point, but we are critical of the field of public administration on two grounds. This research literature is short on systematic investigations of the bureaucracy-democracy link, including the issue of values, and the literature also offers many—and somewhat conflicting—injunctions as to just which values are to be embraced.

This book seeks to bridge the gap between these two worlds. It challenges both perspectives by arguing that the techniques featured in the political control literature can be used in interesting ways to address questions relevant to both groups of scholars and in ways that have not previously been attempted. The book also shows that both fields have ignored important developments in the kinds of institutional arrangements that have almost universally been treated too simplistically in the standard notion of "bureaucracy."

The two fields, and audiences, are bridged in this study through a governance perspective, a thematic emphasis that focuses on the need to consider both broader, institutionally complex systems of governance and also the nitty-gritty details involved in managing the bureaucracy. The book, in short, speaks to both audiences in their native language but brings a message intended to discomfort rather than reassure.

To make our arguments suitably general, we build on a general perspective regarding governance, which is introduced in the first chapter and used as a reference point throughout the volume (in our own longer-term research program we used a more specific model of governance, which is discussed in the appendix). To make our arguments more tangible and persuasive, we include empirical analyses drawn from operating governance systems. The systems tapped for this purpose are at two levels of U.S. government: local and national. For the former, we take advantage of data drawn from hundreds of school districts in one large, diverse state; this set of empirical settings offer opportunities to explore systematically many key features of the bureaucracy-democracy question. For the latter, we tap data available in legislation and administrative rules for national policy and the institutional arrangements established to produce program results. These allow us to draw some pertinent conclusions about the shape of governance systems in recent decades.

The origins of this book date to a 1973 seminar taught by Dwight Waldo on public administration and democracy; we were both students in that class. We then went our separate ways, O'Toole in public administration and Meier in political science, although we frequently addressed similar questions. In 1999 we joined forces to address a set of key empirical questions about organizations and governance. This book represents part of our broader joint research agenda, which concentrates on two persistently important themes: the public management and operation of complex governance systems designed to deliver policy results, and the intersection and mutual influence of politics and administration in contemporary systems of governance.

As with the writing of any book, this project has caused us to incur substantial debts to others. School-district superintendents in Texas served as respondents as we sought to tap information about the management of these uniquely American forms of government. We acknowledge with gratitude the contributions of coauthors, particularly John Bohte, Thad Hall, and Sean Nicholson-Crotty, who worked with one or both of us on some of the analyses included here. PhD students at Texas A&M University and the University of Georgia, particularly those who survived a jointly taught combined seminar offered by us during fall 2002, stimulated and provoked us, with productive results for this project—and, we hope, for them. Sandy Gordon, Tom Hammond, Kim Hill, Greg Huber, David Lewis, Terry Moe, John Scholz, and B. Dan Wood offered helpful comments on the analyses in chapter 4. George Krause, LeeAnne Krause, Paul Teske, John Scholz, Dan Carpenter, and John Brehm provided comments on earlier versions of chapter 5. George Boyne, Stu Bretschneider, Amy Kneedler Donahue, Sergio Fernandez, H. George Frederickson, Holly Goerdel, Carolyn Heinrich, Patricia Ingraham, J. Edward Kellough, Laurence E. Lynn Jr., H. Brinton Milward, David Peterson, Hal G. Rainey, Bob Stein, and Richard Walker offered helpful ideas on various aspects of our research program. Diane Jones Meier and Mary Gilroy O'Toole have had to tolerate our preoccupations and distractions for a very long time; thanks to them above all.

Bureaucracy in a Democratic State

CHAPTER ONE

Governance and the Bureaucracy Problem

One of the most important and persisting challenges of modern government is how to reconcile the demands of democracy with the imperatives of bureaucracy. In many countries around the world, politicos and pundits bash "bureaucracy," frequently in the name of popular governance (Suleiman 2003). Bureaucrats, meanwhile, often look to protect their decision making from uninformed or polemical interference by amateurs who seek influence without having the expertise or experience to handle technically complex policy issues.

Bureaucracies are hierarchical institutions that can provide the capacity and expertise to accomplish complex social tasks, but they are frequently characterized as undemocratic and even threatening to democracy. Democracies are systems of government that are based, directly or indirectly, on the principle of popular control. They attend in differing measures to principles of majority rule and deference to the perspectives of intense interests among the public. But as such, they need not necessarily show keen attention to the values of efficiency, effectiveness, or specialized expertise.[1] Bureaucracy may be thought of as government's tool to exercise coercion as an instrument for productive action. As institutional forms designed to emphasize different values, bureaucracy and democracy sit in an uneasy relationship with each other.

---

1. In the abstract, democracy is a form of government resting on the popular will and thus has no linkage to questions of effectiveness or efficiency (Dahl 1970). In the practical world, however, we know of no modern democracy that does not also have an effective bureaucracy. Suleiman (2003) contends that effective policy provides legitimacy for democratic governments. Meier (1997) argues that only bureaucracy can provide the efficiency needed to absorb the large transaction costs of democracy.

In the classic terms of German sociologist Max Weber (1946), bureaucracies can serve any master. As an abstract institutional form, bureaucracy is thus indifferent to whether that master is authoritarian or democratic. In the United States, Woodrow Wilson suggested the American importation of Prussian bureaucratic approaches (although he urged, rather ambiguously, that Americans should "distil away" the "foreign gases" [1887, 219]). Current reform advocates urge similar action; the latest bureaucratic approaches, including the "New Public Management," continue to stir interest internationally and are borrowed wholesale across dozens of nations worldwide without any concern for democratic issues. Still, in debates from Beijing to Boston, proponents of popular government argue that bureaucracy and its administrative apparatus limit the promise of democracy. Relying on bureaucracy in governance, therefore, can generate challenges to legitimacy in democratic systems (Nye, Zelikow, and King 1997).

Underscoring the bureaucracy problem is the institution's use of expertise and judgment to exercise what are deemed political powers—the determination of who gets what, when, and how—by unelected and insulated decision makers. This well-known feature of bureaucratic decision making is regularly pilloried by politicians (Hall 2002), and the drumbeat of bureaucratic criticism in popular culture encourages the development of skeptical and negative public perspectives on bureaucracy. Nevertheless, decades of research have demonstrated that excising this discretion from the bureaucracy is impossible. Its inevitability poses an apparent threat to democracy.

This book reexamines and reframes this classic question.[2] Several reasons justify such a project. First, while specialists in bureaucracy and public management have extolled the value and contributions of public bureaucracy to governance, they have generally been unsuccessful in clarifying the role and place of bureaucratic discretion in terms of democratic governance itself (e.g., Wamsley et al. 1990). Second, a substantial literature under the rubric of "political control of the bureaucracy" (e.g., Moe 1985; Scholz, Twombley, and Headrick 1991; Scholz and Wood 1999; and Wood and Waterman 1994) has provided some empirical evidence that elected officials influence and perhaps even "control" some of the actions of bureaucracy, but

---

2. One dimension of the issue that will not be covered in this volume is the democratization of decision making *within* the bureaucracy. Researchers in organizational development and change have long explored the impact of more participatory schemes within bureaucratic systems (Golembiewski 1995), and a long tradition of research and debate has considered democratic themes as they might apply to the design and operation of the permanent civil service. As Waldo noted decades ago, it is simply not credible to claim that "autocracy during working hours is the price to be paid for democracy after hours" (1952, 87). Still, redistributing influence within public agencies, while important, is not the same as democratizing a political system (Mosher 1982).

this line of work exhibits some serious limitations. The subject therefore needs to be examined afresh. Third, the evolution of both popularly controlled and bureaucratic institutions of governance continues. In fact, the classic portrait of "bureaucracy" as the institutional form for turning policy preferences into action offers a distorted image of today's realities of governance, which often involve networked combinations of public, private, and nonprofit organizations jointly implementing public programs. These changes mean that the political-control literature underestimates the difficulty of controlling bureaucracy because analysts have not recognized current developments in program design and because typical formulations of the issue have not adequately considered the full range of existing bureaucratic forms.

As this volume demonstrates, while the bureaucracy-democracy challenge remains important across nations and circumstances, the issue cannot be effectively analyzed in the abstract. A clear understanding of how the challenge can actually be addressed, and where its most tendentious elements may lie, must follow from an engagement with the specifics of a particular political system and its bureaucratic institutions. Many kinds of regimes treat the democratic ideal seriously, and "bureaucracy" appears in quite distinct forms in different policy fields, levels of government, and national contexts. These differences matter greatly in any effort to assess the performance of a system. In short, the issue must be engaged by framing it in one or more particular governing systems (Hood 2002).

In this volume, we conduct such an empirically grounded analysis. In doing so, we seek correctives to the difficulties identified above and sketch what we regard as a more accurate and useful perspective on both the particular context and the general issue. Before delving into those specifics, however, we first situate the coverage in the broad bureaucracy-democracy problematic as it has typically been understood among the social sciences and show that most of the discourse can be seen as consistent with one of two partial, albeit abstract, perspectives. We then indicate why a more context-specific approach is necessary. We outline a particular kind of setting for systematic analysis and frame the subsequent coverage in terms of the developing literature on governance. Finally, we sketch the plan of this book.

BUREAUCRACY-DEMOCRACY TENSION: A CONTINUING LEGACY

The difficult relationship between the institution of bureaucracy and the ideal of democracy has been a broad and persistent theme across the social sciences. In sociology, a field that has dissected the institution of bureaucracy for nearly a century, the power implied by the expertise and near-permanence of such structures has been a prime topic of analysis. Bureaucrats facing political leaders are like experts confronting dilettantes, as Weber (1946) indicated. Early astute analyses pointed to a bureaucratic dynamic in which power slowly accretes to insiders at the center of the organizational action: the "iron law of oligarchy" (Michels 1999). This pessimistic insight hypothesizes a tendency for organized arrangements to move in a less accessible and less democratic direction over time, despite contrary preferences expressed during institutional design. Studies of informal organization, as well, and of actions taken by administrators under pressure to generate support from external events, echo a similar thesis: bureaucracies engage in co-optive strategies to protect themselves and aid their survival. Even the most well-intentioned and "democratic" approaches to administration can produce results in which powerful interests exert disproportionate control over bureaucratic action, and broader but more diffuse majoritarian preferences are cast aside (Selznick 1949). Bureaucratic politics and luck, some have argued, rather than responsiveness or even effectiveness, can account for the survival rates of most government bureaus (Kaufman 1985; Pfeffer and Salancik 1978).[3]

Economists have also grappled with bureaucracy, albeit in quite a different fashion. Here the focus has been less on democracy and more on efficiency, although some public-choice analysts would argue that these two concepts converge (Ostrom 1989). Stimulated by analyses of "nonmarket failure" in bureaucratic institutions, economists have identified a range of possible problems entailed by bureaucratic forms, and some of these are directly relevant to the bureaucracy-democracy theme. For instance, economic analysis based on an assumption that bureaucrats are self-interested actors explores the ways that bureaucratic behavior is likely to generate "rent seeking" as opposed to public-interested action. Information asymmetries have been explored by economists, and the results of such analyses have buttressed the sociologists' point about the power of expertise (Niskanen 1971; but see Blais and Dion 1991). The contract notion from principal-agent theory has been especially influential.[4] Political leaders as principals, it is argued, inevitably face a slippage of control when dealing with bureaucrats as agents. The latter constitute a constant threat to principals' control—and thus to democratic governance. This is one reason that many economists prefer market-based policy instruments to bureaucratically managed programs. Another argument voiced by economists that also touches upon the bureaucracy-democracy challenge is that the extensive variety among individual citizen preferences is unlikely to be satisfied by means of a rule-governed, centrally directed bureaucratic apparatus. The implication is that even were the bureaucracy

---

3. Many scholars might feel that the ability to coopt the environment is an essential component of any definition of bureaucratic effectiveness.

4. This body of work receives considerable attention later in this book.

entirely altruistic, it could not possibly deal in a sufficiently variegated fashion with the full range of citizens' or clients' utility functions (Ostrom 1989; Tiebout 1956). Bureaucracies seek regularity and consistent application of rules. Clearly, a bureaucratic process will meet only some citizens' utility functions as a result of this regularity and consistency.

The sociological and economic treatments of the bureaucracy-democracy problematic are provocative. Still, the main lines of analysis rely on either a depiction of selected general tendencies or a heavily deductive argument with little grounding in the actual empirical settings of interest. More direct treatments of the bureaucracy-democracy challenge have been developed in the fields of political science and public administration. These are sketched next and serve as particularly important foci for analysis and critique in the ensuing coverage.

Political science has long considered the feasibility of achieving democracy and has debated, for instance, the extent to which pluralistic or corporatist political systems impede or facilitate popular control. In most of political science, democracy has been interpreted operationally as popular electoral control of political decision makers (for a classic statement, see Schumpeter 1950). This definition is typically interpreted to include such features as political competition, basic individual rights, and transparent mechanisms of accountability within the political system. In this light, bureaucracy can be seen as a potential challenge—particularly to the extent that major decision making devolves to it and to the extent that various protections insulate it from control by the people. As Mosher put the issue in his important study, "The accretion of specialization and of technological and social complexity seems to be an irreversible trend, one that leads to increasing dependence upon the protected, appointive public service, thrice removed from direct democracy. Herein lies the central and underlying problem . . . : How can a public service so constituted be made to operate in a manner compatible with democracy?" (1982, 5).[5]

As we attempt to demonstrate in this book, *all* institutions of governance—not merely those outside the electoral system and separate from the "political" branches— can appropriately be assessed for their contribution to democracy. Political science, on the other hand, has typically viewed bureaucracy ipso facto as a problem because of its independence from political overseers.

---

5. "Reliance upon popularly elected representatives is one step removed from direct participative democracy. A second step occurs when officers so chosen select and delegate powers to other officers, appointed and removable by them. . . . A third step away from direct democracy is taken with the designation of personnel who are neither elected nor politically appointive and removable, but rather are chosen on bases of stated criteria . . . and, once appointed, are protected from removal on political grounds" (Mosher 1982, 4–5).

The main model of the democratic ideal operating in political science has been some version of "overhead democracy" (Redford 1969). The public chooses political leaders in competitive elections, with successful leaders then assuming power and responsibility for enacting and executing policy. Successful leaders—that is, those able to attract popular approval for their program of action—can thus be rewarded with reelection, whereas those seen as failures can be unseated at periodic intervals. In this depiction, those with responsibility to lead must have control over the bureaucracy. Otherwise, bureaucratic autonomy would subvert the political will and make a mockery of the democratic principle. In key respects, therefore, the conventional political science framing of the issue has much in common with principal-agent ideas in economics.

From the perspective of mainstream political science, bureaucracy is inherently problematic for democracy. The "solution" follows directly from the logic of overhead democracy: to ensure that political leaders are effectively able to direct, constrain, and control the bureaucracy. A significant stream of empirical research has sprung up around this topic, particularly in the United States, with the goal of seeing whether bureaucracy is in fact responsive to the policy initiatives from above. We examine this literature in some detail in chapter 2. For now it is sufficient to note that the political science approach is to assume a particular form for the resolution of the issue. That is, control by political leaders is essential. Reconciling democracy and bureaucracy means maximizing control by politicos over bureaucrats. As we shall see, however, bureaucracy itself can sometimes facilitate democracy, and political leaders can sometimes impede it (Meier 1997).

The field of public administration has also long considered the bureaucracy-democracy issue. The U.S. literature is particularly noteworthy. From its coming of age as a self-aware field near the beginning of the twentieth century, American public administration has grappled with the place of administrative institutions in a democratic regime. Woodrow Wilson's (1887) early essay on the field represented a classic argument for distinguishing politics from administration. Advocating for this dichotomy, both normatively and in terms of specific reforms to effectuate it (council-manager city governments, civil service reform, etc.), was a widely adopted way of trying to handle the problem. In this approach, democratic norms were applicable in the political realm, whereas bureaucracy was to be structured and overseen internally by scientifically driven principles of administration, which should be identical for all governments, whether democratic or autocratic (Waldo 1948; for an alternative interpretation, see Bertelli and Lynn 2006).

This tidy manner of resolving the problem and defanging bureaucratic independence was the conventional wisdom in this field for decades. The perspective had only one problem, but that was fatal: It bore no relationship to the real world. Analysts could talk about the separation of politics from administration, and vice versa, but researchers and practitioners began to proclaim in the 1930s and 1940s that the reality was much more a seamless web (Appleby 1949; Herring 1936; Simon 1947).[6] The collapse of the dichotomy was followed by a succession of efforts to find a more effective way of reconciliation. As demonstrated in chapter 2, some of these initiatives have helped in developing important insights on the issue. Nonetheless, none of the reformulations in and of themselves adequately handle the challenge.

Between the 1940s and the late 1960s, the dominant normative stance in the field was what might be termed administrative pluralism. If politics is no stranger to the bureaucracy, the argument went, that fact does not necessarily entail a threat to democracy. Rather, administrators properly socialized in the requisites of democratic governance can use their discretion to grease the wheels of the system by facilitating the virtually endless rounds of bargaining characteristic of pluralistic democracy. In this depiction public administrators, as the lead bureaucrats, are necessary, albeit benign, partners in pluralistic politics (Appleby 1949; Kaufman 1956; Long 1949).

During the late 1960s and the 1970s, in particular, U.S.-style pluralism came under heavy criticism, and the role of the bureaucracy was part of the issue. Analysts and activists argued that the U.S. political system systematically benefits well-organized and well-financed special interests at the expense of the general public and that the bureaucracy is complicit in this pattern (Lowi 1969). Bureaucratic decision makers typically forge alliances with the most powerful interest groups and legislative committees to stabilize their jurisdictions and facilitate smooth policy making and implementation. The critique is aimed at the relatively closed character of policy making—agribusiness is in on the action but not, say, tenant farmers—and the injustice that results. If professions are conspiracies against the laity, as George Bernard Shaw once said, then the bureaucracy, in league with its allies, might be considered a conspiracy against the public.

In the field of public administration, as in other parts of the social sciences, this normative stance represented a theme of the political left. A version of it that made a distinctive mark was the so-called New Public Administration,[7] whose proponents advocated a view of the administrator as free, and obliged, to make a social-equity stand on behalf of the poorly represented rather than the well-represented special

---

6. A careful reading of Goodnow (1900), conceded to be one of the originators of the dichotomy, shows that he did not propose the dichotomy as an empirical reality but rather suggested that it was a normative idea.

7. The ideas of the New Public Administration are not all of a piece (O'Toole 1977), despite efforts to offer an overarching interpretation (Frederickson 1980).

interests (Frederickson 1980; Marini 1971). Some advocates would go so far as to say that the bureaucracy should right the undemocratic wrongs of the political system. The general stance, in any event, is for the democratically inspired exercise of discretionary decision making.

The New Public Administration has been challenged as having been not very new (Mosher 1992) and, in particular, as itself threatening the basic tenets of democratic governance by interposing bureaucratic notions of the public's needs in place of those determined by means of the explicitly political process (Thompson 1975). Still, in one form or another, some such approach has remained attractive to many in the field of public administration. Most who focus primarily on public bureaucracy are inclined to interpret the bureaucracy in relatively positive terms and public bureaucrats as contributors to the public weal (e.g., Denhardt 1993). One of the best-known volumes in this specialty, *The Case for Bureaucracy* (Goodsell 2004), explicitly aims to debunk virtually all aspects of the negative stereotype. Goodsell claims that, particularly in the United States, the "problem" has been vastly overblown. And in the "Blacksburg Manifesto," coauthored by several scholars at the Virginia Institute of Technology, Wamsley and colleagues argue that "the Public Administration" is an extraordinarily positive institution that heals some of the defects in the American constitutional design (1990; see also Wamsley and Wolf 1996). While some critics challenge this argument and emphasize its implicitly undemocratic tenets (Cooper 1990; Kaufman 1990), a significant part of the scholarly community in public administration remains inclined to believe that bureaucracy as an institution offers support for democratic principles.

A portion of the field lies outside this fold. In the 1980s and thereafter, economics has influenced public administration, and public-choice arguments about reframing the bureaucracy-democracy issue have taken root (Ostrom 1989; see also the discussion of the New Public Management, below). Nonetheless, the modal view is much like this: Overhead democracy is a simplistic rendering of the issue; and bureaucracy itself, if infused with appropriate values,[8] can support democratic governance.

While scholars of public administration can be faulted for not treating the potential conflict between bureaucracy and democracy as seriously as it deserves—and for too often dealing with the issue in its abstracted form (as do researchers in other fields as well)—some particularly helpful work has been done. An example of this kind of effort is the maturing scholarship on "representative bureaucracy." Those

8. Several different kinds of values have been seen as attractive or crucial by theorists. A number of these are examined in the next chapter.

aspects of public administration research that do contribute in a helpful fashion to framing and addressing the bureaucracy-democracy question are discussed systematically in chapter 2.

TOP-DOWN AND BOTTOM-UP DEMOCRATIC IDEAS

This brief review shows that across numerous social sciences, the bureaucracy-democracy theme has been considered to be an issue worthy of significant attention. How the topic is framed and analyzed has varied by discipline and also within discipline. If one considers the full set of perspectives, however, two broad logics can be seen. Each of these, in general terms, sketches a way of conceptualizing the challenge, as well as a strategy for addressing the issue. Outlining the two reveals some commonalities across a range of approaches and also sets the core issue in a context that this volume systematically examines.

One basic approach to the bureaucracy-democracy problem is to conceive of the democratic impulse as essentially emanating from "above." The "top" of the political system, in this view, consists of the central or most formally authoritative positions and organs of the governing system: those directly chosen by the electorate and those entailing the broadest and most encompassing jurisdiction. Because of the direct link to the public via periodic competitive elections, bodies like parliaments and elected chief executives have a special claim to represent the agenda of the people. One challenge facing these political leaders, then, is to monitor and control the bureaucracy so that the agents do not replace the democratically chosen principals as the key decision makers.

This depiction is in clear harmony with the political control literature of political science. It also fits the perspective of the new economics of organization. In some of its refinements, it can incorporate the notion of multiple principals as well (Chubb 1985). Although some top-down proponents are particularly positive about parliamentary systems (Finer 1941), in the United States the separation-of-powers design renders the top-down perspective more complicated. At the national level, there is no single constitutionally privileged "top." Similarly, a federal system that permits autonomous state and local elected officials adds additional complications to the perspective.

Outside the United States, other variants on a top-down design include neocorporatist systems, which frame policy agreements as legitimately the province of the "top" conceived as political officials, in conjunction with the key sectoral leadership, like business and labor peak-associational decision makers. The views of individual firms and industries, as well as of laborers and particular unions, are channeled to the top of their respective sectors, where agreements are forged across the social partners, who then have a common interest in monitoring and controlling execution by the bureaucracy.

Why would the bureaucracy respond to the "top"? The main theme in top-down depictions is a reliance on coercion, at least as a default condition (even if not often exercised or visible). In addition, although less often emphasized by analysts of political systems, socialization could play a role. Inculcating bureaucrats with agency missions, emphasizing responsiveness to political authority, and socializing civil servants into the mores of a top-down democratic ethos could also be important forces. The principal-agent approach narrowly frames the response in terms of the incentives offered by the principal, although in practice even the actual incentives are often not specified.

The other broad notion of democratic governance reflected in the set of perspectives sketched earlier is what might be called bottom-up democracy. The reference is not to some naive version of grass-roots or direct democracy, nor to an injunction to maximize discretion in the hands of the administrative "bottom," the legions of street-level bureaucrats. Rather, the logic is that popular control is most effectively achieved through channels other than the political "top." In other words, the bureaucracy as a political institution might best be checked by direct popular oversight (citizens' review boards monitoring police departments, clients controlling some aspects of agency decisions) or by institutional arrangements that deviate from a standard monocratic authority structure and instead incorporate incentives for bureaucratic actors to be directly attuned to popular preferences.

One way that these might operate is via openness of the bureaucracy itself to pressure and control by organized interests that may care greatly about the actions of administrative units. Some analysts have been critical of "excessive" influence through such pluralistic channels (Lowi 1969); but the advocates of administrative pluralism, mentioned earlier in this chapter, saw the democratic ideal advanced by interest groups becoming directly involved in the "pulling and hauling" that characterizes the decision-making process of public bureaucracies.

Other versions of such generally bottom-up institutional designs are sympathetic to the public-choice perspective, including the use of quasi-markets. Such systems ideally transmit signals from consumers of policy, or at least public services, to bureaucratic producers in such a way that the latter are strongly encouraged to follow preferences as conveyed by consumer choice or consumption patterns. The notion here is to use marketlike forces to shape bureaucratic behavior rather than rely upon command and control by standard political authority. Public-choice advocates therefore argue that quasi-market forces can simultaneously improve both governmental efficiency and democracy, with the latter being defined operationally largely in terms of maximizing the match between consumer preferences and governmental production or supply (Ostrom 1989).

Recent reform efforts rely on a modified version of this argument and, in effect, combine features of top-down and bottom-up logics. Thus the so-called New Public Management (NPM), as it has been advocated in several countries, argues in favor of "liberating" government bureaucratic managers as they do their job, thereby reducing some of the direct administrative controls upon them, largely by tapping market forces to encourage greater attention to the production and provision of services. Treating the citizen like a customer is part of the perspective. Liberating the managers, furthermore, has typically been encouraged at the same time that renewed attention to productivity by political leaders has been emphasized. Whether in the U.S. variant of this reform movement, especially popular during the Clinton-Gore presidency through the National Performance Review, or as developed in the United Kingdom, New Zealand, Australia, and a number of other countries, the main emphasis has been on the bottom-up portion of the logic, with government bureaucrats largely cast as efficient contract administrators. This emphasis suggests that it would be a mistake to conclude that the NPM is mostly a bundle of technocratic initiatives, divorced from the political realm. Rather, it appeals broadly in part because of its apparent connection with a key theme of the democratic ethos.[9]

In general, why would the bureaucracy actually respond to bottom-up pressures? Political pressure or economic incentives are typically singled out as major parts of the explanation. Political pressures from clientele can be aggregated to provide political support for bureaucracies in their dealings with electoral institutions; efficiently delivering such services can contribute to being able to increase the total volume of services and thus also add to political support (Meier 2000). Furthermore, as students of bureaucracies like the U.S. Department of Agriculture or the Tennessee Valley Authority have pointed out, socialization of the bureaucrats can also play an important role. Agencies staffed by people trained to consider the public, or certain relevant portions of the public, as their primary constituents are likely to be deferential to direct pressures and inputs from those groups.

These two broad perspectives on democracy and bureaucracy both have some merit. In general, nonetheless, they can be faulted on at least three grounds. First, proponents of one tend to caricature or ignore the other. In particular, political scientists focused on the issue of political control of the bureaucracy seem to have the issue, or aspects of the issue, half right. They treat well and carefully the top-

9. The ideas sketched in the last two paragraphs are revisited later, after several chapters of empirical analysis.

down accountability challenges, but they ignore the ways in which the pressures and incentives from the other direction can aid the cause of democracy. In this latter regard, they pay little attention to the actual incentives operating on the bureaucracy, or they assume that bureaucratic values and socialization constitute threats to democracy. They also tend to assume that the legitimacy of the actions of unelected decision makers are automatically suspect, whereas the actions of elected and politically appointed leaders are necessarily legitimate—this despite widespread evidence that the legitimacy of explicitly political institutions of government is equally (or more) questionable in the eyes of the public (see, e.g., Inglehart 1997; Orren 1997). In this regard, they may misspecify the challenge.

Second, proponents of each perspective tend to ignore the disadvantages of an exclusive emphasis on its features. For example, the transaction costs of leading the administrative apparatus are already very high even without wholehearted efforts to exert detailed control (i.e., to "micromanage") the bureaucracy. Proponents of a top-down variant of democracy have generally not dealt with such important constraints (for a formal demonstration that principal-agent control cannot be effected by the use of incentives alone, even within a single bureaucratic organization, see Miller 1992). Further, the bureaucratic hyperresponsiveness sometimes implicitly endorsed as an element of democratic control—with the bureaucracy expected, in effect, to respond "how high?" to any political injunction to "jump"—distorts the considered meaning of democracy. Bureaucratic institutions and their programs themselves represent institutionalized aspects of responsible government that are politically designed, in part, to provide some stability and regularity to governance; drastic shifts in governmental direction in response to episodic blips of public opinion are not consistent with most careful treatments of democratic governance (note Madison's reference to the "permanent and aggregate interests of the majority" in *Federalist,* no. 10).

Advocates of bottom-up democratic governance generally avoid dealing with the deliberative and collective aspects of democratic consensus building and control, either by focusing on individuals' utility—public-choice approaches—or by assuming that administrative agencies are appropriately general forums for the resolution of public problems—the administrative pluralists or the Blacksburg proponents. The requisites of political control are typically insufficiently depicted and inadequately worked into the logic of bottom-up democratic governance within bureaucratic systems.

The third problem with these perspectives is that they are overly broad and abstract. The arguments in support of overhead democracy tend to be framed to head off the anticipated difficulties of the ideal-typical bureaucracy, sketched generally and in forms that are not much advanced from the Weberian picture formulated nearly a century ago. Whether actual, functioning administrative agencies much resemble the abstract depiction is not a research question among such analysts. Some forms of bottom-up argument are more empirically grounded in the realities of bureaucratic operations, including the values of bureaucrats in particular settings and the access of stakeholders to bureaucratic decision makers in concrete situations (see chap. 2). Still, these perspectives tend to treat politicians and political control from the top in an overly general and abstract fashion—as if political control does or should have little to do with effective democratic governance.

A key premise of this book is that neither line of reasoning about democracy and bureaucracy offers a fully satisfactory picture, that elements of each must be incorporated clearly into the analytical picture in any assessment of how well any actual governing system comports with the democratic principle. The top-down arguments framed in the logic of political control offer an important piece of the puzzle, but an incomplete one. Bottom-up analysts alert us to crucial modes and channels of popular influence but likewise omit elements that must be included. Any valid perspective must necessarily be grounded in the empirical features of actual governing systems.

As one moves from abstract theory to a particular governance setting, the problem becomes more complex because one is no longer dealing with the ideal-typical "bureaucracy" or with unambiguous commitment to an abstractly general "democracy." Bureaucratic units shaped by particular political and cultural forces populate the institutional landscape. A German ministry is an organization very different, in many dimensions, from a postsocialist Russian bureaucracy, and these are both far cries from bureaus of the U.S. Department of Agriculture. These differences—in patterns of bureaucratic recruitment and socialization, decision making, links to interest groups and arrays of formal and informal advisory committees, degrees of decentralization and rule-boundedness, and so forth—definitely matter in any assessment of the fit between bureaucracy and democracy. Some versions of bureaucracy and some contexts are much likelier to facilitate popular influence than others.

Similarly, Westminster-style institutions of top-down popular control reflect a very different realization of "democracy" than do separation-of-powers forms. Grassroots channels of influence over bureaucrats—as visible, for instance, in hundreds of U.S. intergovernmental grant programs—reflect yet another reformulation of "democracy."

We argue, therefore, that the bureaucracy-democracy challenge is central, but it must be addressed in an empirically grounded fashion for any valid conclusions to be drawn. Many varieties of democracy and many kinds of bureaucracy inevitably mean that many different assessments are possible. Understanding the particular challenges and vulnerabilities of a governing system requires analyzing how its particular institutions and patterns of action operate. In this volume, we embed the bureaucracy-democracy discussion in one specific kind of context (the United States) to facilitate this kind of assessment, and further productive discourse on this theme must, we argue, be similarly embedded.

This argument does not mean, however, that the conclusion to be drawn about bureaucracy and democracy consists of the maxim "It all depends." Rather, we suggest that significant advance on this question requires context-specific analyses framed within a more general theoretical perspective, so that different contexts and institutions can ultimately be compared systematically and explicitly. For that reason, we also situate our analysis in a more general way by clarifying what is meant by a governance perspective and then employing it in an approach to understanding public program performance in a governance setting. The next section covers these topics briefly and explains the empirical settings on which the analysis of this book is conducted. The section following then sketches the plan of the volume.

A GOVERNANCE PERSPECTIVE: A GENERAL APPROACH AND AN EMPIRICAL SETTING

A governance approach seeks to integrate political and bureaucratic forces at multiple levels to indicate how programs are designed, adopted, implemented, and evaluated in terms of both effectiveness and democracy. Such a point of view clearly recognizes that only with effective implementing institutions can societies generate the fairness and slack resources that permit democracies with their large transaction costs to exist and prosper. Governing institutions, in turn, operate at multiple levels of government and take a variety of forms; a governance perspective (see Heinrich and Lynn 2000; Kettl 2002; Kooiman 2003; Pierre and Peters 2000; Rhodes 1997) sensitizes one to the fuller array of these. Some are traditional electoral institutions such as legislatures; others operate outside of government—interest groups, political parties, social movements, private organizations. Similarly, implementing institutions, commonly denoted simply as "bureaucracy," actually take a wide range of forms, from the traditional government agency, to nonprofit organizations, private organizations, or elaborate networks composed of all of these forms.

In this book we frequently use the shorthand "bureaucracy" to reference the institutional arrangements used for implementation in a governance system. We do so for two reasons: for economy of expression and also to connect our analysis to the longstanding and important line of debate and research on bureaucracy and democracy (for further coverage see the appendix). As emphasized earlier, however, the actual institutional arrangements operating in any given governance setting can vary considerably. One particularly important dimension of such institutional arrangements is the extent to which, at one extreme, public programs are carried out through a classic and stable hierarchy, on the one hand, or through a set of actors tied together in a less hierarchical and less stable fashion: a "network." Networks consist of two or more actors linked by some degree and type of interdependence, in which the actors are not connected simply by a set of superior-subordinate relations. We refer to the full range of these as "bureaucracy"; but, as will be clear in later chapters, the range of variation in such arrangements is much broader than that encompassed by the usual types of administrative agencies, each separately managing its own straightforwardly structured programs.

This perspective sets the contemporary debate on bureaucracy and democracy in the context of twenty-first century governance arrangements. Governance is a broad topic; governance models range from relatively loosely structured logics of governance (Lynn, Heinrich, and Hill 2001) to highly specific models that specify sets of testable hypotheses (see the appendix; O'Toole and Meier 1999). Rather than examine the literature in detail, for purposes of establishing the context for this book a relatively simple heuristic will be adequate. Governance systems cover three basic functions: the aggregation of preferences, decisions on policy options, and the implementation of policies. Each merits discussion in turn.

The aggregation of preferences, whether of the general public or of highly motivated elites, is accomplished through processes of representation. Although the most common form of representation occurs when legislators take mass public values and express them in the policy-making process, additional representational processes can also be noted. In addition to representation via legislatures and elected chief executives, similar functions can be performed when other institutions, such as interest groups, political parties, private firms, and nonprofit organizations, represent interests. This broader notion is important for our purposes since it suggests that bureaucratic institutions can also serve a representational function. In fact, at least two such forms can be identified: active representation, in which the representational role is explicitly established in authorizing legislation or other initiating pronouncements (e.g., the U.S. Department of Agriculture, which was created to serve the interests of farmers), or more passive representation, the incorporation of values or common experiences by those who populate the administrative apparatus. We examine the bureaucratic representational function empirically later in this book.

The governance perspective is also sensitive to the point that the locus of decision making can vary. Policies can be established in what may be considered the traditional way, by legislative action, but a governance perspective also attends to the point that policies can be made when government defers action to nonstate actors. From this perspective, policy decisions can be made by private-sector organizations whenever government decides not to decide. Policy decisions can also be delegated to elected executives, bureaucratic organizations, or networks comprising a wide variety of actors (see chap. 3). Although a more traditional perspective might trace such decisions to legislative action or inaction, in many cases bureaucracies initiate policies without legislative approval (e.g., airline deregulation, the nonbank loophole in financial regulation) or networks self-organize and set policies (e.g., early AIDS policy; see chap. 3).

Implementation, or generating tangible results from such systems, has perhaps seen the greatest influence of the governance perspective. This impact has become increasingly visible as the institutional arrangements involved in delivering governance have evolved (in academic recognition if not in practice) from solitary government bureaucracies, to more variable networks of multiple organizations, or parts of organizations, including government agencies at the same or different levels of government, nonprofit organizations and associations, and private-sector companies. The clusters of networked units may be charged with varying types and levels of coordination, or they may self-organize to do so even if not explicitly required. Because achievement of public policy objectives takes place within a context of culture, laws, and traditions, some policies might even be relatively self-implementing. Many others will rely on some co-production with citizens, whether the institutional implementing apparatus is a bureaucratic agency or a more complex network.

The governance perspective treats these three functions not as a linear progression from preference aggregation to decision making to implementation, but rather as a set of interrelated and temporally overlapping functions. In addition to the obvious feedback that develops from policy implementation, which can influence both decisions and the aggregation of preferences, each of the elements in this triad of functions influences both of the others. In other words, all the relationships are reciprocal. A wide variety of political institutions or combination of institutions can perform any of the three functions. One important advantage of a governance perspective is that it encourages a consideration of how the various key processes are actually carried out, rather than examining only formal arrangements and formally stipulated tasks.

Many empirical contexts could be useful as settings for the systematic analysis of the bureaucracy and democracy theme. We choose to emphasize evidence from the United States; as a developed nation with substantial commitment to public programs and a long history of serious attention to democracy, it is an appropriate context. At the same time, exploring the bureaucracy-democracy issue for the United States is no substitute for systematic attention to the issue elsewhere. To be productive, analysis must be grounded in the particular democratic and bureaucratic features of a given governance setting. In some respects, particularly with regard to its administrative experience, the United States is a highly unusual case (Stillman 1991); and Europeans or Latin Americans, for example, need to adapt this kind of analysis to the circumstances that are played out in a variety of other cases.

Within the United States, many interesting settings could be candidates for analyses. The Tennessee Valley Authority is a national agency with a substantial history of attention to democratic values, as is the U.S. Department of Agriculture. The former has been known to interpret democracy heavily in terms of local preferences and grass-roots democracy (Lilienthal 1944; Selznick 1949); the latter has emphasized attention to its core sectoral constituency using bottom-up processes of preference aggregation, decision making, and implementation by and among the agricultural community, with some management from above. Many other national bureaus could provide instructive material. Further, there are more than eighty-five thousand governments within the United States, all but fifty-one of which are local.

In this volume, we offer some limited but systematically framed and gathered data from the national level to elucidate some aspects of the bureaucracy-democracy challenge. The bulk of the empirical coverage, however, is drawn from the local level, and in particular from that uniquely American form of special governmental form, school districts. On issues of democracy and bureaucracy, the governance of school systems is a key forum; public education represents a significant channel of socialization and civic development. How such systems perform can be considered one of the critical challenges of democratic governance. Of the more than fourteen thousand U.S. school districts, we select the thousand-plus districts of the state of Texas for detailed examination. While a focus on so many different governance systems precludes detailed attention to any one of them, the tradeoff is sensible. Analyzing bureaucracy and democracy in many different governance systems, each providing similar and important public services in the same state at the same time, provides ideal research settings for systematic analyses of some of the key aspects of this topic as outlined earlier. Texas is a large, diverse state, and the availability of high-quality and detailed data on many of the most salient issues gives us a chance to make some empirical headway.

PLAN OF THE VOLUME

Thus far we have framed the subject to be tackled in this book in terms of attention to it by various social sciences and reform perspectives, empirical settings, and dimensions. We have also connected the issue to the contemporary discussion of governance (see the appendix for our formal model of the governance process).

Chapter 2 emphasizes the political-control theme, which has been such an important part of the dialogue on bureaucracy and democracy in political science. We use four alternative streams of literature to show that the standard political-science control framework is incomplete and at times even inaccurate. The chapter demonstrates conclusively that political control is only one of many environmental inputs to bureaucracy and that "political control" or overhead democracy is only one relevant form of democratic governance.

Chapter 3 begins the empirical analyses. Most studies of political control of the bureaucracy assume a simple principal-agent model; even more complicated models, which allow for multiple principals, only examine a single, unitary bureaucracy. This chapter demonstrates that traditional models of political control are inaccurate and underestimate the problems of top-down political control. The analysis presents national U.S. empirical findings to show that public programs are increasingly implemented not by single, hierarchical bureaucracies but by complex intergovernmental and interorganizational networks. In such networks, the ability of a lead bureaucratic agency to coerce compliance is limited. Instead, bureaucracies must use resources, political skills, and strategic efforts to entice other governments, private organizations, and citizen groups to cooperate to implement policy. Such relationships imply that while Congress may have some hierarchical influence over a federal bureaucracy, the bureaucracy often does not have sufficient institutional control over other relevant policy actors to carry out the intent of Congress. These networks characterize a wide range of U.S. policies, thus validating the importance of a governance perspective and implying that top-down political control faces a structural system that is not especially amenable to such control.

Chapter 4 then asks and provides an answer to the following important question: If one were to examine a more "ideal" structural situation (ideal, that is, from the standpoint of the logic of political control), how effective would overhead control actually be? Here the treatment moves to the subnational level for some systematic exploration of the factors that shape bureaucratic results in these relatively simple and straightforward settings. The chapter argues that political control itself can only be assessed when one knows the goals of both the politicians and the bureaucrats. This assertion is justified with two different theories: representative bureaucracy and spatial modeling. The chapter then provides a critical test by using school districts and the interests of Latino citizens to demonstrate how little control political institutions have over one set of implementing institutions. The chapter probes various methods of political control, such as relying on political appointments and setting general policies, in addition to undertaking simple majoritarian efforts. All prove to be marginally effective. In short, even in situations of optimal structure, from the standpoint of advocates of political control, top-down control is problematic. At the same time bureaucracy appears to be highly responsive to citizen demands; this responsiveness, however, is a function of bureaucratic values, not political-control efforts. This chapter thus develops the bottom-up theme from what began as a top-down portrayal.

Chapter 5 sets up a second situation in which political control over bureaucracy should be at a maximum: the use of standardized testing to hold schools accountable. In such circumstances political principals tend to be unified, monitoring is done relatively cheaply and openly by parents and the media, and bureaucratic shirking should be minimized. Even in such ideal situations, however, bureaucracies can "cheat"—that is, use their own devices to comply with the letter of accountability schemes but avoid the substantive intent of political controllers—in clever and difficult-to-counter ways. The analysis and findings are then linked to a theoretical framework that predicts when an implementing organization facing multiple goals is likely to cheat in this manner and when it is not. Two implications follow. First, in a situation that should be optimal for political control, bureaucracies can subvert that control by relying on techniques that emphasize their expertise. Second, bureaucracies can adopt such strategies not because their objective is to subvert political control but because their professional values lead them to believe that such testing policies will have major deleterious effects on students. The bottom line is that in a situation that appears to be ideal for political control, there is substantial evidence of bureaucratic discretion and that a professionalized implementing institution is no guarantor of democratic governance.

The concluding chapter interprets these empirical findings within the context of contemporary governance research. The basic themes are two. First, top-down political control of the bureaucracy has only modest impact at best on the activities of bureaucracy in the United States. The book shows that overhead democracy in such settings is not an effective way to ensure the responsiveness of bureaucracy in a democracy. If overhead democracy is limited in these "ideal" situations, its impact in more challenging situations, circumstances that are clearly not uncommon, is substantially less. Second, at the same time bureaucracy in the United States can be highly sensitive to the needs and desires of citizens. Shared values and commitments to democratic norms, along with political control, produce a bureaucracy that is often responsive to the American people. These themes are then used to speculate on the role of bureaucracy in a democratic society, both in the United States and elsewhere. A brief review of contemporary notions of bureaucratic reform, in the context of the present analysis, suggests that caution be used before adopting wholesale some of the most popular current notions for "reinventing government." In fact, the requisites of democracy require an extended critique and reappraisal of such ideas.

CHAPTER TWO

Democracy and Political Control of the Bureaucracy

Chapter 1 demonstrates that the political-control theme has been an important component of the discussion about bureaucracy and democracy. This subject merits careful examination, particularly from the political science and public administration perspectives. Here we analyze both, beginning with the former, and demonstrate that each suffers from considerable deficiencies. Our objective is to show that these limits stem from taking an incomplete view of the governance process and thus focusing on only one aspect of the problem. This coverage establishes the context for the empirical analyses in chapters 3, 4, and 5.

Within political science, particularly since 1982, a distinct line of research has emerged on what has come to be known as "political control of the bureaucracy" (see table 2.1 and references therein). Taking its cues primarily from political and journalistic claims that bureaucracy can run amok and must be held in check by overtly political forces if democracy is to be served, the literature seems to demonstrate in a variety of ways that bureaucratic actions are correlated with political stimuli. Indeed, the portrait painted of the political process suggests a bureaucracy not only responsive to political pressures but also generally passive in the face of such challenges. In fact, however, bureaucratic values and variables themselves are generally ignored in the most prominent studies of this genre (see table 2.1, cols. 2, 3). Ironically, then, the modal test of political control of the bureaucracy omits everything, or nearly everything, regarding the allegedly problematic institution itself.

This chapter was co-authored with Sean Nicholson-Crotty.

TABLE 2.1
A Review of the Literature on Political Control of the Bureaucracy

Citation	Political variables measuring preferences?	Bureaucratic values?	Bureaucratic variables?	Number of agencies in study?	More than one dependent variable?
Moe 1982	no	no	no	3	yes
Gormley, Hoadley, Williams 1983	yes	yes	yes	12/50	yes
Moe 1985	yes	?	no	1	no
Scholz and Wei 1986	no	no	no	1	yes
Wood 1988	no	no	no	1	yes
Wood 1990	yes	no	no	1	yes
Eisner and Meier 1990	yes	yes	yes	1	no
Scholz, Twombly, Headrick 1991	yes	no	no	1	yes
Wood and Waterman 1991	yes	no	no	7	yes
Wood and Waterman 1993	yes	no	no	1	yes
Hedge and Scicchitano 1994	yes	no	no	1	no
Ringquist 1995	yes	no	no	1	yes
Sabatier, Loomis, McCarthy 1995	yes	yes	yes	1	yes
Carpenter 1996	yes	?	no	2	yes
Krause 1996	yes	yes	yes	1	yes
Balla 1998	yes	no	no	1	yes
Chaney and Saltzstein 1998	no	yes	yes	145	no
Meier, Polinard, Wrinkle 1999	yes	?	yes	1	yes
Scholz and Wood 1999	yes	?	yes	1	yes
Balla and Wright 2001	yes	no	no	1	no
Mete 2002	yes	no	no	1	yes
Whitford 2002	yes	yes	no	1	yes
Canes-Wrone 2003	yes	no	no	1	no

As others might put it, it is time to bring the bureaucracy back in—to the investigation of its own politically relevant actions (Evans, Rueschemeyer, and Skocpol 1985). At the same time, we reject the idea of drawing the bureaucracy back in only to throw out discussion of political institutions (Wamsley et al. 1987). This chapter directly challenges the literature on political control of bureaucracy by arguing that the empirical studies have misrepresented the policy process and thus encouraged misleading inferences about the forces shaping bureaucratic action. It also challenges the public administration literature that places its faith almost completely in the beneficence of bureaucracy.[1] Because the literature on political control of the

1. In a sense, therefore, we are developing a theme not dissimilar from that sketched by Golembiewski (1995), who pointed to the weaknesses of theoretical arguments developed by ardent defenders of the bureaucracy as well as strident critics of the same institution. He referred to those developing such ideas as the "hallowers" and the "hollowers" (i.e., those favoring a hollowing out of robust bureaucratic institutions of the state), respectively.

bureaucracy is somewhat larger and has not been subjected to rigorous criticism, this chapter focuses primarily on that literature. Secondarily, it also discusses the bureaucentric view of politics that grows out of the public administration literature. These examinations then support an argument for a balanced approach to the question of bureaucracy and democratic governance.

EXPLORATIONS OF POLITICAL CONTROL

Within the discipline of political science, the study of bureaucracy and democracy has been narrowed to a concern with political control over the bureaucracy.[2] Political scientists generally cluster into two broad groups reflecting distinct approaches to the field: those interested in institutions and those interested in behavior. Only modest intertribal communication occurs between these two. This gulf, coupled with the relative paucity of political scientists interested in bureaucracy (as opposed to legislatures, chief executives, or courts), means the subject of study has been focused, laserlike, on how well the president and/or Congress can "control" the bureaucracy.[3] Assumed in the process is the notion that elected officials are responsive to the general public (a topic in political behavior that is subject to substantial dispute; see Erikson, MacKuen, and Stimson 2002), and dismissed in the process is the idea that mass political pressures, either directly from the public or from interest groups, could manifest themselves on the bureaucracy without the mediation of one of the political institutions.[4]

Political science scholarship has produced both formal-theoretical and empirical literatures on political control of the bureaucracy. While the latter is our primary concern, the former illustrates some interesting questions and provides the justification for much of the empirical work. The formal-theoretical work, alluded to briefly in chapter 1, starts with the unconventional notion that relationships between a political official and a bureaucrat should be viewed in terms of a contract between the two.[5] This view allows scholars to import the principal-agent model from law and economics, a model that was used extensively to investigate relationships between

2. Historically, political scientists had broader concerns. The work of Dahl, Waldo, Simon, Herring, Gulick, Friedrich, and others shows a concern with governance and the design of administrative systems in a democracy.

3. The great bulk of this literature is centered on the United States at the national level.

4. We use the term *political institution* to refer to institutions in which key decision makers are elected. We recognize that in any broader definition of political institution, bureaucracy would easily be considered a political institution (Meier 2000).

5. Whether the application of a model designed to explain voluntary relationships between peers is appropriate for describing mandatory relationships between unequals is an open question.

physicians and patients, used car dealers and customers, and a variety of other marketplace relationships (e.g., Evans 1980; Ross 1973).

As Terry Moe (1984, 756) frames the problem (substitute *politician* for *principal* and *bureaucrat* for *agent*),

> The principal-agent model is an analytic expression of the agency relationship, in which one party, the principal, considers entering into a contractual agreement with another, the agent, in the expectations that the agent will subsequently choose actions that produce outcomes desired by the principal. . . . The principal's decision problem is far more involved than simply locating a qualified person—for there is no guarantee that the agent, once hired, will in effect choose to pursue the principal's best interests or to do so efficiently. The agent has his own interests at heart, and is induced to pursue the principal's objective only to the extent that the incentive structure imposed in the contract renders such behavior advantageous.

The above excerpt shows that the model, reflecting its roots in studying market exchanges, starts with an assumption of an inherent conflict between the goals of the principal and the agent (Mitnick 1980; Perrow 1972). This antagonism means that the principal cannot be certain that the agent will follow the wishes of the principal; this uncertainty is further exacerbated by the greater knowledge and experience of the agent, experience gained either in day-to-day activities or in specialized education (Jensen and Meckling 1976; Mitnick 1980; Moe 1984; Ross 1973). Information asymmetry and goal conflict, therefore, are the driving theoretical concepts behind the principal-agent model and its subsequent application to the question of political control.

The theoretical literature takes the assumptions of goal conflict and information asymmetry and formally demonstrates the difficulty that political officials are likely to have in attempts to control the bureaucracy (Banks and Weingast 1992; Bendor, Taylor, and Van Gaalen 1985, 1987; Niskanen 1971; Woolley 1993; for coverage in terms of the emerging themes of governance, see Lynn, Heinrich, and Hill 2001). Although an extensive literature can be found on this question dating back at least to Max Weber, much of this work is purely theoretical and pays little attention to earlier empirical or other theoretical scholarship. A conclusion from this literature is that attempts to monitor the bureaucracy after the fact are likely to be expensive and inefficient, thus comporting with early empirical work on the lack of formal congressional oversight into bureaucratic operations (Ogul 1976; Scher 1963).[6] The

---

6. More recent empirical work (Aberbach 1990) finds that congressional oversight has increased dramatically and occurs in forums other than traditional oversight committees. Oversight is nothing more than an information-gathering process, and political institutions exist in information-heavy environments. From an organizational perspective, political institutions likely face a situation of too much rather than too little information.

theoretical question then becomes, Could one design an incentive system for a principal-agent relationship that overcomes these problems?[7]

The first theoretical solution was proposed by McCubbins, Noll, and Weingast (1987), who argued that Congress could design structures and processes that would determine bureaucratic actions. Although they did not cite the traditional public administration literature on structural design of organizations (Seidman 1970), they implied that the environment of the organization was extremely important. The controversial portion of their argument contended that administrative procedures, such as those under the Administrative Procedures Act, were not designed to guarantee fairness at all but to generate biases, to make sure that the same interests that pressured Congress would act similarly on the bureaucracy (see also Rosenbloom 2000). With only modest empirical evidence (see Weingast and Moran 1983), this theoretical argument evolved to become known as the "congressional dominance" theory, which contends that Congress not only influences the bureaucratic process but actually dominates it (for a compelling critique, see Moe 1987). Owing to the emphasis on organizational design and the contention that designed structures *determine* bureaucratic actions, this approach might be termed *organizational creation science.*

The second theoretical solution was to find ways of reducing the costs of gathering information on what the bureaucracy is doing. McCubbins and Schwartz (1984) argued that congressional casework is a cheap way to acquire information about bureaucracies. Interest groups that are interested in a policy area have an incentive to monitor bureaucratic actions closely. When displeased, these groups are then likely to inform Congress, thereby providing information that is valuable even if biased. McCubbins and Schwartz called this form of oversight "fire alarms" to distinguish it from oversight hearings, or "police patrols."[8]

The empirical political science work in the United States took a different tack by focusing initially on the president rather than Congress as a bureaucratic control. The typical political-control study begins with a brief allusion to theory, often framing the questions under examination as within the realm of principal-agent theory but not directly engaging the theory. In Moe's (1982, 1985) seminal works in this area, for example, he presents no statement about theory at all in the first article, and in

---

7. For a formal argument demonstrating that principal-agent relationships *within* the bureaucracy cannot be established and then operated basically on autopilot, see Miller 1992.

8. The problem with the McCubbins and Schwartz argument is the general lack of policy content to casework. The noise-to-information ratio, as a result, is fairly high. At the same time, the general argument does hold because Congress is in an information-rich environment with a variety of informants willing to provide it with data. McCubbins has not returned to this subject to reconcile the conflict between McCubbins and Schwartz (1984) and McCubbins, Noll, and Weingast (1987).

the second he devotes a single paragraph to the suggestion that his approach draws from agency theory and the behavioral tradition in organizational analysis (1985, 1987). Researchers who followed Moe generally assumed that agents/bureaucrats have goals that conflict with those of the principal/politician and that politicians will take a variety of actions to get the bureaucrat to respond as the politician(s) desire(s) (e.g., Balla 1998; Hedge and Scicchitano 1994). As the literature demonstrates, such politically triggered actions can range widely, from direct orders (Chaney and Salzstein 1998) to the use of political appointments (Wood and Waterman 1991) to "deck-stacking" procedures like the notice-and-comment process for regulatory agencies (Balla 1998). Although much of the literature focuses on the president, following Moe's example and a series of follow-ups by Wood and colleagues, as a group the studies cover most of the institutions that interact with bureaucracy.[9]

After the empirical study is introduced, however, the bureaucracy itself is usually left behind. In most cases, a set of political variables are measured (often as surrogates), and correlation of outputs with these is taken as evidence of political control.[10] The limits of this research, however, can be clarified and surmounted by a focus on four streams of literature that address similar problems: public administration, bureaucratic politics, organization theory, and network analysis.

Public Administration

Within public administration, an extensive literature examines similar questions under the rubric of "public administration and democracy" (Finer 1941; Friedrich 1940; Redford 1969). This scholarship is explicitly focused on bureaucracy and how that institution with its nondemocratic orientation might be reconciled with democratic governance. One stream of work advocates overhead democracy, the notion that elected political actors oversee and perhaps influence the actions of bureaucracy (Finer 1941; Redford 1969). Although this literature is normative (e.g., Hyneman 1950) as well as empirical, it parallels somewhat the principal-agent/political-control work within political science.

9. We have not included the delegation literature (e.g., Epstein and O'Halloran 1999; Huber and Shippan 2002) in this discussion because that literature is interested in the types of authority that legislatures delegate to the bureaucracy. While that question is related to political control, this literature is really about how legislatures make decisions and contains no effort to consider bureaucratic variables in the analysis or to assess the effectiveness of various delegations.

10. The accumulated studies are not all of a piece. Research has explored a wide range of external political institutions and stimuli, employed several methods, examined a number of (usually U.S. federal and regulatory) bureaus, and sought to explain a number of bureaucratic actions. Some of the studies have found only limited support for a simple version of the political-control hypothesis (e.g., Balla 1998; Carpenter 1996; Wood 1988), and some suggest complex and possibly reciprocal causal paths (Krause 1996) as well as subtle and multiple bureaucratic response repertoires (Ringquist 1995; Wood and Waterman 1993).

One distinct point of divergence in the two literatures is that the public administration studies are concerned with the circumscribed reach of political control. Friedrich (1940), perhaps most eloquently, notes the limitations on elected officials in terms of time, but especially with regard to expertise. Political control as a process is no different from the internal managerial question of how one gets subordinates to comply with the wishes of superiors (Brehm and Gates 1997; Miller 1992). Within public administration, that relationship is addressed in more interesting ways than is acknowledged in the empirical principal-agent literature. Several arguments suggest that superiors will not be able to control subordinates easily.

First, the public administration literature sees the principal-agent model *as applied* as a serious oversimplification of reality because it focuses only on top-down relationships. Simon (1947), using the prior work of Barnard (1938), argues that authority must come from below, that subordinates must accept authority for it to function. Bureaucrats have a "zone of acceptance"; requests to act outside that zone in normal circumstances are rejected. Simon conceptualizes the relationship between superior and subordinate as a reciprocal relationship with both actors shaping aspects of their joint action.[11] Politician-bureaucratic relationships can clearly be seen in similar terms. In both theoretical and empirical terms, Krause (1996) extends this argument and shows that the Securities and Exchange Commission (SEC) exerts far more influence on both the president and Congress than either institution does on the SEC. The failure to grapple empirically with the reciprocal relationship issue before Krause is surprising because principal-agent theory in its original form focused on the need of the principal to respond to actions of the agent—in short, the theory implies a dynamic, reciprocal relationship, not a top-down hierarchical one.

Second, the problems of information asymmetry between the bureaucracy and the political institutions are likely far more severe than portrayed in the literature. Friedrich (1941) first systematically analyzed this issue and concluded that politicians simply could not cope with the differences in expertise without a fellowship of science to vet information. Even such a fellowship (or hiring their own experts, as both Congress and the president have done) does not necessarily solve the problem, because most politicians lack understanding of the fundamental scientific questions; prominent examples include the British decision over whether or not radar could be used to land planes in World War II (Snow 1961) and the more recent fraudulent research on AIDS by the National Institutes of Health (Crewdson 2002).

---

11. The fourth edition of Simon's *Administrative Behavior* (1997) is especially skeptical of contract-based explanations of organizational behavior. Simon argues that without understanding values and the normative orientation of employees and employers, much behavior will appear unexplainable (see also Golden 2000).

Information asymmetry might be at its most severe in the case of research and science-based policies, but it is found in all policy areas and extends even to political questions. Because bureaucracies interact with clientele and interest groups far more frequently than do politicians, agencies have far more information about what will work and what might be politically feasible. As programs rely more on intergovernmental networks for policy implementation (see below), bureaucratic information advantages extend to state and local political climates and increase correspondingly.

Third, the information advantage of bureaucracy is intensified by the time constraints operating in and on each of the institutions. Any given politician can spend only a modest amount of time overseeing any administrative unit. Bureaucracies, in contrast, are institutions that stretch operations out through time by disaggregating tasks and using specialists on small parts of the problem. Bureaucrats gain a further advantage because they are permanent employees, unlike either the president—who has, at most, an eight-year tenure—or the perpetually changing Congress. Politicians are faced with the need to accomplish tasks before the next election; bureaucrats know a problem can be revisited over an extended period of time.[12]

Fourth, most of the tools that political institutions have to exert control over a bureaucracy are fairly blunt instruments. Budget cuts or increases rely on the discretion of the bureaucracy to make the precise changes that the political institution desires. With few exceptions, legislation establishes only the broad outlines of policy and leaves numerous opportunities to alter or subvert the policy during its implementation (Lowi 1969; Rourke 1969). At times, political appointments can be an effective and precise tool (Wood and Waterman 1994), but that result is contingent on having political appointees with sufficient expertise and political skill to use the means at their disposal. The generally poor quality of appointees in some recent administrations creates severe limits in this regard (Golden 2000; Ingraham 1995).

The reciprocal nature of the bureaucracy/politician relationship, the greater expertise possessed by the bureaucracy in both political and technical terms, the time constraints on politicians, the relative longevity of bureaucratic actors, and the general bluntness of political tools of control—all these factors suggest that overhead democracy will face severe limits. As Robert Dahl (1947, 1970) notes, the pri-

---

12. A comparison with political appointees is particularly clear. At the national level, these appointees typically average 1.5 years in office. Even this figure overstates their stability and thus likely impact, since it omits the fact that key positions often go unfilled for extended periods. Consider a recent presidential transition. By the end of 2001, nearly one year into the administration of George W. Bush, only 306 of 508 key positions had been filled by new appointees. Another 42 from the Clinton administration had been retained, and 160 possible appointments were still unaddressed or in process (www.appointee.brookings.org/ as of December 21, 2001).

mary control on administrative behavior is the inner check, the values held by the bureaucrat; or in the words of Brehm and Gates (1997, 69), "The overwhelming evidence . . . indicates that bureaucrats' own preferences have the greatest effect on performance." These can operate beyond the decisions and actions that can reasonably be monitored by political overseers and may even enable bureaucrats to "respond" in an anticipatory sense to broad public preferences without explicit intervention or signaling from politicians (cf. here Friedrich's [1940] "law of anticipated reaction").

Dahl's position is not unusual; it is endorsed by a wide range of public administration scholars who then seek to define either what these values are or, more often, what they should be. A research agenda focusing on the values held by public servants has generated literatures on a "public service ethic" or "public service motivation" (Brewer and Selden 1998; Crewson 1997; Perry 1996, 2000; Perry and Wise 1990; Rainey 1982), the differences between public and private sector employees (Brewer 2001; Nalbandian and Edwards 1983), and how well public employees represent disadvantaged segments of society (Selden 1997). Another more normative literature, often under the rubric of administrative ethics, focuses on what the values should be (Appleby 1952; Terry 1990, 2003; Wamsley et al. 1987; Wamsley et al. 1990).[13]

Without knowledge of the values held by the bureaucracy, it is futile to attempt any full determination of the degree of political control. The notion of political control entails the concept of power—that *political officials get bureaucrats to act in a way that they would not otherwise have done.* Only by knowing how the bureaucracy would act, independent of the efforts of would-be political controllers, can the idea of political control have real meaning. Measuring bureaucratic values, therefore, is essential to resolving the issue of how much political control is available or possible, and under what conditions.

Unfortunately, the literature on political control rarely measures any bureaucratic variables, let alone bureaucratic values (see table 2.1, cols. 2, 3). In general, goal conflict between politicians and bureaucrats is assumed rather than directly measured, despite substantial evidence that many relationships are marked by goal consensus (Golden 2000; Meier, Wrinkle, and Polinard 1995).[14] In a few cases, some

13. The public administration and democracy literature can even be used to challenge the notion that democracy is what political institutions practice (Wamsley et al. 1987). This position is consistent with our arguments about governance in chapter 1. At times the political-control literature recognizes that responsiveness to a political appointee might not further the interests of democracy (Wood and Waterman 1994).

14. The common notion of "iron triangle" or "triple alliance" highlights the observation that agencies often remain in sync with certain key external political actors over extended periods. The referents here, of course, are legislative committees and interest groups.

authors use the notion of revealed preferences and infer bureaucratic values from agency outputs (Krause 1996; Scholz and Wood 1999) or simply assume that values are captured in a lagged dependent variable (Meier, Polinard, and Wrinkle 1999; Wood 1992). Neither approach is particularly useful given that outputs should be jointly determined by bureaucratic values and a wide variety of other factors including political forces (see our governance model in the appendix). Three exceptions in the research can be noted. Sabatier, Loomis, and McCarthy (1995) used proposed forestry plans to estimate bureaucratic values and concluded that bureaucratic values are a significant predictor of agency policies. Eisner and Meier (1990) employed professional training and found that the addition of economists to the antitrust enforcement agencies was associated with predictable changes in the types of antitrust cases filed. Gormley, Hoadley, and Williams (1983) used surveys to gather information on the values of public utility regulators and then linked these to policy decisions. Despite the findings of these three studies, however, for the most part the political-control literature fails to adequately measure bureaucratic values and, as a result, limits what can really be said about how well political officials can direct the actions of bureaucracy.

Bureaucratic Politics

The political-control literature also limits its utility by focusing attention on single agencies or a few agencies of a similar type. The work of Wood (1988) and colleagues has used advanced time-series techniques to show how political actions are associated with changes in agency activities (controlling for the history of the organization). The focus on a single agency over a period of time gives analysts leverage by transforming some variables into constants and permitting others to be easily measured. Political forces, as a result, can often then be measured as dummy variables representing a presidential appointment, a committee hearing, or a shift in partisanship. The literature has provided some interesting findings; for example, the Environmental Protection Agency's (EPA) average response to Senate hearings takes 8.9 months while the response to House hearings averages only 5.5 months (Wood and Waterman 1994, 95–96). Why this difference exists and what difference it makes are not addressed. Attempts to overcome the limited number of agencies generally involve adding additional time series cases with another agency.

The advantages of a limited number of agencies in terms of measurement and tractability come at some cost, however, particularly in terms of generalizability. Results could well be idiosyncratic to the agency. Why did the political appointment of William Ruckelshaus to head the EPA during the Reagan administration matter (Wood and Waterman 1994), whereas the appointment of Susan Kennedy to the Consumer Product Safety Commission did not? Of the political-control studies listed in table 2.1, only those of Chaney and Saltzstein (1998) and Gormley, Hoadley, and Williams (1983) incorporate more than a handful of agencies.

Perhaps as limiting as the small number of agencies has been the reliance on agencies generally of the same type—federal regulatory agencies (exceptions are Corder 1998, 1999, and Meier, Wrinkle, and Polinard 1995 at the federal level, and Chaney and Saltzstein 1998, and Gormley, Hoadley, and Williams 1983 at the subnational level). The bureaucratic politics literature suggests that the ability of bureaucracy to take independent action is a function of having both resources and autonomy. Resources and autonomy are in turn a function of the bureaucracy's political support (clientele, the public, elected officials), expertise, organizational cohesion, and leadership (Carpenter 2001; Meier 2000; Rourke 1969). Limiting studies to federal regulatory agencies is likely to truncate variation on many of these factors, thus suggesting either greater or lesser political control than would be the case for most other agencies.[15]

Discussing how regulatory agencies compare with others on three key dimensions—political support, expertise, and cohesion—will show how regulatory agencies might be more amenable to political influence than other types of agencies.[16] Strong political support, for example, is a resource that permits agencies to resist the efforts of political officials to redirect agency missions (Rubin 1985). With a few exceptions, political support for regulatory agencies is relatively limited because regulatory agencies are charged with restricting the behavior of individuals or firms. Since the regulatory industry is unlikely to be a strong supporter of an effective regulatory agency and since political elites look askance at regulatory agencies that are popular with their clientele, the opportunities to generate political support are relatively rare. Interest group support for regulatory agencies generally lags well behind that of other agencies, particularly the distributive policy agencies that exist to serve rather than regulate their clientele (Meier 2000, chap. 4). As regulatory environments have become more supportive of general consumer advocacy groups, regulatory agencies are buffeted by pressures from both sides; attempts to please the industry bring the ire of consumer groups, attempts to placate consumers bring industry opposition. With such weak overall political support, regulatory agencies

15. We think that regulatory agencies are more "controllable" than distributive agencies but less controllable than redistributive agencies. These are merely hypotheses that need to be empirically verified.

16. Leadership can probably make a difference in regulatory agencies, but this variable is not discussed here because leadership appears to be somewhat independent of agency type. Just as in other agencies, strong leaders (e.g., William Ruckelshaus, Alfred Kahn, Eleanor Holmes Norton) do head regulatory agencies.

such as the Equal Employment Opportunity Commission are generally at the whim of the political branches of government, when those political branches actually care (Wood 1990). Although a regulatory agency can develop a strong clientele base (e.g., the Federal Deposit Insurance Corporation or the EPA), they generally rank among the weaker federal agencies on this dimension.

Expertise has its roots in either scientific/technical knowledge or detailed political experiences. In neither case are federal regulatory agencies relatively advantaged. The professions that receive deference for expertise—medicine, the sciences, engineering—are rarely the dominant professions in a regulatory agency. Lawyers and a modest number of economists are more likely to be the dominant professionals. The result, with the exception of such regulatory agencies as the Food and Drug Administration or the EPA, is a general lack of technical expertise. Expertise is also generated in the implementation process as agencies learn what will and will not work both technically and politically. While regulatory agencies can pick up implementation expertise, federal regulatory agencies are subject to a variety of procedures that limit how they implement policy. At best, regulatory agencies do not gain any advantages over other types of agencies as a result of their implementation experiences.

A structural reason also suggests that regulatory agencies are less likely to be among the most cohesive federal agencies. Congress has shown a distinct preference for structuring regulatory agencies as independent commissions, headed by a bipartisan set of political appointees. The bipartisan requirement for regulatory commissioners means that political conflict is built into the decision-making process of the agency; the ability to build cohesion in such an organization is more limited.

The limited set of bureaucracies in the political-control literature are also all characterized by a similar structural factor; none operates in an interdependent network setting where the agency must co-produce regularly with other units or gain the cooperation of other agencies, governments, and private organizations to actually implement policy (O'Toole 1997b, 1998, 2000c). Some evidence suggests that these more complicated structural arrangements are fairly common settings for new public programs (see chap. 3 and Hall and O'Toole 2000, 2004). In fact, what the notion of political control means in a situation in which policy is implemented through a network is unclear (see Light 1999b). Does it actually matter if a political institution "controls" a bureaucracy but that bureaucracy is enmeshed in a network of actors over which the bureaucracy has little if any control?

One structural variation for regulatory agencies that is linked to the network theme, however, illustrates fairly well the problems with controlling networks. Several federal regulatory agencies rely on state governments to implement part or all of their programs; prominent examples are workplace safety and environmental protection. Empirical studies of these agencies that include the actions of state-level regulators in the analysis show that the state agencies generally respond to political pressures at the state level rather than to national pressures (see Ringquist 1995; Scholz and Wei 1986; Wood 1992; Wood and Waterman 1994). In these realms, multiple political principals, each with different policy objectives, interact with multiple bureaucratic agents who respond to a variety of forces in addition to those emanating from political institutions. The meaning of political control in such circumstances boils down to "control by whom?"—a normative question that has not been adequately addressed.

Organization Theory

Government bureaucracies, like all other organizations, are goal-oriented collectivities. Unlike the stereotype of private sector organizations, government agencies have multiple goals (Downs 1967; Rainey 2003; Thompson 1967). This feature renders the interaction of political officials and bureaucracy more complex, simply because the bureaucracy can respond to political officials in terms of one goal while simultaneously moving away from political intent on another. The general issue of political control, therefore, is more complicated than is often apparent. A review of numerous studies of political control shows that a range of bureaucratic activities are examined, each perhaps linked to different goals. Most of the relevant control literature follows Wood and examines enforcement activities (Scholz and Wei 1986; Wood 1988; Wood and Waterman 1994); other studies assess whether agencies respond in terms of the content of regulation (Balla 1998), internal resource allocations (Scholz and Wood 1999), or proposed plans (Sabatier, Loomis, and McCarthy 1995).

Despite this diversity of activities across different research projects, each individual study tends to limit itself to a narrow range of indicators. We do not know, for example, whether while the EPA was responding by enforcing regulations, the agency might have been taking the opposite tack as it issued regulations or oversaw state clean air plans. A lesson of organization theory is that studies need to consider a wide range of agency activities, a set of behaviors consistent with the multiple goals the agency has to consider (see Wood 1988). This full set of actions should include not just internal decisions and policy outputs but also policy outcomes. After all, the most critical political question is whether or not EPA actions result in cleaner air, not whether the total number of enforcement actions rises or declines. While the latter may relate to the former, and while it may garner attention from political overseers (and researchers), one can think of ways that an agency could manipulate enforcement actions so as not to affect policy outcomes (see Bohte and Meier 2000, and chap. 5, below).

The second lesson of organization theory for this literature is the obvious one. Organizations are open systems (Thompson 1967) and as such both influence their environments and are influenced by them. Political institutions are a key part of the environment of government bureaucracies; political institutions create bureaucracies and for the most part also supply them with resources. The foil established in the political-control literature—of autonomous, out-of-control bureaucracies—is clearly a straw man, just as such organizational creation-science ideas like congressional dominance are an overstatement. In addition, the influence that bureaucracies have on their environments cannot but affect political institutions either directly or indirectly by affecting constituents. For example, the effectiveness of the Department of Veterans Affairs is quite likely to influence the political fortunes of members of Congress with a large number of veterans as constituents. Shortcomings in administration are likely to be translated into congressional casework; positive actions should lead to constituent communications in regard to increasing the department's budget. A recent book by Suleiman (2003) makes a similar argument more broadly: that democratic institutions gain their legitimacy from the effective performance of bureaucracies.

In addition to the role that bureaucracy plays in the establishment of effective democratic institutions, the role that political institutions play in bureaucratic actions can be overestimated. Political institutions are only one factor in the environment of an organization that affects performance. In addition to the many other environmental actors (including bottom-up influences of democracy), management, structure, and personnel also influence what an organization does (see the appendix). Political institutions, to be sure, are a crucial component of the organization's environment, but they compete for attention with numerous other forces, and all these forces are mediated through the management, procedures, and structure of the organization.

The Networked World of Public Organizations

Public programs in the United States are increasingly implemented in complex networks composed of government agencies at multiple levels as well as private and nonprofit organizations. Numerous reasons for the choice of networks to implement policy are discussed in chapter 3. For the purposes of this section the appearance of networks rather than the reasons for them are important and greatly complicate the question of political control. The political-control literature has struggled to deal with the multiple-principals problem, the fact that the president, Congress, the courts, or even interest groups could be a principal to the bureaucracy's agent (Ringquist 1995; Wood and Waterman 1994). The literature has also started to address the question of chains of principals and agents rather than a single principal and a single agent. In this case, the implementation of regulatory programs that permit state agencies to become the primary implementation agency (see Scholz and Wei 1986; Wood 1992) means that federal political institutions (principals) affect a federal bureaucracy (agent), which in turn becomes a principal to the state bureaucracies.

The complexities of multiple principals or of a principal-agent chain pale in comparison to the complexity of some program networks, as the following illustration from family-planning policy demonstrates. The federal government funds family-planning services for low-income individuals through not one but four different statutes. Title X of the Public Health Service Act creates a categorical grant for family-planning services that is administered by the Public Health Service regional offices, which contract with state health or welfare agencies or private organizations (such as Planned Parenthood) to provide family-planning services to low-income women. The services themselves are delivered either by nonprofit organizations or by local county health departments. Title XIX of the Social Security Act (Medicaid) provides the largest share of family-planning funds. These funds go to welfare departments to reimburse physicians for specific services. The actual administration of these funds is often done via nonprofit organizations such as Blue Cross. Services are provided by private physicians. Title XX of the Social Security Act is a block grant to state welfare agencies; funds from these grants are used for family planning but may also be used for other social services. Title V of the Social Security Act, also known as the Maternal and Child Health and Crippled Children Act, is a formula grant to state health departments; federal law specifies that a minimum percentage of such funds be spent on family planning. In addition to the four federal sources of funds, approximately half of the states fund their own family-planning programs (McFarlane and Meier 2001).

The complexity of funding sources is matched by the complexity of the implementation process. The interdependence among units and activities in the process of converting policy intention into action creates plenty of opportunities for collaboration—or, for that matter, for shirking. Family planning is a policy with a known and effective technology; the basic problem is getting individuals to co-produce "family planning." Programs as a result rely on a network of physicians who treat Medicaid patients, county health departments that interact with poor women who are not Medicaid patients, nonprofit organizations such as Planned Parenthood that primarily treat a similar group, health clinics at universities, and some private health care providers. Carrying out family-planning policy, therefore, is a good example of why the governance theme, as sketched in chapter 1, is of considerable importance.

The problems of federal political principals in influencing this network are well known (see McFarlane and Meier 2001). During the Reagan administration, the data-collection efforts under Title X were abolished; as a result, while there is information on how much money goes to each state, there is no information on what services are actually delivered. Medicaid closely monitors the services received (since reimbursement is on a fee-for-service basis), but the delivery of services is not subject to any coordination. Title V and Title XX monies are loosely monitored, and no systematic, government-collected information for family-planning services under these programs is in place. Services provided with state funds are also not reported to the federal government.

The difficulty that federal political principals have in influencing this network can be illustrated with a couple of high-profile cases involving access to abortion. Nonprofit vendors such as Planned Parenthood believe that access to abortion is an essential part of family-planning services. Several federal government efforts have tried to eliminate federal funding for abortions for medically needy women; at the same time several state governments explicitly fund such abortions and private groups also provide financial support in this area (McFarlane and Meier 2001). In 1988, the Reagan administration issued regulations, referred to as the gag rule, that prohibited any organization that receives family-planning funds from also counseling about abortion services. Opposition, particularly from the nonprofit members of the network, was vehement; and the federal government was soon sued by Planned Parenthood and other service providers, who won at the trial court level before the Clinton administration rescinded the rule. The case illustrates not only that political principals do not control the agents but also that agents can sue principals to stymie control efforts.

In the family-planning policy network, scores of political institutions at various levels of government represent the full gamut of views on family planning. At times even for the federal government alone, Congress (or one house of Congress) holds a policy position different from that of the president or the courts. With the rise of abstinence-only programs in the late 1990s, the implementation arrays show almost as much diversity. Most implementing agencies receive funds from multiple government sources and have access to private funds as well. Compliance with political directives in such a network requires extended negotiation, especially given the virtual absence of monitoring, and then is likely to be only partial. Linking policy changes in such an area to changes in who is president or the partisan composition of Congress is possible, but only by means of some fairly complex processes that do not always operate effectively.

Family planning, we should emphasize, is not an unusual case. Provan and Milward (1991), for example, have documented networks for the provision of services to the seriously mentally ill in medium-sized American cities that encompass several dozen organizations per urban area, and many of the same kinds of issues sketched here for family planning arise in these instances as well. Additional illustrations would be easy to outline, and the theme has also been prominent in democratic settings beyond the United States (see, e.g., Bogason and Toonen 1998; European Commission 2001; Kickert, Klijn, and Koppenjan 1997). In networked situations, the issue of "control" as framed in the research literature of political science is paralleled by a literature in network analysis focusing on the themes of "management" and control, as elaborated in the literature of public administration; both sets, in turn, can be conceptualized in terms of governance models that are significantly different from the simple principal-agent models in the political science literature (see also Meier and O'Toole 2003; O'Toole and Meier 1999, 2003; and the appendix).[17]

POLITICAL CONTROL FROM THE PUBLIC ADMINISTRATION SIDE

Our focus of attention on the political science literature thus far should not be taken as an unqualified endorsement of the public administration literature on the same topic. That body of work too is problematic, although it does consider the bureaucracy more carefully. The relationship between political institutions and bureaucracy is a central question within public administration, but in general that literature is skeptical of the notion of overhead democratic control, as explained earlier in the chapter. Some in the field view political control as potentially a bad thing, on the grounds that abuse of power might arise as often or more often from the political institutions of government as it does from the bureaucratic ones (Goodsell 2004; Meier 1997).[18] The distinct difference in the public administration literature is that it generally seeks solutions to the bureaucracy-democracy problem within and through the bureaucracy itself rather than through reforms to electoral institutions.

17. One clear sign of the emerging salience of the issue of democratic governance in network settings is that a Danish university recently established a research unit dedicated solely to this topic: the Center for Democratic Network Governance at Roskilde University (see www.ruc.dk/demnetgov_en/). The center has begun to develop a series of publications exploring the normative, methodological, and empirical aspects of this subject.

18. The political-control literature thus ignores the problem of the moral hazard of the principal (i.e., a politician can take actions that are harmful to the politician—e.g., the extent of corruption under Mobuto) or shirking on the part of the principal (e.g., by failing to reveal all of his or her preferences).

Bureaucracy, in this view, is a political institution that takes on uniquely "political" roles such as representation, governance, and policy design.

This section of the chapter examines the most typical public-administration approach to the bureaucracy-democracy question by exploring more carefully one particularly well-developed and distinctive version of this gestalt, that embodied in the so-called Blacksburg Manifesto.[19] After a brief summary of the basic tenets of the manifesto (Wamsley et al. 1990) and how it relates to other similar intellectual traditions, we show that this approach exhibits weaknesses that resemble those plaguing the political-control literature.[20]

The Blacksburg Manifesto begins with an argument that bureaucracy is a legitimate institution of governance, perhaps one on a coequal basis with those established explicitly by the U.S. Constitution.[21] This quaint argument serves as the basis for contentions that a larger and independent role for bureaucracy is both necessary and legitimate.

The issue of the legitimacy of bureaucracy rarely troubles scholars who appear to be pragmatists and simply recognize that contemporary government or governance without bureaucratic institutions is simply not possible (Meier 1997; Suleiman 2003). Some might even go so far as to argue that societies are only able to absorb the high decision and transaction costs of democracy because they have effective and efficient bureaucracies that provide the surplus political and social capital to fuel these democratic processes. The Blacksburg Manifesto, in contrast, argues that the bureaucracy performs the constitutional function that was envisioned for the U.S. Senate, that of executive advice, consultation, and policy oversight and imple-

19. So named because the coauthors of the argument were all associated with the Center for Public Administration and Policy at the Virginia Institute of Technology, in Blacksburg, Virginia: Gary Wamsley, John Rohr, Charles Goodsell, Orion White, James Wolf, and Camilla Stivers.

20. Other proposed solutions to the bureaucracy-versus-democracy dilemma are to (1) stimulate citizen participation directly in bureaucratic processes and have the bureaucracy become the institution that aggregates citizen demands (Redford 1969); (2) create competing bureaucracies so that the actions of one can serve as a check on those of others (see Friedrich 1940; Lowery 2000; Ostrom 1989; note also the themes of the New Public Management, as in Barzelay 2001); (3) encourage a role for the bureaucracy as one political contestant in a larger pluralistic struggle, which includes additional political institutions as well as interest groups and others (Herring 1936); (4) require adherence to the rule of law in bureaucratic actions (Rosenbloom 2000); and (5) create a bureaucracy representative of the basic origins and values of the general population (Mosher 1982). Both the fourth and fifth approaches come down to the same values questions that are addressed in this section. Representative bureaucracy differs from the other inner-check approaches because it has developed a robust empirical literature. Still other approaches to the bureaucracy-democracy conundrum seek answers in efforts to democratize the bureaucracy itself. Some parts of the literature on organizational development in the public sector are clearly framed in this manner. As indicated in chapter 1, however, we focus our analysis on the broader perspective traditionally offered by democratic theorists, one examining democratic governance in the large, rather than the sharing of decision-making authority only within the bureaucratic organization itself.

21. The Blacksburg Manifesto is clearly U.S.-centric, but much of the rest of the literature is also overly focused on the United States, either empirically or theoretically.

mentation (Rohr 1986). As the Senate evolved into a second legislative institution, the federal bureaucracy was pressed into service to perform those key constitutional functions.[22]

Establishing a legitimate role of the bureaucracy permits the Blacksburg advocates to argue that bureaucratic discretion is a positive force. Rather than seeking to limit bureaucratic discretion and subject it to political control, administrators in particular must be encouraged to exercise discretion, albeit wisely, and at times to use that discretion to counter the excesses of the political branches. Although the Blacksburg Manifesto is an original approach to the bureaucracy-democracy dilemma, it has deep roots in the tradition of public administration, including other formulations that have sought one or another version of administrative guardians to protect the public interest (see Appleby 1952; Marini 1971).

How does one guard the guardians? In essence, the Blacksburg Manifesto suggests that we not guard the guardians but train them, or rather inculcate them with values such that they make decisions responsive to citizen needs while considering both the democratic process and the rights of minorities. Specifically which values, one might ask? At least five different approaches to sets of values have grown out of the Blacksburg Manifesto or have been proposed separately but are compatible with the overall orientation of the manifesto.

First, Blacksburg contributor John Rohr (1986, 1990, 2002) argues that what are important are regime values—that is, those values that undergird and support the current political regime. These are the values that are found in the Constitution or evolve from it as it is interpreted via the political system. Understanding these normative standards is best achieved, according to Rohr, by reading and understanding the decisions (including dissents) of the U.S. Supreme Court. Rohr clearly has in mind rules about access, due process, fairness, majority rule, protection of minority rights, etc.

Second, Gary Wamsley (1990), also a key Blacksburg contributor, advocates what he calls the agency perspective. Taking the basic principal-agent model (discussed above), Wamsley examines the relationship from the perspective of the agent, an agent with substantial expertise concerning both administrative and political matters. The agency perspective means that the bureaucrat must advocate the agency's mission while taking into consideration the demands as well as the needs of political actors. Recognizing that political demands can differ from political needs, the agency perspective requires the bureaucrat to exercise discretion for the good

---

22. A constitutional flaw in Rohr's argument is that even if one concedes a legitimate Senatelike role, there is no reason why that role should fall to the bureaucracy rather than, say, the Cabinet or the Executive Office of the President.

of the principal. Wamsley has an all-encompassing and plural concept of principals that includes not just political institutions but also citizens. This perspective puts the bureaucracy in the role of balancing the competing interests of principals, not in the manner of a neutral referee but rather as an active participant in the process.

A third set of values, compatible with the Blacksburg Manifesto but developed in advance of it by decades, can be derived from the "New Public Administration," with its focus on social equity (Marini 1971; Waldo 1971). An initial indictment offered from the New Public Administration was that bureaucracy was biased in its decisions and actions and that it systematically discriminated against those citizens without resources (see Frederickson 1996 for a review of the empirical literature debunking this claim). The corresponding obligation placed on the bureaucracy, in this view, is therefore to counter such biases of the larger political system with the goal of furthering social equity. In short, the bureaucracy would become an advocate for disadvantaged clientele, and in this fashion the institution should discard its facade of "neutral competence." The implication of the New Public Administration is that bureaucracy should take an open and political role, a role fraught with risks given that it would represent the least politically powerful elements of society and that other political actors might question the appropriateness of such a role for bureaucracy (Daley 1984).

A distinctly more conservative approach to values, but one proposed by a scholar with strong ties to the Blacksburg tradition, is the notion of administrator as conservator, as sketched by Terry (2003). Rather than offering a notion of bureaucrat as a high-profile advocate for the disadvantaged, Terry proposes a Burkean conservative role whereby the bureaucrats are charged with preserving the capacity of the bureaucracy to support public-policy decisions.[23] Bureaucracy's advocacy role, in Terry's view, is to retain the skills, support, and resources to allow it to act and deal with problems. Conserving these capacities serves the broader polity because doing so allows for modifications in policy as needs or political priorities shift. Terry's proposal might be interpreted as seeking a British-style civil service, equally adept at serving different political masters, but without actually creating such a system.

The fifth alternative set of bureaucratic values comes from the feminist critique of bureaucracy (e.g., Ferguson 1984; Stivers 2002). While some feminist scholars link their work to traditional public administration and the early contributions of

---

23. In this respect, Terry's argument bears similarities to Wamsley's (1990). Wamsley's agency perspective grounds key deliberative and knowledge-preserving functions in the public agency per se, and he sees the administrative role as critically tied to supporting and maintaining the institution as a locus of wisdom, precedent, and consideration of the long-term public interest.

Follett (1987), most of the literature is tied more closely to postmodern political theory and contemporary feminist theory. Although characterizing the full range of feminist theory is not possible here (see Stivers 2002), the basic argument is that bureaucracy and bureaucratic hierarchy drive out feminist values, forcing all bureaucrats, including women, to take on masculine roles to survive in the institution. Feminists propose that bureaucracies become decentralized, with greater worker and clientele participation. The different sex roles in society should be accepted and the bureaucracy adapted to them, rather than the reverse—forcing women to adapt to the bureaucracy. The feminist bureaucracy advocates for client interests and simultaneously breaks down gender-based values and structures in the organization.[24]

This brief review of several proposals for instilling values in the bureaucracy illustrates the difficulty such suggestions face. The range of values that could be proposed, and the range that has been discussed, is extensive. The sets of values frequently conflict with one another, and their application to practical public administrative decisions is not always clear. Even within the Blacksburg group, individual authors (Stivers, Rohr, Wamsley) put individual twists on the general approach, thereby implicitly specifying or pulling the manifesto in myriad directions.[25]

In addition to the lack of agreement on which values should permeate the bureaucracy, a key empirical question is not addressed. What are the values actually held by the bureaucracy? That is, how closely do bureaucracies in practice come to the theoretical ideals proposed by the various theorists? The short answer is that we do not know.[26] Advocates of instilling values in public administrators frequently reject research approaches that would seek to measure bureaucratic values (either because these approaches could not tap the nuances that are deemed important or because empirical epistemology is rejected out of hand). Those who do attempt to measure bureaucratic values (see Brewer 2001; Garand, Parkhurst, and Seoud 1991; Lewis 1990) are trapped by existing survey research instruments that measure general political values. So even though we know that bureaucrats generally hold values similar to those of the general population on contemporary political questions (or are slightly left of center and more communitarian; see Brewer 2001), we

24. Some feminist perspectives are more varied, complex, and nuanced than suggested here. We emphasize a values-based version that is recognizable in the literature of the field.

25. This discussion ignores the point that one Blacksburg scholar has raised questions even about the general formulation, largely on empirical grounds. Kronenberg (1990) analyzes one important case and finds the benign characterization of bureaucratic values at the core of the manifesto to be inconsistent with the evidence. We can add that this point seems to hold, whether for the general manifesto version or the several more specific formulations identified in the current chapter.

26. Again, Kronenberg (1990) raises the question and offers challenging case-study evidence, but more complete and systematic data have not been presented.

have no idea how bureaucrats think about the values advocated by the Blacksburg Manifesto. It could well be that bureaucrats in general or, more likely, bureaucrats in specific agencies hold values that are inimical to democracy.

In addition to the lack of knowledge about current values, all proposals are vague about how one instills the correct values and, more importantly, how one enforces conformance with the values. Making sure that the correct values fit within a set of decisions is a compliance problem or, in the contemporary ideas of economics, a principal-agent problem. In situations in which one can disagree about how values might be applied or what the values actually are, making sure that the correct values permeate the bureaucracy is no easy task.

CONCLUSION

Studies of political control of the bureaucracy suffer from a number of drawbacks, as we have shown in this chapter. The work appropriately frames the bureaucracy-democracy question in terms of whether and how bureaucratic units conduct themselves in a fashion consistent with popular governance. Nonetheless, the bulk of relevant scholarship in political science characterizes the issue in terms of principal-agent models that are seriously flawed, as demonstrated by much work in public administration. Most of the empirical evidence adduced in support of the idea that political principals control bureaucratic agents is drawn from distinctive kinds of settings such that external validity is quite limited. Furthermore, almost all the relevant work of this sort ignores some basic features of organizational theory and behavior long established in other literatures, and it assumes that political principals themselves surely and regularly speak for the people. Overall, almost all the relevant political science research work ignores the real world of bureaucrats, bureaucratic agencies, and the values infusing them, even as it addresses the themes and necessity of bureaucratic control.

Yet while the research field of public administration has provided a much more plausible and nuanced picture of bureaucracy, along with a considerably more sanguine view of the potential for its internal, or value-grounded, control in accord with the requisites of democracy, serious questions can be raised about this perspective as well. Much of this work either ignores the question of how legitimate political institutions like legislatures or an elected chief executive can and should shape bureaucratic action, or it actually views such externally driven influence as an interference with business as usual.[27] Internal bureaucratic values can potentially be quite

27. A variant on these alternatives can be seen in the work of Rohr (1986, 1990), who argues that, constitutionally speaking, the bureaucracy is subordinate to legitimate political principals; but the designed reality of multiple and conflicting principals means that bureaucrats are operating appropriately as long

important to take into account when exploring the actual fit, or misfit, of bureaucracy with democracy. Scholars seem not to agree on what value grounding is the critical one, as can be seen by an examination of even a relatively coherent subset of suggestions: those developed through and consistent with the Blacksburg perspective. Even if there were such agreement, and valid practical knowledge about how to effectuate and maintain an appropriate base of values in the bureaucracy, we know very little about how closely today's actual administrative settings approximate any such ideal.

Finally, both lines of discussion ignore an important empirical complication which, we argue, needs to be taken into account explicitly in dealing with the bureaucracy-democracy question: the multiorganizational, or networked, character of many public programs and much bureaucratic activity. If the "agent" in the principal-agent is really many actors and unlikely to be coordinated hierarchically, most political science work on political control is off the mark. If the "bureaucracy" is not one unit but multiple ones, bureaucratic values as a simple basis for democratic fit may easily be challenged. Plural bureaus, perhaps cutting across plural governments and the private sector, are a standard part of the mix when policy is brought to life in practice. If so, then, it is reasonable to expect that the "agency perspective" of Wamsley (for instance) is more likely a cacophony of views and values rather than a coherent map forged in the crucible of long-term, stable agency deliberation under the care of an administrative conservator.

The bureaucracy-democracy problematic quite clearly requires reframing. Both political science and public administration research should contribute to the reformulation, but we should take care to avoid the more serious deficiencies of either. The next three chapters contribute to the reframing to explore systematically how political principals actually shape what bureaucracy does, how management matters for bureaucratic performance, and how bureaucratic values can drive what bureaucracy produces as results. Chapter 3 demonstrates how both the political science and public administration approaches, with their simple politician-bureau-

---

as they consciously pick and choose from among their principals and their (conflicting) preferences on an issue-to-issue basis. In this view, administrative actors can legitimately be subject to external control while also, in effect, operating with free rein to choose which controls are most appealing at any given time. As Rohr puts it, the "Public Administration . . . choos[es] which of its constitutional masters it will favor at a given time on a given issue in the continual struggle among the three branches as they act out the script of *Federalist* 51." This pattern is invested with principle: "The normative theory I am suggesting deals more directly with attitudes than behavior. Administrators often do choose among constitutional masters, but they usually do so as a matter of fact and seldom as a matter of constitutional principle. Their preoccupation with the low arts of organizational survival blinds them to the brighter angels of their nature" (1990, 81). We view this framing of the issue as one that does not deal effectively with the requirements of democratic governance, even if it takes into account key features of the U.S. constitutional design.

cracy models, miss the real-world problems of control. Many governance structures diffuse authority by creating complex interorganizational and intergovernmental networks with few hierarchical controls. Chapter 4 brings the bureaucratic values question to center stage and finds that much of what passes for political control is really bureaucrats doing what they would do anyway. Chapter 5 examines a simple principal-agent structure with unified principals and clear goals for bureaucrats. Even in an ideal situation for political control, the results show that bureaucracy can and will implement policies in ways unintended by the political principals. While this systematic work focuses on one kind of government and a limited set of empirical circumstances, it provides a beginning for additional and more complete explorations of the bureaucracy-democracy question.

CHAPTER THREE

Structural Barriers to Political Control

As chapter 2 documents, most studies of political control from a political-science perspective assume a simple principal-agent model; even somewhat more complicated models, which allow for multiple principals, only examine a single, unitary bureaucratic organization. Similarly, most research from a public administration perspective also assumes that individual agencies are the modal institutional form for implementing public policy. Public administration specialists may disagree about what values should infuse public agencies, but they largely agree that the values nurtured by or within bureaus are crucial in connecting bureaucracy to democracy.

The present chapter presents empirical work that challenges both perspectives. Rather than the simple governance structures assumed in the literature (usually top down by one principal of a single agent), public programs are very often implemented via complex intergovernmental and interorganizational networks. In such networks, the ability of the "lead" bureaucratic agency—if any—to coerce compliance is limited; and the involvement of multiple organizational actors also reduces the likelihood that a common core of values infuses the full scope of administrative action. Instead, bureaucracies must use resources, political skills, and strategic efforts to entice other agencies, governments, private organizations, and citizen groups to cooperate to implement policy; and they must often find ways to do their work while also operating interdependently with others who have different

This chapter was co-authored with Thad E. Hall. Portions were published in Hall and O'Toole 2000 and 2004.

goals and values.[1] These empirical realities of this type of governance structure thus indicate that the bureaucracy-democracy challenge is more serious and more difficult to address than either political scientists or public administrationists have anticipated.

Cases of such complex and interdependent institutional arrangements for implementation abound. Extensive work has been conducted, for instance, on the collaborative management of local watersheds and estuaries (Lubell 2004; Lubell et al. 2002; Schneider et al. 2003). Similarly, interagency collaboration has been well documented in the fields of social policy, environmental enforcement, and fire prevention (e.g., Bardach 1998). Other instances make the headlines; consider the controversies about complex and expensive patterns of contractor and subcontractor interaction in support of the American military and reconstruction efforts in post-Saddam Iraq.

We use systematic U.S. national-level data to develop the point. At this level such relationships imply that while Congress, for instance, may have some hierarchical control over a federal agency, that bureau does not have sufficient institutional control over other relevant policy actors to carry out the intent of Congress. While federal agencies are intimately involved in converting policy into action, they must do so in league with others who may have vastly different perspectives. The resulting networks for execution characterize a wide range of U.S. policies, from mental health to family planning to environmental protection to drug abuse treatment. The main conclusions for present purposes are, first, to call into serious question the whole body of literature on political control, since that work specifies the issue in a strictly hierarchical fashion that ignores the structural realities of many, probably most, public programs and public agencies; and, second, to challenge conventional notions of an "agency perspective" (Wamsley 1990) as an antidote to unaccountable implementers.

AGENCIES AS AGENTS? UNITS OF ANALYSIS FOR EXPLORING OVERSIGHT AND CONTROL

Scholars interested in political control of the bureaucracy have devoted considerable attention to exploring whether and how political bodies like Congress and the chief executive exert influence over and limit the unmonitored discretion of the bu-

---

1. In terms of our governance model specified in the appendix, this chapter shows how varied the stabilizing, or S, factors actually are. A significant portion of the S vector can be expected to consist of structural elements; the exceptionally broad range in structures for implementing policy means that the opportunities for relatively straightforward political or even managerial control are more limited than the political science literature has suggested. Note that as S moves away from the value of 1 toward 0, designating a less hierarchical and more networked setting, the likelier the administrative system is to be shaped by a broader range of forces, and its performance is less likely to be predicted by what has happened recently through the system.

reaucrats charged with implementing public purposes. A variety of associated issues have been explored, including the motivations of political principals, the means and effectiveness of oversight channels, and the influence of institutional arrangements and procedural constraints in controlling administrative discretion. Scholars of public administration, on the other hand, have sketched the value bases they believe can infuse public agencies with perspectives grounded in democracy. In this chapter we concentrate especially on the former cluster, since its external-control perspective has been extensively developed and elaborated. Both research traditions, nonetheless, rely on a particular assumption about single-agency action for their persuasiveness; and both can be critically assessed on the basis of the same kind of systematic empirical examination.

Within the external-control literature, some analysts have offered interesting and largely encouraging principal-agent theoretical claims about the general effectiveness of oversight and control (see chaps. 1 and 2). Critiques and challenges have also been directed against the assertion that principals can exert significant control over administration. Some appraisals have probed the theoretical bases of the control logics offered by scholars; others have explored the issue empirically and found evidence that control and oversight are, variously, impressively evident or greatly limited, at least under some important circumstances (see also chap. 4). In general terms, the questions continue to be debated and explored, with mixed evidence and a clear need for further investigation. What all these perspectives have missed, however, is a basic issue about the appropriate unit of analysis to be considered when framing the subject; in particular, what is the relevant object or agent for oversight and control?

The research discussion about administrative control by political principals has been premised on an unexamined assumption that the relevant unit capable of exerting independence and thus subject to the potentially constraining influence of political principals is the administrative agency or bureau. Similarly, internal-administrative solutions tend to concentrate attention on the bureau-centered value bases of administrative action. In short, from both directions the analysis of the control issue has assumed agencies (and their staff) as agents—the presumed objects of attention from political actors are the administrative unit defined in structurally formal terms and the presumed administrative actor exerting influence via policy action.

In the political-control literature, the precise kind of administrative unit has often been rather ambiguous, whether cabinet-level department, for instance, or main subunit (e.g., the Food and Drug Administration within the U.S. Department of Health and Human Services), or independent regulatory authority. Still, the analysis of oversight and control at the national level has assumed consistently that the challenge is for political principals to exert or arrange influence, one way or another, over a *single* administrative apparatus of the federal government.[2]

The preceding chapter explored the considerable weaknesses and gaps of the research literature on political control. Here we single out one of those limitations for special empirical attention: we argue that the "agent" has been misspecified. Very often, the most relevant unit of analysis for the challenge of oversight and control (or, alternatively, for proactive policy action) is not the administrative agency but, rather, a network of interagency, perhaps intergovernmental, and increasingly intersectoral ties. Public programs, we can show, are frequently implemented via institutional arrangements that bridge between or among administrative structures rather than sit nested within them; and these typically involve discretionary, potentially collaborative relations among the units in the networked array. To the extent that this claim is correct, the analysis of administrative oversight, control, and policy action needs to be fundamentally reframed. Under extant conditions, the ability of any set of political principals to control those involved in program implementation can be called into question, in ways that have been undiscussed in the main treatments of the subject. And the ability of administrators to infuse their organizations with values may touch only a relatively small portion of the relevant implementation apparatus for public programs.

To describe this line of reasoning, we first sketch briefly the standard way in which oversight is considered by scholars. We use one particularly influential treatment as a way of demonstrating the premise on which the discussion thus far has rested. We then suggest why treating the agent as a single agency in the principal-agent model does not comport with reality. To do so we draw from recent empirical scholarship on the full reach of federal program employment, our own investigations, and analyses by an important congressional agency.

THE STANDARD POLITICAL-CONTROL PERSPECTIVE

Researchers have long been concerned about how actions of public agencies can be constrained so that these units perform their duties within the confines of law and according to the preferences of elected officials (Finer 1941; Friedrich 1940). A significant body of literature suggests means by which agencies can be made more politically responsive by congressional or presidential activity (e.g., Aberbach 1990; Bendor 1988; Cole and Caputo 1979; McCubbins 1985; McCubbins, Noll, and Weingast 1987, 1989; Moe 1984, 1993, 1998; Moe and Howell 1999a, 1999b; Ogul

2. The literature frequently considers federalism and extends the single-agency concept to the individual states (see Ringquist 1995; Scholz and Wei 1986; Wood 1992).

and Rockman 1990; Rockman 1984; McCubbins 1985; Wood and Waterman 1991). The causal stories are varied and intricate.

Students of oversight have typically investigated how Congress or the president seeks to control the way in which new public programs are implemented. Ex ante controls are designed to limit or influence agency choices prior to any final administrative action (McCubbins 1985). The Administrative Procedures Act (APA) is a classic example (but see Rosenbloom 2000 for a different interpretation). Ex post controls are crafted to limit or influence an agency after it has already taken action; congressional committee oversight hearings are an obvious example.

The need for formal control mechanisms for reining in agency discretion has long been recognized (e.g., Finer 1941). Scholars have argued, however, that there are severe limits to the use of oversight hearings as a means of control (Dodd and Schott 1979; Ogul 1976; Schattschneider 1960; Scher 1963). The reasons for this argument go beyond the current study, as does empirical work that shows the amount of oversight activity by Congress increasing over time (e.g., Aberbach 1990, 34–39).

In addition to oversight hearings, Congress also uses both structural and procedural tools to seek control of agency action, and these have been explored by scholars as well. When Congress delegates a problem to an agency, especially a regulatory agency, scholars of legislative control argue that Congress intends to "control . . . the exercise of delegated authority by administrative entities" (McCubbins 1985, 723) and reduce problems of shirking and slippage (e.g., McCubbins and Page 1987). Many different mechanisms can be used for achieving these objectives, including selecting an institutional setting for regulatory action, specifying regulatory scope and targets, stipulating implementation tools (market mechanisms, direct provision of goods, and so forth), and adding procedural requirements for informing Congress about agency actions. Congress enforces the arrangements chosen, it is argued, by using its legislative powers, including the ability to provide rewards or impose sanctions on the agency. Further, agency discretion can be controlled by the selection of an appropriate agency head (Calvert, McCubbins, and Weingast 1989) and by the way in which the hierarchical structure of the agency is designed (see Hammond 1986; Cook 1989). Presidential control of the bureaucracy is often framed as a matter of control via appointment of agency heads. Presidents also exert control over the bureaucracy by reviewing agency rule making (e.g., Moe 1998). Because presidents can act unilaterally—unlike the Congress, which must act collectively—presidents can often work nominally through agencies to achieve their policy objectives (Moe and Howell 1999a, 1999b).

Perhaps the most influential argument regarding how agencies can be controlled through procedural channels has been advanced by McCubbins, Noll, and Weingast (esp. 1987). They argued that because traditional oversight mechanisms, such as monitoring and the threat of sanctions, are not very effective and indeed impose costs on members of Congress, the legislature nonetheless instead uses administrative procedures and institutional arrangements to constrain administrative activities. Procedural requirements placed upon an agency allow Congress to induce policy outcomes without having to bear the full cost of enforcement. By structuring the "rules of the game" and sequencing agency action, the argument goes, Congress can limit an agency's choices regarding the way a policy will be implemented.

One way in which Congress could use procedures to overcome information asymmetries is by forcing an agency to reveal its policy preferences before implementing a new policy. The APA does so by requiring an agency to publish proposed rules and receive comments from interested parties before implementation (elaboration of this stricture was developed by PL 104-121, The Contract with America Advancement Act of 1996; see subtitle E, Congressional Review). Yet, as West has shown, even the APA exerts limited influence, since many important discretionary decisions have already been made by the time these requirements are triggered in a given case (West 1995, 42–46). Macey (1992) also notes that there is often an extended delay between the time when the law is passed and implemented and when the administrative rules are actually promulgated.

A second type of control procedure sketched by McCubbins, Noll, and Weingast is "deck stacking," which manifests itself in several ways, including (1) enfranchising new interests, an effort that often manifests itself through crosscutting mandates (one set of requirements that apply to many different agencies, like environmental or civil rights requirements); (2) subsidizing or mandating participation by specific groups in the legislative and rule-making processes; and (3) limiting the agenda-setting capabilities of agencies, for instance, by requiring multiple agencies to confer and agree on a policy before a final decision is made and implemented. These procedures are seen as constraining agency activity so that continuing and intrusive oversight by Congress is rendered unnecessary. By establishing these procedural "rules of the game" at the outset, Congress can ensure that certain outcomes are favored; only a limited range of outcomes should result.

The legislative "creation-science" logic sketched by McCubbins, Noll, and Weingast is provocative and suggests that substantial congressional control might be induced by strategically crafted structural and procedural means. The claims have been widely cited by supporters of the notion that procedural controls are an effective way to control an agency, especially the regulatory agencies that are frequently the focus of analyses (e.g., Bawn 1995; Hammond and Knott 1996; Hopenhayn and

Lohmann 1996; Lupia and McCubbins 1994; Spulber and Besanko 1992). The impact of the argument on research has been considerable. Several empirical studies, nonetheless, suggest that certain regulatory agencies are able to circumvent the procedures that Congress develops to constrain them (e.g., Balla 1998; Hamilton 1996; Hamilton and Schroeder 1994). One scholar noted that, in the case of the Federal Energy Regulatory Commission, "each time the Congress or the courts imposed a new procedural requirement . . . the agency was able to construe the new requirement narrowly and use its retained substantive discretion to minimize the policy effects of the new procedures" (Spence 1999, 425).

One reason for such findings would seem to be that agencies with different types of structures are affected differently by pressures from their environment (Macey 1992). This fairly straightforward point offers a hint about a more fundamental question: Are administrative agencies themselves really the appropriate units of analysis for investigating the typical control issue?

The entire range of theoretical and empirical explorations referenced in this section is based upon the unexamined assumption that public programs and the discretionary action they trigger during implementation are housed within individual administrative units, which are then (and prospectively) influenced by political principals. Researchers implicitly assume a clear, unequivocal hierarchy and a standard administrative unit as the object of such hierarchical control. The bulk of their analysis then explores how administrative procedures executed by such units can be structured by political actors so as to limit or direct discretion in intended directions. Although scholars of executive and legislative oversight and control differ with each other on a number of particulars, they are alike in specifying the challenge of control as one having to do with influencing administrative units.

Similarly, as chapter 2 demonstrates, researchers in public administration focus on the values undergirding the work of particular administrative units. The arguments, particularly Wamsley's agency perspective, presuppose that a single, cohesive organization is responsible for policy implementation. Very different perspectives, in other words, converge on an assumption about single-agency action. Is this presumption accurate? In empirical terms, what kinds of structures are actually charged with the responsibility for executing policy? Later in this book, particularly in chapters 4 and 5, we explore the subjects of political control and also bureaucratic values in structurally simple and straightforward settings; even there, we show that the standard political-control and benign-bureaucratic-values notions do not resolve empirically the bureaucracy-democracy challenge. First, however, it is valuable to know whether such single-agency assumption covers most of the relevant settings of interest.

STRUCTURES FOR PUBLIC PROGRAMS: AN EMPIRICAL SKETCH

Unlike the literatures reviewed above, the research field of policy implementation has devoted considerable attention to more complex, multiactor structures for program execution (Mazmanian and Sabatier 1989; O'Toole 2000b; see also Kettl 1993). Indeed, the world of policy implementation is populated by a wide variety of arrangements for program execution. Even if one leaves aside the range of institutional variation across administrative units themselves—regulatory commissions, single-headed agencies, government corporations, and the like—any effort to identify the structures for carrying out public tasks is likely to yield a huge range of types. Similarly, the recent literatures on governance (Kettl 2000a, 2002; Lynn, Heinrich, and Hill 2001; Pierre and Peters 2000; Rhodes 1997) and networks (Agranoff and McGuire 2003; Bogason and Toonen 1998; Kickert, Klijn, and Koppenjan 1997; Klijn 1996; Mandell 2001; McGuire 2002; O'Toole 1997b; Provan and Milward 1995) suggest that programs often require arrangements that are not encompassed within individual agencies. What does the empirical evidence actually say about this issue? While the theme has been developed in the literatures of several countries, as these citations suggest, we follow here our own admonition sketched at the beginning of this volume to ground the treatment carefully in the specifics of particular contexts. It is useful in this regard to draw from experience at the U.S. national level in addressing this question.

Hidden Agents

One way to begin to get a sense of the issue is to explore the actual size and scope of hiring undertaken by government or effectively driven by it as part of the requirements to carry out policies. The best systematic recent study of this question is Light's *The True Size of Government* (1999b). Light examines the important phenomenon that policy requirements are often executed by a mass of personnel beyond the direct employ of the federal government. How many? It is impossible to say with any real precision, but Light (38) estimates a "shadow" federal workforce in 1996 of almost 12.7 million personnel beyond the 1.9 million in the federal civilian employ of Washington. (These figures omit more than 850,000 postal workers and the 1.5 million in the military.) The exact figures are impossible to verify, but precision on this point is much less important for present purposes than the general scale of the shadow phenomenon.

Where are these additional millions? They work under contract with the government, indirectly carry out federal policy in their capacities on the receiving end of grants (e.g., to state and local governments) or are involved in executing national mandates via subnational authorities. Light's estimate of the number of contract-created full-time jobs is more than 5.6 million; grant-created work takes up another 2.4 million positions, and state and local mandate-created jobs are estimated at approximately 4.6 million.

The calculations Light undertakes are especially helpful in getting a handle on the notoriously difficult-to-determine impact of national policy requirements on the private sector. Further, he estimates that, aside from the Departments of Energy and Defense, most agencies have been experiencing an increase in contract employees. It is clear from these data that the national government cannot hope to carry out most of its policies without extensive reliance on other governments and other sectors. A wide variety of incentives combine to make it in the narrow interests of nearly all direct stakeholders, including political principals, to impose tight limits on direct federal employment but then to move a huge portion of the public work into the "shadow" government elsewhere. As Light conclusively demonstrates, repeated efforts to determine the precise size of this auxiliary apparatus and just who is doing what for which federal program have gone for naught. Neither Congress nor the president, for instance, has required the data or the analyses needed to answer such basic questions.

Therefore, despite the notion that perhaps contract language frames principal-agent terms clearly enough to eliminate the control issue as it might apply to the shadow government (deck stacking at one remove, so to speak), and despite the occasional complaints from state and local officials about heavy-handed federal intrusion, the chains of agency reaching outward and downward into these varied niches are loose, often poorly documented, and exceedingly important. Clearly, for many programs, substantial amounts of policy-relevant, discretionary decision making have moved out into the nonfederal workforce. The results are multiple. Of particular relevance for the present analysis is what Light calls the "illusion of accountability":

> The shadow of government clearly changes the nature of accountability between government and its agents. In theory, the principal-agent relationship should hold regardless of where the final point of delivery occurs. Principals would give instructions to their agents all the way down the hierarchy, both formal and virtual, thereby assuring faithful execution of the task. In reality, the shadow adds to the mix multiple layers of agents, many of whom have divided loyalties between their government principals . . . and their organizational principals . . .
>
> One does not have to go too far down the accountability chain to find mixed motives, diffused responsibilities, and general confusion about who is accountable to whom. (Light 1999b, 184–85)[3]

3. Even simple principal-agent chains of single principal to single agent, who in turn becomes the principal for a subordinate agent, and so on, create problems of control. See Downs (1967).

Most of the procedural constraints that, for instance, McCubbins, Noll, and Weingast identify as useful in political control over agencies are absent in these shadow-located portions of implementation arrangements. As one prominent example, the Administrative Procedures Act does not apply to private or nonprofit organizations implementing federal policies at the end of a networked chain of relationships. Similarly, reporting requirements are often eased (under the guise of reducing paperwork or other management reforms) or, in the case of federal family-planning programs, disappear completely (McFarlane and Meier 2001). And—crucially—several of the main variants of the "shadow" phenomenon involve heavily voluntaristic transactions rather than compelled ones. Public-private collaboratives and partnerships are self-evidently noncoercive. Intergovernmental programs rarely have sanctions, such as the cutting off of federal funds, for noncompliance among participating units (see, e.g., Derthick 1970; O'Toole 2000a). Furthermore, even contracts are often bundled into "omnibus packages" that combine many activities and objectives into large and longer-term arrangements, with diminished possibilities for control by a lead federal agency. Such larger contracts are increasing rather than diminishing. As Light reports, for instance, the Environmental Protection Agency has moved in this direction with much of its contracted work, in part because of cutbacks in EPA's in-house procurement staff. "The result is fewer but bigger contracts, many of which involve multiple agents bundled together in towering relationships that may displace EPA as an active principal" (185). The standard scholarship on oversight and control has missed these significant aspects of the subject by framing the authoritative federal administrative unit as the relevant unit of analysis.

Some analysts would point out that in certain of these instances, those that are designed primarily as relatively diffuse relational contracts, trying to force the pattern into a narrowly principal-agent mold might also diminish trust among the parties and reduce the likelihood of productive collaboration (Milward 2001; for analytical grounding along with some evidence, see Williamson 1985; 1996; Kettner and Martin 1990; Bennett and Ferlie 1996; Smith 1996; Sclar 2000). Evidence has been developed to suggest that this sort of contractual link may be more common than most specialists in government contracting have realized (Fernandez 2004). If so, an additional conclusion beyond that in the preceding paragraph would be that it could be counterproductive to tighten the contractual leash in many circumstances, even if it were possible to do so.

Complex Structures of Agency

Some of our empirical work bears even more directly on the unit-of-analysis question. In research conducted on this subject, we analyzed federal legislation enacted in two Congresses, as well as regulations flowing from these enactments, to see what kinds of structural arrangements have actually been adopted to carry out new or substantially revised national initiatives. This work is particularly relevant to a consideration of the subject of control and oversight, since formal policy as enacted in law reflects, clearly, the actual choice by political principals, whereas some might argue that at least a portion of the shadowing phenomenon has emerged as a byproduct of various forces rather than by conscious choice of Congress. (Nevertheless, Light's analysis also demonstrates that Congress has abetted the trend for decades.)

We first cover the legislative aspect of formal structuring and then provide information on what happens to such structures during the rule-making phase of policy action. We review the full set of laws passed by two Congresses: the 89th (1965–66) and the 103rd (1993–94); and on the basis of an initial sorting we isolate those statutes that either created new programs or substantially modified existing ones. Both Congresses were controlled by the Democrats during a term of a relatively activist, first-term Democratic president. The statutes creating or significantly modifying public programs, of course, constitute a small minority of the overall totals (97 of 714 laws for the earlier Congress, and 40 of 293 for the later one). We analyzed the statutory language of all laws establishing or influencing the shape of national programs to determine the kinds of structures for implementation explicitly required or encouraged by the formal mandate. In each case of a new or revised program, we recorded information on certain features of the structure, the type of interdependence specified among implementing units, the kind(s) of institutional participants to be involved, and a few other kinds of data (for details, see Hall and O'Toole 2000, 2004). By "structure" we mean not only the creation or reorganization of individual administrative units but also interagency, intergovernmental, and public-private arrangements (or combinations of these). In short, we sought to ascertain whether the structural choices selected by Congress for policy execution were typically single administrative units, which enhance hierarchical control, or more complex arrays—including parts of what Light calls the shadow government, along with options not encompassed by the shadow phenomenon, such as federal interagency collaborations.

Of course, national legislation is only one source of mandates. Executive orders and other formal directives can also be important—and a whole range of other influences can shape the actual institutional arrangements that emerge in operating programs (for a discussion of a number of these, see O'Toole 1997b).[4] But for purposes of determining what arrangements political principals, especially legislative

4. These other influences tend to complicate rather than simplify relationships. As a result, the structural problems addressed in this chapter get more severe as one accounts for the other influences on governmental programs.

TABLE 3.1
Structures for Implementation, as Stipulated by Law

	89th Congress	103rd Congress	Total
Single agency	16.5%	10.0%	14.6%
	(16)	(4)	(20.0)
Multiactor	83.5	90.0	85.4
	(81)	(36)	(117)
Total	100.0	100.0	100.0
	(97)	(40)	(137)

ones, actually design for the execution of national programs, we should start with legislation.

For present purposes, we concentrate on a few of the most relevant findings. What proportion of new or substantively revised programs during these Congresses required or encouraged the involvement of more than one institutional actor during implementation? Table 3.1 displays the answer. An overwhelming majority of programs called for involvement on the part of two or more actors rather than a single administrative unit. A comparison between the two time periods, furthermore, shows that the more complex arrangements are not a new phenomenon.

Examining the various patterns shows that a number of laws stipulated the involvement of more than one federal agency during execution. In the 89th Congress, as table 3.2 indicates, one-third of the cases explicitly involved more than one federal agency; this circumstance increased to 52 percent in the 103rd Congress. These laws involving multiple federal agencies frame program design so that implementation requires participation by individuals ensconced in different organizational cultures, influenced by different sets of incentives, often reporting to different oversight committees in Congress, and directed toward somewhat different organizational objectives. In situations such as these, political principals will have a difficult challenge overseeing or controlling overall performance. Indeed, in the influential argument set forth by McCubbins, Noll, and Weingast (1987), one of the tools they point to as a means of procedural control—crosscutting mandates—can also be seen as one of the kinds of fragmenting mechanisms evident in modern legislation. Evaluating the overall success of environmental or civil rights mandates would require scrutiny of a panoply of different agencies and programs. Similarly, the internal controls of a strong agency culture steeped in a coherent set of values is also diluted in such multiple-agency cases.

Beyond interagency circumstances, what kinds of institutional actors are required or encouraged to be involved in the execution of national programs? Table 3.2 shows the results on this score for 89th and the 103rd Congresses. Clearly, programs with an intergovernmental dimension are extremely common, composing a majority of

TABLE 3.2
Actors Involved in Program Implementation, as Designated by Law

	89th Congress	103rd Congress	Total
Interagency (federal)	34.0%	52.5%	34.9%*
Intergovernmental	52.6	55.0	53.3
Business actors	28.9	27.5	28.5
Nonprofit actors	39.2	10.0	30.7*

*Difference in means significant $p < .05$.

the relevant laws in each of the two-year periods. Indeed, we know that hundreds of intergovernmental grant programs in virtually all policy fields, along with significant numbers of underfunded and unfunded intergovernmental mandates, have been a staple of American administrative policy for decades. In addition, businesses and not-for-profits are important components in some programs, as would be expected given the data on "shadow" government reviewed earlier. Mandated nonprofit involvement in new or revised programs seems actually to have declined between these two Congresses; why that might be the case is not clear. The earlier, Great Society Congress may have been unusual in seeking to avoid the biases of existing administrative agencies (Waldo 1971), or the routine involvement of not-for-profits in recent years may mean that Congress now simply assumes that such units will be part of the picture and thus does not feel compelled to stipulate such links in law. In any event, the data we are examining do not track existing programs or established involvement by other parties in program implementation; table 3.2 displays only mandated or explicitly encouraged involvement for new or newly modified programs.

The mere identification of implementing actors is only part of the answer to the structural question, for the data reported thus far say nothing about just how multiple actors must deal with each other while executing public policy. For instance, if two federal agencies are required to play a role in the implementation of a given program but each is able to do its own compartmentalized task without coordinating with the other unit, political principals could direct and constrain the actions of each independently, even if overall program success requires both to perform. The separate agencies might also be able to infuse their own actions with values without having to cope with the potentially contrary value-bases of other units. On the other hand, if the product of implementation action is to be some kind of jointly produced output that calls for interunit coordination, it would be much more difficult for political principals or agency managers to control or oversee such combined production. We coded the sample of legislation, therefore, to reflect the distinction between the former case (called "pooled interdependence," after Thompson 1967) and two

TABLE 3.3
Relationships between or among Actors

	89th Congress	103rd Congress	Total
Pooled	17.5%	25.0%	19.7%
	(17)	(10)	(27)
Sequential	47.4	32.5	43.1
	(46)	(13)	(59)
Reciprocal	18.6	32.5	22.6
	(18)	(13)	(31)
Single agency	16.5	10.0	14.6
	(16)	(4)	(20)
Total	100.0	100.0	100.0
	(97)	(40)	(137)

types of higher-order interdependence: "sequential" (interunit action is structured as an assembly-line arrangement, with the outputs from one organization serving as the inputs for another) and "reciprocal" (two or more units pose contingencies for each other; see Thompson 1967). Of the multiactor cases in our sample, most reflect the higher-order kinds of interdependence, as table 3.3 shows. The practical implication is that principals are even likelier to experience difficulty constraining the combined actions of organizations involved in executing many programs. Most of these programs seek to induce patterns of collaborative ties rather than to place control over the broader program structure in the hands of an authoritative actor (note also the argument of Miller 2000, who indicates that even bureaucratic managers can see only total outputs rather than individual ones). Instances of reciprocal interdependence in particular would seem most clearly to involve joint production without much prospect of unilateral control by any particular actor.

In short, these findings confirm from a somewhat different perspective the general theme developed by Light concerning the true size and shape of government. While national administrative agencies serve as the institutional "home base" for federal bureaucrats, and while a number of programs are indeed housed within the structural boundaries of individual agencies, a great many programs cross boundaries, involve other actors, bridge governments and sectors, and rely at least partially on voluntary commitments rather than coercion as a stimulus to concert efforts. Further, the collaborative links frequently signal complex production processes that are likely to be difficult to monitor and control from outside—or, indeed, from the inside of any one of the units. Agencies, in other words, are not the modal agents of governance, at least when considering national public programs and their execution; nor are they independent and autonomous value-grounded actors. They are bound by legislation, and likely by other means as well, to each other and to additional actors as they perform their tasks.

Structural Adjustments during Administrative Rule Making

The law is not the last word about structural arrangements for the execution of public policy. While legislation can stipulate institutional ties, the law is often simply unclear on important issues. Similarly, the agency may find it necessary to formally include new actors in the implementation process to ensure that all the actors needed to implement the program effectively are allowed to participate. The reasons could be technical, political, or both. Adjustments accomplished by agencies through the rule-making process can be given the force of law. Whether and how rule making supplements the structural arrangements stipulated in legislation, therefore, is worth examining. Again, we restrict ourselves to the U.S. national government.

Agencies issue rules on an ongoing basis; more than four thousand rules are produced annually, and these fill, on average, more than fifteen thousand pages in the *Federal Register* (Kerwin 2003). Substantive rules have the force of law and are binding on both the agency and on regulatory targets. They must be issued in accord with stipulated procedures, such as those prescribed by the Administrative Procedures Act. Other rules explain to regulatory targets how to interpret an existing law or regulation. A law or extant body of regulations may be dense and difficult to understand, especially in light of changes in circumstances over time. An interpretive rule explains how the law or rules should be understood in the new environment. Procedural rules are issued to define an organization and its processes. These rules can clarify for the public the roles of different actors within an agency, and they can set forth how the public can interact with the agency.

Despite their importance, the impact of rules on administrative structure has rarely been explored systematically by researchers. Of particular interest for our purposes is the fact that rules often clarify the primary target of the law as well as those who are to be involved in the implementation process. For example, the law creating the National Voter Registration Act (NVRA) places certain burdens on "the state"; the rules for implementing the NVRA, on the other hand, define the specific actor at the state level who is responsible for implementing the law. Regulations may also add actors to the process by specifying that certain types of participants—corporations, nonprofits, and specific governmental actors not named in the law—be a part of the implementation network. Rules also clarify what specific terms mean, and such elaborations help to elucidate participation in the implementation process. For example, the rule issued to implement the Family and Medical Leave Act specifies what it means to be a health care provider, a parent, an employee, and an employer. Such clarifications clearly help to determine the shape of the institutional arrangements for implementation.

In short, rule making helps to define when networked patterns are employed during implementation, as well as the shape of those patterns. How might we expect structural arrangements sketched in legislation to be adjusted in the process of agency rule making? In particular, how might we expect the number and kinds of actors structured into program operations to be shifted, and in what ways are these likely to be linked—or to have their interunit arrangements shifted—via rule making? We expect that structures stipulated in rule making are likely to call for larger numbers of networked actors, or at least the number of types of networked actors, than does legislation; and that more demanding forms of interdependence among multiparty arrangements are also likely to be established (for detailed rationale, see Hall and O'Toole 2004). Formerly excluded actors are apt to press for inclusion during rule making, and organizations or types of organizations formally included in legislation have an incentive to push for a more ongoing, mutual relationship with the other unit(s). In short, we would expect to find some of the "simple" (single-agency) implementation arrangements rendered more complex as a result of rule making. In addition, we expect some of the more complex cases will become further complicated through the rule-making process, with more parties or types of parties stipulated in the rules adopted than were identified in legislation.

What does the evidence show? We examined all regulations adopted in support of the 137 laws referenced above and analyzed their content to record many of the same factors as had been done in the earlier analysis of legislation. Using the *Code of Federal Regulations*, we began by noting details about each regulation, including who issued it, what type it is, and who the target is. The rules were also coded for all actors explicitly required or encouraged to be involved in implementation, including federal agencies, state or local governments, businesses, not-for-profits, Native American tribes, and international actors (e.g., secretariats of international organizations). For those cases involving multiple institutional actors, we also sought information on how much these parties were required by regulation to rely on or coordinate with one another during implementation.

Of the 137 laws considered in the earlier work, 97, or 71 percent of the total, involved the subsequent development of rules to elaborate and clarify the policy sketched in legislation (see table 3.4). Rule making was somewhat more likely for policies developed in the 89th Congress (75.3%) than for those passed in the 103rd Congress (60%). The incidence of rule making, however, does not much vary by whether the law specifies a single-agency implementation arrangement or a multiactor structure.

Each row of table 3.5 shows the implementation structure created by law. Following rule making, each program retained *at least* the same level of structural complexity as stipulated in law; for example, the regulatory process did not restruc-

TABLE 3.4
Rules Issued to Modify New Programs, 89th and 103rd Congresses

	89th Congress	103rd Congress	Total
Yes	75.3%	60.0%	70.8%
	(73)	(24)	(97)
No	24.7	40.0	29.2
	(24)	(16)	(40)
Total	100.0	100.0	100.0
	(97)	(40)	(137)

ture formerly reciprocal arrangements into a pooled variant. Each column shows the types of implementation structures that were added to those already established in law. The data show that the regulatory process often crafts new, more complex interactions. For example, twenty-one of the laws in the earlier data set contained language suggesting, in effect, a pattern of pooled interdependence for the multiactor units involved in implementation. In two-thirds of these cases, the rule-making process created more complicated, reciprocal implementation links than were provided for in the law. For instance, in some cases an agency rendered the ongoing interactions between it and regulatory targets more complex by adding a process of negotiation or review to an ostensibly unilateral link as established in the law. Similarly, thirty-one of the laws created reciprocal implementation structures and twenty-two laws were subject to the rule-making process. In 54.5 percent of these cases, the rules either reinforced the reciprocal implementation structures already created by law or added new reciprocal links. Thus, even complicated cases were subject to increased complexity through the rule-making process.

The rule-making process can also lead to actors being added to the implementation networks stipulated in law. Table 3.6 shows that despite the strong multiactor tilt given

TABLE 3.5
New Complexities Added to the Implementation Process through Rule Making

Structure established in law	Additional links established via rules				
	Pooled	Sequential	Reciprocal	Intra-agency	Total
Pooled	14.3%	9.5%	66.7%	9.5%	100.0
	(3)	(2)	(14)	(2)	(21)
Sequential	19.5	7.3	63.4	9.8	100.0
	(8)	(3)	(26)	(4)	(41)
Reciprocal	28.6	14.3	52.4	4.8	100.0
	(6)	(3)	(11)	(1)	(?1)
Intra-agency	42.9	0.0	57.1	0.0	100.0
	(6)	(0)	(8)	(0)	(14)
Total	23.7	8.2	60.8	7.1	100.0
	(23)	(8)	(59)	(7)	(97)

TABLE 3.6
Actors Added to the Implementation Process through Rule Making

Actors	89th Congress			103rd Congress			Total	
	In law	By rules	Total	In law	By rules	Total	Before rules	After rules
Intergovernmental	52.6	15.5	68.1	55.0	10.0	65.0	53.3	67.2
Business	28.9	12.4	41.3	27.5	10.0	37.5	28.5	40.2
Nonprofit	39.2	4.1	43.3	10.0	5.0	15.0	30.7	35.0

to implementation arrangements in legislation itself, the rule-making process adds additional parties to the implementation arrays of a number of programs. There are no cases of actors who had been included during legislation being omitted in the more detailed characterizations in rules, although the roles of actors sometimes shifted. These changes are not dramatic, but they indicate a further complicating of the networked settings for program implementation. Further, they appear during both Congresses.

Agencies craft an implementation process from congressional legislation. Often such efforts entail adding more actors or more elaborate structures than Congress proposed. The end result should be obvious. Rule making adds to the structural complexity of bureaucratic action and exacerbates the control challenge faced by any political principals.

Challenges for Oversight and Control

Logically these complex structures make the basic hierarchical control implied in principal-agent models extremely difficult. Theory and practice often diverge, however. Is there any empirical evidence that such arrangements do indeed render external control and oversight difficult? Anecdotal findings to this effect are frequently reported, but systematic evidence is more difficult to uncover. Still, a careful examination of a series of reports published by the U.S. General Accounting Office (GAO), now renamed the Government Accountability Office, within the last several years provides enlightenment. The reports focus on cases in which two or more federal agencies must work together during implementation. The GAO analyses have been triggered in significant measure by the Government Performance and Results Act (GPRA) (Public Law 103-62).

Among other things, GPRA requires federal agencies to develop performance measures and performance plans, with the goal of measuring policy achievement and improving opportunities for monitoring and effective control. The implicit assumption is the same as that in the research literature on oversight and control: Individual administrative units are the loci of implementation action.

But GAO quickly noted the challenges of effective implementation under the conditions documented earlier in this article, as the following comments, garnished with some of the jargon of the National Performance Review make clear: "An agency's customers are the individuals or organizations that are served by its programs. That is not to say that contact between a federal agency and its customers is always direct. Many federally mandated or federally funded services are dispensed through third parties, such as state agencies, banks, or medical insurance providers. In such cases, federal agencies face the particularly challenging task of balancing the needs of customers, service providers, and other stakeholders, who at times may have differing or even competing goals" (GAO 1996, 15). Relatively early, as well, GAO assessed progress on this front among federal agencies and found uneven execution of GPRA requirements, particularly because some programs are structured in more complex fashions (GAO 1997). In a series of investigations undertaken in recent years, the theme is developed at length and with considerable evidence.

A 1999 study, for instance, concluded that a key weakness in Fiscal Year 2000 performance plans submitted by agencies was their failure to address the coordination of crosscutting programs (GAO 1999a, 3). The agency noted that the 2000 plans constituted an improvement over the preceding year in that the more recent ones included "further identification of crosscutting efforts and more inclusive listing of other agencies with which responsibility for those efforts are shared." Still, "similar to the situation with the 1999 plans, few agencies have attempted the more challenging task of establishing complementary performance goals, mutually reinforcing strategies, and common performance measures, as appropriate" (17).

The GAO offered a similar assessment in considering early efforts to link planning with budgeting, in this case by taking explicit note of the intergovernmental dimension to many programs: "Allocating funding to outcomes presumes that inputs, outputs, and outcomes can be clearly defined and definitionally linked. For some agencies, these linkages are unclear or unknown. For example, agencies that work with state or local governments to achieve performance may have difficulty specifying how each of multiple agencies' funding contributes to an outcome" (GAO 1999b, 32). As is well known, there are hundreds of such programs in place.

Some of the more recent analyses of the GAO frame the issue even more broadly. Although the agency seems to express an almost wistful preference for a clear and straightforward design of principal-agent chains to alleviate the complications (including fragmentation and diffusion of responsibility) inherent in the present arrangement, its studies document the fact that structures for the implementation of programs now routinely extend far beyond individual agencies or even tightly coupled interunit arrays, with consequences for the tractability of the oversight and control problem. "Our work has identified widespread mission fragmentation and program overlap in the federal government," GAO reports. "The broad scope of this fragmentation and overlap—ranging from social programs to defense efforts—indicates the inherent complexity of national problems that the federal government traditionally has addressed in a piecemeal approach" (GAO 2000a, 11; see also table on 12–13).

The GAO documents succinctly some of the results of such an arrangement: "Virtually all of the results that the federal government strives to achieve require the concerted and coordinated efforts of two or more agencies. Yet our work has repeatedly shown that mission fragmentation and program overlap are widespread and that crosscutting federal program efforts are not well coordinated" (GAO 2000b, 19–20).

The institutional arrangements for carrying out national policy, in other words, are typically broader than the individual agency that has served as a focus of research on oversight and control. The descriptor "virtually all" in the last-quoted excerpt may be a modest overstatement—at a minimum it is unsupported by a comprehensive analysis; but as a summary statement from Congress's principal performance and accountability agency, it is telling. The chronic lack of coordination documented by the GAO is evidence that the more complex program arrays cannot be assumed to operate as if in response to a common point of control. Consequences of this state of affairs include difficulties in ensuring concerted action, challenges to effective implementation, and gaps in accountability. Lead agencies themselves face serious limitations in imposing a control regimen where Congress and others have allowed and encouraged the widespread use of more complex arrangements.

The great bulk of such analyses have focused on the external-control aspects of the situation, but the data arrayed in this chapter raise serious questions about the internal-control, or "values," perspective as well. If public programs are typically executed not through solitary bureaus but by a mix of multiple units—across agencies, governments, and often from the private or nonprofit sectors as well—then the "values" mix shaping the discretionary decision making of implementing actors almost certainly becomes more diffuse, plural, and even contradictory, when taken across the full set of organizations involved.[5] Even within the U.S. federal government, there is nothing approaching the old-style British civil service, with its com-

5. Family-planning policy provides a good example of the increase in heterogeneity of the values involved. With the rise of abstinence-only policies, implementing organizations run the gamut from Planned Parenthood, which advocates unrestricted access to abortion services, to the abstinence-only groups, which espouse a right-to-life philosophy. Also included in the mix are the various values possessed by state and local bureaucrats in both welfare and health agencies, as well as the values held by local school districts (which both teach sex education and sometimes participate in contraceptive counseling).

mon socialization and ethos. Rather, different bureaus draw from different pools of talent and interest, and even the employees of individual agencies are more likely these days than ever before to move in and out of government rather than rise slowly in the bureaucracy over a period of years, even decades (Light 1999a). Those expecting some straightforward values-based solution to the bureaucracy-democracy conundrum, therefore, have their perspective seriously challenged by the institutional forms of most public programs—if these national data from the United States represent the universe of administrative arrangements actually operating in government these days.[6]

These observations might seem to amount to mere hand-wringing about complexity or perhaps a nostalgic preference for the good old days. But the data from the 89th Congress at least raise the query as to whether such good old days ever existed, at least in modern times. Furthermore, since there are several important reasons for the continued use of such complexly networked implementation arrays, the most interesting question is likely not to be how to restructure implementation arrangements to reflect principal-agent chains that better resemble the models widely used by scholars, but rather, given the more complex arrangements that have actually emerged, with substantial support by political leaders themselves, How can we understand and perhaps improve the capacity of the governance system to effect the democratic ideal?

CONCLUSION

The scholarly discussion of oversight and control, as well as the usual perspective on democracy emanating from the field of public administration, has assumed a set of institutional arrangements for policy execution that is out of sync with the arrays that have actually been designed and adopted by government. Both assume a single administrative agency with one or more political principals, a situation that is no longer the norm. This is not to say that administrative agencies are like the mastodons of an earlier era. Agencies continue to be an influential presence; they retain substantial legal authority and political weight, and they remain the prime employers of millions of civil servants. Agencies, furthermore, serve as a kind of institutionalized niche for organized interests seeking to press their claims on government over extended periods. In addition, as the next chapter attests, there are

---

6. Actually, we intend to argue in the next chapter that there are simpler, less structurally complicated cases; and we systematically explore the subject in one sample of such cases. Still, the national data presented in this chapter do indicate, at a minimum, how much the usual discussions of external and internal control miss the mark for many important instances.

less networked cases, and in some policy fields these are particularly important. For these reasons and more, single administrative units need to be given weight in both scholarly discourse and policy considerations.

But if most of the effective national governmental agents are not in the federal government's employ; if most national programs are administered by multiple organizations rather than through a single institutional agent; if these more complex networked arrays involve substantial discretion on the part of constituent units in contributing to the potentially collaborative effort; and if the results of such arrangements include real difficulties specifying coordination patterns, designating performance targets, motivating actors toward a unified public purpose, and clarifying mechanisms for accountability and external or internal control, then the investigation of "bureaucracy" and democracy in action needs to take such realities into explicit consideration. The challenge of oversight and control would seem to be more tendentious than most extant research has acknowledged.

This chapter has documented the structural complexities of any efforts to control the bureaucracy by electoral institutions. The next chapter steps back to examine a policy area with a simple structure that should maximize the ability of politics to control bureaucracy. Even in structures that eliminate these structural barriers to political control, however, just considering the role of bureaucratic values reveals how difficult it is for elected institutions to impose their will on bureaucracies.

CHAPTER FOUR

Political Control versus Bureaucratic Values

Representative Bureaucracy and Latino Representation

Chapter 3 provided a detailed examination of the structural barriers to political control over the bureaucracy. The weak basic models used in the political science literature assume a simple principal-agent structure with a modest number of clear relationships. In the United States and other systems, however, programs are frequently implemented in networks of public, private, and nonprofit organizations with no single unit having the ability to coerce others into taking a given action. Political institutions seeking to control such a network, especially a network that is intergovernmental and relies on private and nonprofit organizations at the street level, face a daunting task. Such institutions cannot issue orders, since the legitimacy of such orders is open to question; they can resort to monitoring, but monitoring without some ability to take focused corrective action is of little value. Political institutions can restrict funds or even abolish governmental funding, but neither strategy effectively forces the implementing organizations to do the bidding of political principals. And indeed, political institutions may have no effective recourse to relying on networks of governance, since these may garner more support than do standard-issue administrative agencies and may also be more effective. The arrangement is likely to be one of interdependence between principal and agent(s) rather than a simple one-way street.

In the U.S. situation, the separation of powers at the national level creates additional uncertainty with regard to political institutions and policy objectives, simply because Congress and state legislatures often have goals different from those of the presi-

A subsequent analysis of this issue, with more data, can be found in Meier and O'Toole (forthcoming).

dent (or governor) or those of the courts. Such uncertainty creates further difficulties since the bureaucracy might be asked to do contradictory things, or the bureaucracy itself might be overlooked in the battles between branches of government.

Given the numerous structural barriers to effective external control of bureaucracy in the United States, our strategy of analysis is to select a case that is structurally highly *conducive* to such control. We do so to give the political principals the largest possible potential to demonstrate their influence. In effect, the approach we adopt focuses on the best-case situation as far as the chance for political control is concerned. If political institutions are not unambiguously driving results in this sort of situation, it should be clear that the standard political-control perspective is seriously flawed for virtually all empirical circumstances.

Another reason to adopt this approach has to do with feasibility. Tracing the influence of political institutions in complicated networked settings is an extremely difficult task. Even explaining program results for a very small number of such cases requires a huge commitment of resources and is subject to alternative and equally plausible explanations (e.g., see Provan and Milward 1995; also Pressman and Wildavsky 1984). An urgent but clearly long-term task is to trace the opportunities for and realities of control by popularly elected public authorities of the outputs and outcomes of governance networks (O'Toole 2006). The foregoing analysis indicates that such situations definitely face attenuated principal-agent control (see esp. the review of studies by the GAO in chap. 3), but determining exactly what is or is not possible regarding democratic decision making awaits the accumulation of a great deal of evidence through many careful studies.

All the more problematic is the objective of showing the results for networked contexts by systematic analysis involving large numbers of cases and the use of careful controls. The sheer variety of networked arrays is itself an impediment to rigorous exploration of the causal forces at work. For this reason, as well, it is appropriate to focus on the most straightforwardly simple and controllable kind of case, a strategy that offers the best near-term approach for clarifying the core issues at stake. In particular, for the instances configured to facilitate optimum political control, we are interested in learning whether the preferences of the putative controllers really drive results and also whether the impact of bureaucratic values, to the extent that these are visible in the pattern, is supportive of democratic governance.

The case we select for investigation is local public education organizations, or school districts. School districts do not face the separation-of-powers problems that most other U.S. public bureaucracies do. School districts are generally established as single-purpose governmental units governed by an elected school board that combines both legislative and executive powers in a single body.

School districts are numerous, they constitute a set of crucial governments for delivering results in a salient policy field, and they can also be seen as important institutions for educating citizens in the civic values of democracy. For these reasons, they are an appropriate focus for empirical investigation. The particular sample of school districts to be examined in this chapter are drawn from the state of Texas, a large and diverse context. School districts are hierarchies—that is, they have primary control over the actual education of students. While school superintendents—the top managers of the districts—often engage in networking behavior and schools have relationships with a variety of other organizations (see Meier and O'Toole 2001; O'Toole and Meier 2003), the actual production of education takes place within a single organizational pattern. Within a bureaucracy a good deal of performance is inertial and can be traced to organizational and other forces that change but little from year to year. While a number of such inertial elements are bundled into the bureaucratic unit, one that is especially worth considering is the values held by the bureaucrats and administrators in the organization. As suggested in chapter 2, these values are seldom studied but can be expected to be critical in determining what happens through administrative units.

In this chapter we use the theory of representative bureaucracy rather than principal-agent "theory" because the former provides some advantages in providing an effective empirical test. Despite this focus, all the work fits within the logic of principal-agent relationships simply because it centers the analysis on values and value conflict. Without understanding the values held by the bureaucracy relative to the values held by the political institutions, one cannot determine whether correlations between policy outputs and political actions are the result of political control or simply the result of administrative units doing what they would have done anyway. Because the theory of representative bureaucracy explicitly relies on bureaucratic values, it works well in determining the extent of political control. The theory of representative bureaucracy also provides a way to bridge across agencies so that the empirical results do not apply to just a single agency as it interacts with a single set of political actors. Comparing results for a relatively large number of instances strengthens the findings.

The analysis takes place in several steps. First, we introduce the theory of representative bureaucracy as a way to solve, for purposes of investigation, the values problem in the political-control literature. Second, we provide some background information on our substantive case, Texas school districts. Third, we introduce the data and methods. Fourth, we set up the initial portion of our study to mimic the studies of political control and observe that policy outcomes do correlate with political values. Fifth, we introduce bureaucratic values into the analysis and demonstrate that these values in most cases simply overwhelm the influence of political factors. Finally, we present and analyze a variety of alternative explanations for our findings and show how they cannot adequately explain the evidence provided in this chapter.

SOLVING THE VALUES PROBLEM: REPRESENTATIVE BUREAUCRACY AS AN INTEGRATIVE THEORY

One problem in the political control research conducted thus far is its use of a truncated version of principal-agent theory (see chap. 2; Waterman and Meier 1998). As a result, the literature cannot consistently present falsifiable hypotheses. Even in its most robust form the principal-agent model cannot predict in advance either how a principal will attempt to control an agent (e.g., legislation vs. oversight) or how an agent will respond (compliance, avoidance, outright opposition). Although a variety of theories might be used to flesh out the question of political control over the bureaucracy, we think the most promising is representative bureaucracy.[1] The theory of bureaucratic representation provides an attractive alternative to the principal-agent framework because it can offer predictions about the most crucial question in the political control puzzle: how the bureaucracy would act in the absence of political pressures.

Representation is a process that occurs both in political and bureaucratic institutions (Long 1952). In political institutions representation is often the institution's sine qua non. Legislatures exist to represent the preferences of the public, among other things; as a result, representation is virtually second nature to legislators. Bureaucracies are not considered primarily as representative institutions, yet a long line of scholars have argued that bureaucracies can perform such functions, even

1. The same theoretical implications could be derived via spatial modeling by constructing this problem as one with different ideal points (preferred results) for bureaucracy and legislature, where the legislature stands for all political institutions. In a one-dimensional space, one can denote the ideal point of the bureaucracy with the letter b, the ideal point of the legislature with the letter l, and the current policy with the letter p, as in the following figure:

$$b \qquad p \qquad\qquad l$$

If the distance from b to p is less than the distance from l to p, then one could conclude that the bureaucracy had more influence over (or at least derived greater utility from) current policy than the legislature. Political control might also be established by observing the legislature take some action (e.g., a set of hearings) and then determining if p then moved closer to the legislative ideal point. The model generalizes to a multidimensional space either by assuming all policy dimensions to be relatively equal and thus using Euclidian distances or by weighting the policy dimensions so that the comparison is one of weighted distance. The point is that, in spatial terms, we can conceptualize a test of political control as a sort of tug of war between bureaucratic and political institutions, with the result of the contest providing an indication of which is more influential over a given policy in practice.

if only under limited circumstances (see Keiser et al. 2002; Selden 1997). Historically some agencies, such as the Department of Agriculture or the Department of Veterans' Affairs, were created explicitly to represent a given clientele (Meier 2000; Mosher 1982). Other agencies developed such roles as they implemented policy. Examining the representation process in both a bureaucratic unit and a political institution can provide some leverage on the question of political control, simply because this approach establishes a set of values for each institution.

The representation literature, whether for political institutions or for administrative units, is concerned with the translation of passive representation into active representation. Passive representation occurs when the representative resembles the represented on one or more dimensions (race, ethnicity, political party, social status, etc.). Active representation occurs when the representative acts in the interests of the represented—that is, takes action that the representative thinks will benefit the represented (Mosher 1982; Pitkin 1967).

The theory of representative bureaucracy focuses on this translation of passive to active representation by addressing whether and when a bureaucrat makes decisions that benefit the persons being represented. Representative bureaucracy is a parsimonious theory that considers such questions as when minority bureaucrats are likely to act in ways that benefit minority citizens.[2] A bureaucrat who shares common demographic origins with a citizen is thought also to share values. As a result, if a bureaucracy representative of the public (on all its dimensions) exercises discretion and pursues its own values, it will also pursue the values of the public.[3]

The theory of representative bureaucracy can be reduced to a set of simple premises and assumptions. First, the theory assumes that bureaucrats exercise discretion; after all, if bureaucracy is merely a cipher, then one would not be concerned about whether bureaucrats hold one set of values or another (nor would one care about political control of the bureaucracy). Second, given discretion, the theory assumes that bureaucrats seek to maximize their own policy values within the range of possibilities. This second point does not mean that bureaucrats are unfettered by constraints, only that when facing a choice between option A and option B, they select the alternative that better matches their own values. Values are not limited to economic self-interest,

2. The minority element is not necessary to the theory. Majorities or occupations (e.g., the Departments of Agriculture or Veterans' Affairs) might be involved. See Mosher (1982).

3. This outline of the theory omits numerous complications. Not all individuals in a given bureaucracy have equal power, so aggregate representativeness does not necessarily translate into active representation in important bureaucratic decisions. Agency and professional socialization can also attenuate the passive-active link. These and other issues can be ignored in the analysis that follows. The empirical portion of this chapter focuses on public organizations where discretionary decision making is widely disbursed and on a demographic dimension that is salient to both politicos and bureaucrats, thus affording an appropriate context for an assessment of political vs. bureaucratic control.

as in the budget-maximizing-bureaucrat literature (Niskanen 1971), but include a wide range that could be linked to public policy. Third, values are formed from socialization experiences. Although socialization is a process that continues throughout the life of every individual, the theory of representative bureaucracy holds that social origins continue to play a role—that is, a person's race, ethnicity, gender, social class, and so forth, remain relevant to the values that he or she holds. Not all social origins are likely to matter—only those that become salient in the political process and linked to public policies that the bureaucrat can affect (Keiser et al., 2002; Meier 1993). In the United States this has meant a concern with race, ethnicity, and gender.[4] Finally, the theory holds that a bureaucracy that is descriptively representative (i.e., one that is a microcosm of the polity) is likely to make decisions that are responsive to the needs and interests of the citizens. In the case of race, for example, the theory suggests that black clients will be less disadvantaged if they are served by a bureaucracy that includes black bureaucrats.[5]

Of course, the influences of representativeness in the implementing apparatus are not exclusive, and additional values are likely to be espoused by the bureaucracy—and political institutions—aside from those relevant to represented demographic groups. But comparing the translation of passive into active representation in a bureaucracy with that in a political institution might tell us a great deal about political control. By incorporating some of the values of both institutions, we can determine whether a bureaucracy acts as it does because such actions fit the values of those in the administrative role themselves or whether, alternatively, those in public organizations are being responsive to demands or pressures from political institutions. The answer is directly relevant to any analysis of the bureaucracy-democracy question, but such a direct comparison has not been made by other analysts engaged in the question, either in the political-science or the public-administration community.

The present chapter grapples with the question of political control using the theory of representative bureaucracy within the context of Latino education. Previous literature on legislatures (Espino 2003; Hero and Tolbert 1995; Kerr and Miller 1997; Vigil 1997) and bureaucracies (Hindera 1993; Meier and Stewart 1991; Selden 1997) has examined the ability of Latino legislators and bureaucrats to make decisions that benefit Latinos in general. In both cases passive representation (being a Latino) was associated with active representation (actions that benefit Latino citizens).

4. In other countries the appropriate cleavages might be social class (England), religion (Belgium, Lebanon), or language (Belgium, Canada).
5. The literature indicates that passive representation does not always result in policies that benefit the represented group (see Keiser et al. 2002; Meier and Nicholson-Crotty 2005).

Our specific test here of "politics versus administration" focuses on Latino education in Texas. Designed to address the main limitations illuminated by the review of related literatures (see chaps. 2 and 3), the analysis offers four distinct advantages over the extant research on political control. First, the ethnicity of both elected officials (school board members) and bureaucrats (teachers) can be used to infer values in the respective institutions (a way to tap values that has been used in earlier studies; see Hero and Tolbert 1995; Hindera 1993; Kerr and Miller 1997; Meier and Stewart 1991; Selden 1997). Both political values and bureaucratic values, therefore, are measured on the same metric. This commonality makes such a measure preferable to values measures such as interest group scores or roll call votes, which can be measured only for one institution (see Balla and Wright 2001; Scholz and Wei 1986; Wood 1988). Our approach allows a direct test of which institution is more influential over policy results. Second, schools have multiple goals, and this study exploits that factor by examining eleven different policy measures. Without consideration of the multiple goals of policies, analysts may miss the possibility that bureaucracies could yield to political principals on one policy dimension while resisting on another; for example, a public agency might step up enforcement but simultaneously weaken regulations. Third, the education literature offers a well-developed set of production functions that predict how various inputs lead to specific results. Control variables to ensure that the results are not spurious are therefore readily available, so we can isolate the impacts of representation on results in a way that is not confused by other kinds of influences (resources available to help educate, special difficulties in educating certain groups of students, and so forth). Fourth, the data set we employ contains more than one thousand cases—that is, more than one thousand sets of political principals interacting with a thousand different administrative systems—thus ensuring that the results are not a function of the unique features of a given set of politicians or bureaucrats.

Ideally, we would prefer to examine public organizations that operate in a wide range of policy fields. Finding comparable output indicators in such a situation, however, is probably impossible. By selecting the same types of agency, we improve our measurement at the expense of external validity (generalizability to other kinds of public organizations)—a good tradeoff given that these agencies are extremely diverse even if they are all focused on public education. In short, this study reaches beyond federal regulatory agencies with a sizable number of cases (that is, large-N) test of the relative importance of overhead political control versus the influence of bureaucratic values in shaping multiple policy outputs and outcomes.

DATA AND MEASURES
The Data

The units of analysis are 1,043 public school districts in Texas. Because data on educational results are reported only when at least five students in a district meet the reporting criterion (e.g., at least five Latino students taking an advanced placement [AP] exam), the actual number of cases varies from 988 for student attendance to 158 for pass rates on advanced placement examinations.[6] More general indicators, such as attendance and performance on the required state test, have the most cases; indicators of elite performance such as SAT scores or AP classes have the fewest. All data are for the 1998–99 school year.[7]

Although most studies of political control fail to carefully justify the representativeness of their cases, little will be gained in the study of bureaucracy and democracy without an explicit consideration of organizational characteristics and how they compare to those of other administrative units. School districts, the commonest type of U.S. public bureaucracy, employ more individuals than any other type of government organization. School districts in Texas are highly diverse, as one might expect in a heterogeneous state that contains approximately one out of every fourteen districts in the United States. Districts in the data set cover the gamut from urban to rural, rich to poor, monoracial to multiracial.

School districts are highly professional, decentralized organizations that vest a great deal of discretion in street-level bureaucrats. They fit Wilson's (1989) definition of craft organizations. While such organizations have characteristics that appear to favor bureaucracies in their interactions with politicians (e.g., professional expertise, decentralized structures, a craftlike technology), they are also situated in governance structures that facilitate political control. All districts but one in this study are independent school districts governed by an elected school board.[8] The school board appoints the chief operating officer (the superintendent), establishes the agency budget (and the tax rate), determines such educational policy issues as curriculum, and oversees the operations of the school systems.[9] Because school

6. Technically speaking, there is no universally accepted "pass" or "fail" score for AP tests. Many colleges and universities accept at least partial credit, however, for a student score of three on the conventional five point scale. That shorthand is used in the analysis that follows.

7. The analysis was limited to a single year because school board data were available at the time of analysis only for that single year. Data were cleaned for obvious reporting errors.

8. A dependent school district has a school board appointed by another entity (e.g., the mayor, the city council) and does not have independent taxing powers. Dependent school districts are more likely to exist in large cities in the Northeast and Midwest.

9. Unlike some states that permit voters to act on district budgets, Texas vests this authority fully in the

districts tend to be flat organizations, the principal-agent distance between school board members and teachers actually delivering services is relatively small. The transaction costs entailed by attempting to influence the front-line actors, as a result, should be less than for organizations in which politicians have to penetrate several layers of a hierarchy to influence the appropriate bureaucrats. Earlier research has found that proximity to political overseers enhances control (Chaney and Salzstein 1998; see also Scholz, Twombly, and Headrick 1991; Scholz and Wood 1998); these sorts of local districts, therefore, should be good contexts for picking up political influences. Furthermore, as special districts executing only one type of policy, school districts permit political leaders to pay focused and sustained attention to control and performance in a single policy field without competition from a range of unrelated policy issues.

Finally, no separation-of-powers or structural issues arise to complicate the principal-agent link. Separation-of-powers systems permit legislatures and chief executives to send conflicting signals to the bureaucracy as each institution seeks to further its own policy interests. Such problems mean that political control is more difficult for two reasons. The bureaucracy might play one institution off against the other, thus trying to force the two political bodies to resolve their conflicts before the bureaucracy needs to respond. Alternatively, the bureaucracy might cast its lot with one of the institutions and thus respond (say) to the legislature but not the chief executive (e.g., the EPA during the Reagan administration; see Rohr 1990 for a normative justification for such an exercise of bureaucratic discretion). School systems have only a single governing board, which exercises both legislative and executive powers. The simple structure enhances political control efforts.[10] In short, school districts are not fully representative of the full range of public organizations, but analyzing the relative strength of political and administrative influences on policy outputs and outcomes of such systems offers a reasonable test of the political-control notions.

School districts also deliver services mostly within their own organizations. While they interact with a range of actors in the environment, they have primary control over the education of children. In this sense, school districts are much closer to hierarchies than complex networks, a structural form that facilitates control by political institutions. As indicated earlier, if the typical political-control perspective is likely to be valid anywhere, such standard bureaucratic institutions offer the most likely context for such overhead influence.

---

school board. Voters can play a role in only two cases: school bond referenda and school board elections. Such structures are similar to those that operate in most models of overhead democracy.

10. All other political actors, such as a state legislature or a governor, will have to operate through the school board, which is the formally designated policy maker.

No single study of the relationship between political actors and the bureaucracy is likely to be generalizable to all such relationships, primarily because bureaucracies vary in numerous ways likely to influence these relationships (Meier 2000). While the results of this analysis can be generalized most easily to other school districts and to highly professional, decentralized agencies, the large number of cases, the focus on multiple outcomes, the emphasis on structures that should facilitate political control, and the problems identified in prior research suggest that the findings reported in this chapter should apply more broadly to political-bureaucratic interactions than should those currently available in the literature. In short, school districts may be the optimum situation for a political body to exert control over an administrative unit.

Representation: The Values Surrogate

Any clear and direct comparison of political versus bureaucratic influence on policy outcomes requires that both political and bureaucratic values be measured on the same metric. If we assume, as the empirical literature finds, that both Latino school board members and Latino teachers seek to improve the educational opportunities of Latino students, then the simple percentages of school board members and teaching faculty who are Latino will provide good measures for comparison purposes. No single kind of measure picks up the full preference or effort of political actors to try to achieve an outcome like improved Latino educational performance, but ethnicity itself—the ethnicity of school board members—offers a suitable and perhaps superior alternative to measures employed in earlier studies, which have relied primarily on interest group scores, partisan percentages, or budgetary shifts as proxies for political preference (See Balla and Wright 2000l; Carpenter 1996; Krause 1996; Ringquist 1995; Sholz, Twombly, and Headrick 1991; Sholz and Wei 1986; Wood 1988, 1990). While these measures are not necessarily flawed ways of tapping political preferences, they are also neither theoretically nor empirically superior to ethnicity as a proxy for values. This point holds in particular when the outcomes being examined directly affect clients of the same ethnicity, as they do in this study.

Ethnicity works especially well in studies of public education because Latinos see education as the single most important political issue (Juenke 2005b). Latino ethnicity has been used as a values surrogate for studies of legislatures (Espino 2003; Hero and Tolbert 1995; Kerr and Miller 1997; Vigil 1997) as well as for studies of bureaucracy (Hindera 1993; Meier and Stewart 1991; Selden 1997). The linkage between ethnicity and values is likely to be especially close because our measures of policy results, to be explained shortly, tap how well Latinos perform in school. Although there is some diversity in values among Latinos, most members of this group clearly endorse the value of Latino achievement in education as a clear preference; in particular, Latinos should attend class, do well in school, and go on to college.

Because the variables capturing political and bureaucratic preferences are measured with the same metric, the way we measure the impacts of these (via coefficient sizes; see below) on educational results in a systematic, quantitative study can be directly compared. Here we report on such an analysis. School board ethnicity and school board size were obtained from the Texas Association of School Boards (TASB); because the ethnicity of some school board members was unknown, we made three hundred phone calls to individual districts to supplement the TASB data. The school-board ethnicity data thus provide a measure of support for Latino educational achievement in the districts' political institutions. All other data— including information on bureaucratic values on the same issue (via ethnic representation in the teachers' corps), along with measures of other variables that can influence performance (control variables) and the multiple measures of educational performance—were taken from the Texas Educational Agency (TEA). The average school district in Texas has 8.5 percent Latino board members (with standard deviation, or s, equal to 19.8) and 8.7 percent Latino teachers (s = 18.7).[11] The two measures share approximately 59 percent of their variation; thus, they are related but quite far from perfectly correlated. Therefore, we can indeed check for the impact of each without having to worry that we are actually tapping the other inadvertently.

How might school boards and teachers, respectively, influence the performance of students? This question becomes important because the analysis in this chapter generally focuses on policy outcomes rather than outputs (i.e., on student performance rather than actions of the bureaucracy). School boards can affect student performance by adopting policies that benefit Latinos, such as a comprehensive bilingual program that identifies needs and ensures that all eligible students are served. They might also influence student performance by encouraging administrators to pay attention to the specific needs of Latino students or by providing the political support necessary for program changes. Teachers, the street-level bureaucrats in this research, can influence Latino student performance in several ways. Because Latino teachers are aware of the literature on ethnic differences in learning styles, they might be more willing to adopt a more effective pedagogical technique. Changes in pedagogy might then spread throughout school systems as Latino teachers influence their colleagues by their own practices, so that changes in Anglo teachers' techniques would then also benefit Latino students. Change might even

11. Because the variables have generally the same mean and distribution, a comparison of the slopes yields an indicator of total potential impact in addition to the normal marginal impact.

be informal; Latino teacher influence might be as simple as providing support and encouragement for students having difficulty. Latino teachers might also advocate changes in school practices—for example, more open recruitment of students into advanced classes—that never reach the attention of the school board. Finally, Latino teachers can serve as role models for Latino students (see Keiser et al. 2002; Meier, Polinard, and Wrinkle 1999). In short, Latino school board members and teachers have many channels through which they can exert influence on Latino student performance.

To remain a fair test of political versus bureaucratic influence, this study limits the comparison to these variables. Administrative organizations influence outcomes in a wide variety of ways, and we could easily bias the results by giving the bureaucracy credit for the overall student performance (used as a control, see below), the stability of the system (both inertial aspects and personnel stability, which are basically bureaucratic features), or the level of expertise in the system (see Meier and O'Toole 2001). We ignore these possible bureaucratic influences and effectively create a tough standard on which to compare bureaucratic and political influence.

Dependent Variables

Public organizations have multiple goals (Downs 1967; Simon 1947; Thompson 1967), and school districts are no exception. Even if one ignores the broader educational objectives of creating democratic citizens and focuses solely on student performance, school systems provide numerous programs aimed at a broad range of goals—ensuring attendance, preventing dropouts, mastering basic skills, preparing students for college, and numerous additional objectives. Even though some goals are held in higher regard than others, Latino politicians and bureaucrats are presumably concerned with Latino student performance with respect to all these goals. To provide as complete a view as possible, therefore, we explore eleven different performance indicators for Latino students.

At the low end of the performance scale, students need to attend school and remain in the system until graduation. Three measures tap this part of the performance question: the percentage of Latino students attending class, the percentage of Latino students who drop out of school, and the percentage of Latino students who graduate from high school with their cohort. Of these three measures, attendance is measured with the greatest accuracy and the dropout measure with the least. Dropout data in general are problematic; student populations are highly mobile, and schools may not know if a student has dropped out of school or moved, and they have little incentive to find out.[12] Consequently, we include the measure but incorporate the others as well.

Basic skills test achievement is a moderate-level goal for school districts. Texas administers the Texas Assessment of Academic Skills (TAAS) to students in grades 3 through 8 and as an exit exam. The performance measure we use here is the percentage of Latino students who pass all of the various TAAS tests (e.g., math, reading, writing) at all grade levels. The TAAS score is the most salient of all performance measures. It is a fundamental part of the state accountability system, and results on this test are front page news (see chap. 5).[13]

Within a school system, the quality of education varies from school to school and classroom to classroom. To tap some of this variation in educational quality, we use three indicators: the percentage of Latino students who gain access to advanced classes, the percentage who take advanced placement classes, and the percentage who pass advanced placement exams. AP classes are designed to be college-level classes; students who take these classes and pass the national exam with a grade of 3 or higher can often receive college credit.

For top-end indicators, we include four measures of college preparation. These include the percentage of Latino students who take either the ACT or SAT exam, the average Latino SAT score, the average Latino ACT score, and the percentage of Latino students who score above 1,110 on the SAT or its ACT equivalent. Students who do not take either exam are unlikely to attend college. Texas has large percentages of students who take both the SAT and the ACT, so that results are generally not affected by the performance of a small number of students. The 1,110 criterion has been defined by the state of Texas as indicating potential success in college.

The eleven performance indicators for Latino students are clearly distinct from one another. Of the fifty-five intercorrelations between the indicators, only twenty-six are statistically significant—that is, different from zero. A factor analysis of the eleven indicators, a statistical technique designed to see if these different indicators actually seem to be tapping something in common, revealed four significant factors, with no single factor accounting for more than 30 percent of the variance.[14]

12. There are reasons to be skeptical of the graduation figures also, since they do not include individuals who attain GEDs, nor do they include students who take an extra year or two to graduate.

13. In 2003 the TAAS exam was replaced by the TAKS exam. Whether the two exams are comparable is an empirical question. Prior changes in exams did influence overall pass rates, but the results were strongly correlated across the exams; that is, the average pass rates rose or fell, but the relative ranking of the school districts remained stable. The correlation between the two exams is approximately the same as the year-to-year correlation of the TAAS.

14. The factor scores are not useful for analysis given that the details of the analysis entail list-wise deletion of missing values. As a result, the factor analysis is based on less than 20% of the total number of school districts (those with reportable data on every indicator).

Control Variables

Two distinct types of control variables—other influences on performance besides the representational ones that are of most interest to us—are included in the analysis. The first represents general school district performance, and the second includes the standard education production-function controls (Hanushek 1996; Hedges and Greenwald 1996). Because Latinos, especially recent immigrants, face a segmented labor market that discourages them from pursuing many professions, the literature suggests the possibility that the pool of Latino teachers could be more talented than the pool of Anglo or black teachers (Meier, Wrinkle, and Polinard 1999). Other studies argue that nondiscriminatory bureaucracies are more apt to be effective simply because they do not consider nonproductive factors such as race, gender, or ethnicity (Becker 1993). Both arguments indicate that a control for non-Latino student performance might be appropriate, because Latino teachers could be associated with better performance for all students, not just performance by Latino students. For each indicator, therefore, we control for Anglo student performance on the same indicator (i.e., for Latino SAT scores we include Anglo SAT scores in the model). This control requires that Latino teachers or school board members affect Latino students over and above the impact that they might have on Anglo students (see Weiher 2000).

Additional controls can be clustered into two groups: resources and constraints. Bureaucracies cannot influence outcomes without resources. Five resource indicators, all commonly used in education-production functions (i.e., quantitative analyses aimed at explaining the differences in student or school-district performance), are included in all models: average teacher salary, per student instructional spending, class size, average number of years of teacher experience, and percentage of teachers who are not certified (Burtless 1996). Three measures of constraints include the percentage of African American, Latino, and poor students; the last-mentioned is measured by students eligible for free or reduced-price school lunches.

Although the production-function literature specifies directional hypotheses for each control variable, with more resources expected to contribute to results and constraints to suppress results, the actual direction of relationships in this study is not obvious. Because each equation controls for Anglo student performance, these control variables must affect Latino performance over and above their impact on Anglo performance. For teachers' salaries to matter, therefore, better-paid teachers would need to benefit Latino students more than they benefit Anglo students. While there is a modest literature on differential impacts (Jencks and Phillips 1998), it indicates little consistency in regard to expectations. The controls should be viewed merely as an effort to make sure key factors are not left out of the model rather than to estimate precise impacts for each control variable.[15]

FINDINGS

Our logic of analysis is, first, to illustrate the influence of political factors on bureaucratic performance without any consideration of bureaucracy (see chap. 2)—thus, in effect, replicating the typical approach taken in most work on political control—and then to add the bureaucracy variable, and finally to consider the influence of political appointees. We do so to illustrate why we believe the literature has found a substantial number of positive results and then to argue why those results might be less convincing than they have appeared.

The Case for Political "Control"

Political influence over the bureaucracy, some even suggest political control, is commonly demonstrated by showing that variables representing political factors are correlated with bureaucratic outputs or outcomes. To mimic this argument, eleven regressions were run with the full set of control variables and Latino school board membership as the political variable (the bureaucratic variable was not included). Multiple regression is a key technique to employ at this point in the book, and also in the chapter that follows this one, because we are moving here from *descriptive* analyses, which provided the primary focus in chapter 3, to an effort to explain results *causally*. This form of analysis allows us to isolate the impacts of the variables of interest, for a properly specified model, while controlling for the others that can be expected to contribute to the results. Here, of course, the variables of interest are the impacts of political and bureaucratic actors. The results appear in tables 4.1 and 4.2.

The findings for this analytical step suggest a fair amount of political influence on policy outcomes generated by the bureaucracy. Seven of the eleven relationships are statistically significant and in the predicted direction. Greater Latino school board representation is associated with more Latino students passing the TAAS, attending school, taking advanced classes, taking AP classes, and taking college board tests. Latino representation is also positively related to Latino SAT scores and negatively related to the Latino dropout rate. For Latino AP pass rates, ACT scores,

15. Similarly, we are not concerned with collinearity among the control variables. This statistical point matters in efforts to estimate the impact of these other variables, but it does not bias or impact the results for the variables of concern to this study.

TABLE 4.1

Political Influence on the Bureaucracy, without Considering the Bureaucracy

	Dependent variables: Percentage of Latino students who					
Independent variables	Pass test	Attend daily	Drop out	Take advanced classes	Take AP	Pass AP
Political Control						
Latino board (%)	.052*	.005*	−.006*	.031#	.056*	−.056
	(2.10)	(1.97)	(1.89)	(1.62)	(2.64)	(0.68)
Controls						
Anglo performance	.756	.587	.417	.545	.344	.594
	(15.44)	(13.88)	(10.28)	(18.58)	(10.15)	(7.74)
Teacher salary (000)	.636	−.003	−.028	.170	.428	1.405
	(2.72)	(0.14)	(0.99)	(0.96)	(1.61)	(1.23)
Instructional $ (000)	.604	.147	−.163	−.121	−.289	−.422
	(0.75)	(1.85)	(1.71)	(0.19)	(0.20)	(0.06)
Black students (%)	−.137	−.007	.017	−.077	−.132	−.048
	(3.57)	(1.89)	(3.98)	(2.91)	(3.42)	(0.26)
Latino students (%)	−.168	−.018	.020	−.043	−.133	−.074
	(6.05)	(6.83)	(6.07)	(2.00)	(4.10)	(0.49)
Low-income students (%)	.048	.017	−.008	.002	.060	−.095
	(1.43)	(5.20)	(1.93)	(0.07)	(1.57)	(0.55)
Class size	−.053	.002	.058	−.090	−.596	2.089
	(0.19)	(0.07)	(1.79)	(0.40)	(1.54)	(1.12)
Teacher experience	−.102	−.010	.057	−.217	−.369	−2.393
	(0.48)	(0.47)	(2.19)	(1.35)	(1.47)	(2.00)
Noncertified teachers	.049	−.006	.009	−.001	.025	.539
	(0.61)	(0.80)	(0.96)	(0.01)	(0.21)	(1.08)
Adjusted R-squared	.29	.28	.22	.32	.33	.52
Standard error	10.11	1.05	1.22	7.32	6.31	17.04
F	38.50	37.62	26.64	40.93	18.15	18.17
N	934	988	929	851	350	158

Note: Directional t-tests are not appropriate for the control variables. Critical values are 1.96 for $p < .05$ and 1.65 for $p < .10$.
  *$p < .05$ one-tailed test.
  #$p < .10$ one-tailed test.

students who score above 1,110 on the SAT, and high school graduation rates, the coefficients are not significantly different from zero. While some of the relationships are small, expecting massive impacts from political forces is unrealistic given that most of the indicators are policy outcomes rather than policy outputs.[16] That is, these results are not, for the most part, measures of what the bureaucracy does (an exception might be advanced classes and AP classes) but are measures of actual changes in Latino student performance. Such a set of findings, given the difficulty in influencing such factors (Burtless 1996; Jencks and Phillips 1998), would be considered optimistic in the education policy literature and supportive in the political-control literature.

16. The long-run impacts, however, might be substantial, given that these are highly autoregressive (i.e., inertial) systems. Our cross-sectional research design cannot tap this aspect of influence.

TABLE 4.2
Political Influence on the Bureaucracy II, without Considering the Bureaucracy

Independent variables	Take test	Score above 1,110	Graduate	SAT Score	ACT Score
	Dependent variables: Percentage of Latino students who				
Political Control					
Latino board (%)	.233*	.019	.025	.299#	.002
	(4.20)	(0.63)	(0.94)	(1.30)	(0.48)
Controls					
Anglo performance	.415	.173	.811	.533	.217
	(7.58)	(3.96)	(43.98)	(8.24)	(3.16)
Teacher salary (000)	−.207	.422	.260	−.320	.005
	(0.34)	(1.21)	(1.03)	(0.13)	(0.08)
Instructional $ (000)	6.420	−.622	−1.200	−.012	−.050
	(2.10)	(0.33)	(1.11)	(0.75)	(0.16)
Black students (%)	−.102	.123	−.045	.783	.002
	(1.15)	(2.21)	(1.13)	(2.00)	(0.14)
Latino students (%)	−.058	.028	−.023	.226	−.001
	(0.73)	(0.59)	(0.66)	(0.77)	(0.12)
Low-income students (%)	−.152	−.227	−.011	−1.449	−.041
	(1.64)	(4.08)	(0.29)	(3.57)	(4.52)
Class size	1.756	.540	−.483	1.289	.101
	(2.09)	(1.01)	(1.44)	(0.33)	(1.19)
Teacher experience	−.056	−.386	−.409	−.414	−.026
	(0.11)	(1.15)	(1.68)	(0.15)	(0.45)
Noncertified teachers	−.417	.177	.027	−.997	−.004
	(1.66)	(1.10)	(0.27)	(0.80)	(0.15)
Adjusted R-squared	.20	.29	.79	.44	.40
Standard error	16.72	8.88	8.38	52.08	1.24
F	13.02	15.88	199.43	20.26	19.70
N	490	360	538	248	284

Note: Directional t-tests are not appropriate for the control variables. Critical values are 1.96 for $p < .05$ and 1.65 for $p < .10$.
*$p < .05$ one-tailed test.
#$p < .10$ one-tailed test.

These findings merit additional discussion within the context of that research literature. The results reported in that literature are not massive—that is, one does not find frequent 180-degree shifts in agency outputs.[17] The influences are primarily incremental in size (although not in direction) and often die out over a period of time (Wood and Waterman 1994). Given this context, finding significant political relationships for several hundred agencies using eleven different policy measures that are not easy for policy makers to manipulate would be considered a substantively significant and important finding in the literature on political control.

17. The exception might be the large changes in agriculture and agricultural debt (see Meier, Wrinkle, and Polinard 1995, 1999). There are qualitative cases of large changes associated most frequently with legislation, such as passing welfare reform in the 1990s or the effort to move to a market-based farm system in the 1970s.

The Limits of Political Influence

As is traditional, tables 4.1 and 4.2 have been interpreted as supportive of claims about political control over the bureaucracy. In past studies, these findings would have served as evidence that political principals had exerted influence over the bureaucracy to act in a way that it would not have in the absence of oversight. Fortunately, the current data set permits us to test this assertion by directly measuring bureaucratic preferences. Table 4.3 reports abbreviated results of models *adding the percentage of Latino teachers* to each regression in tables 4.1 and 4.2. The results are stunning. The number of significant relationships for school board members drops from seven to two (taking AP classes and taking the college boards). In contrast, eight of eleven relationships for Latino teachers are statistically significant in the predicted direction. What appears to be political control in tables 4.1 and 4.2 now appears simply to be politicians and bureaucrats holding similar values.

This general summary of statistical comparisons might actually underestimate the contrast between the two lines of influence. Several points support such an interpretation. First, the significant *political* influences in table 4.3 have to do with students taking either advanced placement classes or one of the college board tests; no political influence is evident on how well students perform in class or on these tests, thus suggesting that such indicators could be symbolic and may have little substantive meaning. Given the ability of administrative agencies to manipulate symbolic outputs for political principals (see Bohte and Meier 2000, and chap. 5), these influences by school board members might be ephemeral. In contrast, the bureaucratic influences appear across a wide range of indicators, some more symbolic but others more substantive.

Second, in cases in which both institutions influence the outcomes, the relative size of the bureaucratic influence is far larger; this is clear if one compares the coefficients, which are measures of the degree of impact. By measuring Latino school board representation and Latino teacher representation on the same metric, we can conclude that Latino teachers have twice the impact on Latino students taking college boards and three times the impact on Latino students taking AP classes than Latino school board members do. Even comparing the bureaucratic slopes in table 4.3 to the political slopes (coefficients) in tables 4.1 and 4.2 consistently gives bureaucracy the edge. That is, if all the joint variation accounted for by politics and bureaucracy is assigned to politics (tables 4.1 and 4.2)—and it should not be—the degree of bureaucratic influence (table 4.3) is still larger.

Third, the bureaucratic (i.e., teacher) relationships are supported by a more convincing causal theory than are the school board relationships (see Lynn, Heinrich,

TABLE 4.3
Bureaucratic and Political Impacts

Dependent variables	Political impact		Bureaucratic impact		Adjusted	
	Slope	t	Slope	t	R^2	N
Latino TAAS pass rate	.015	0.56	.106	2.95*	.29	935
Latino attendance	−.003	1.20	.024	6.74*	.30	988
Latino dropout rate	−.002	0.69	−.011	2.53*	.23	929
Advanced classes rate	.002	0.10	.088	3.19*	.33	851
Taking AP classes	.033	1.49#	.103	3.14*	.35	350
Passing AP exams	−.089	0.96	.109	0.79	.52	158
College test rate	.161	2.78*	.315	3.86*	.22	490
SAT scores	.173	0.71	.552	1.47#	.44	248
ACT scores	.003	0.57	−.003	0.33	.40	284
Above 1,110	−.002	0.06	.085	1.84*	.30	360
Graduation rate	.014	0.36	.021	0.73	.79	538

Note: All equations control for Anglo performance on the same indicator, % state aid, teachers' salaries, % black students, % Latino students, class size, teacher experience, and % noncertified teachers.
*$p < .05$ one-tailed test.
#$p < .10$ one-tailed test.

and Hill 2001 on the importance of causal linkages). School board influence on taking AP classes would almost certainly have to be indirect, by either advocating more funds for such classes or perhaps serving as role models. For the most part, school board members do not come into direct contact with students. Teachers, on the other hand, interact with students on a daily basis. Latino teachers can influence Latino student performance by (1) adopting more effective pedagogical techniques, (2) providing support and encouragement for students having difficulty, (3) advocating changes in school policies, many of which never reach the school board, (4) simply serving as a role model, or (5) influencing non-Latino teachers to change their instructional approaches.

One other aspect of table 4.3 merits discussion: the relationship between Latino school board representation and Latino teacher representation. Advocates of political control might contend that political control is so complete that even the values of professional bureaucrats are determined by political activity (see Wood and Anderson 1993). In the present case, they might contend that school boards determine who is hired as teachers; therefore, Latino board members hire Latino teachers and should get credit for those relationships as well.[18]

Three flaws mar this argument. First, the strong influence of teachers is apparent over and above any shared influence with school board members, that is, the unique

18. In fact, school board members do not hire teachers. Teachers are hired by administrators: the superintendent, in very small districts, and principals or specialized personnel units in larger districts. School board members only hire one person directly, the superintendent. They might influence some aspects of hiring, but they do not do the actual hiring.

teacher variance has far more influence than the variance shared with school board members. Second, *even in districts without Latino school board members, Latino teachers are associated with better Latino student performance.* Checking for bureaucratic influence in this subset of districts is a nice way of isolating the bureaucratic representational impact. Table 4.4 presents the teacher representation coefficients for only those districts without Latino representation on the school board. If teachers are not the key causal factor here, then one would expect that Latino teachers would have no influence on student performance unless supported by political representation. Table 4.4 provides clear evidence to the contrary. Again, eight of the eleven relationships for Latino teachers are significant, even in those districts with no Latinos on the school board (roughly three-fourths of the total districts). Third, the political-control argument assumes that the direction of causality between Latino political representation and Latino bureaucratic representation is solely top down—that is, political representation affects bureaucratic representation but not vice versa. Despite the common nature of this assumption in the urban politics literature (see Eisinger 1982; Mladenka 1989), the only systematic across-time study to examine these relationships (using Granger causality methods) concluded that the relationships were reciprocal (Meier and Smith 1994; see also Krause 1996). Some of the impact of the shared variance, as a result, is also a function of teacher influence.

An advocate of political control might still challenge these findings by arguing that the values of school board members, even Anglo members, might be the reason why some school districts have more Latino teachers and more favorable policies than others. Although measuring such a hypothetical attitude unrelated to ethnicity would require a massive survey, one can construct surrogates for such a policy orientation. Presumably school boards favorably disposed to hiring Latino teachers would also be favorably predisposed to hiring Latino administrators. To probe this possibility, we included a measure of Latino administrators in the equations in table 4.3 and present those results in table 4.5. Before examining those results, we should note that using Latino board members, administrators, and teachers in the same equation creates a great deal of collinearity (teachers, e.g., share 70% of their variance with the other two measures). This degree of collinearity creates a fairly difficult test for Latino teachers to remain statistically significant in such an analysis.[19] As table 4.5 demonstrates, the results were essentially the same. Latino teachers are

19. Where collinearity is high, it is more difficult to reach levels of statistical significance. The point can be put differently: the answer to the question of whether there are actual impacts of collinear variables is more difficult to determine through multiple regression than would be the case if the variables were not highly correlated with one another.

TABLE 4.4
Bureaucratic Influence without Political Representation: Districts with
No Latinos on School Board

Dependent variables	Bureaucratic impact		Adjusted	
	Slope	t	R^2	N
Latino TAAS pass rate	.104	1.59#	.27	690
Latino attendance	.023	3.56*	.27	738
Latino dropout rate	−.011	1.46#	.20	684
Advanced classes rate	.159	3.04*	.27	619
Taking AP classes	.187	2.74*	.33	210
Passing AP exams	−.044	0.13	.54	72
College test rate	.503	2.94*	.20	302
SAT scores	.155	0.17	.46	136
ACT scores	.032	1.60#	.34	141
Above 1,110	.211	1.71*	.29	188
Graduation rate	−.044	0.58	.77	340

Note: All equations control for Anglo performance on the same indicator, % state aid, teachers' salaries, % black students, % Latino students, class size, teacher experience, and % noncertified teachers.
   *$p < .05$ one-tailed test.
   #$p < .10$ one-tailed test.

no longer significantly related to taking AP classes, but they gain a significant impact on the percentage of Latino students who pass AP exams. These findings hold even though political forces are being given all the credit for the percentage of Latino administrators, which in reality is a bureaucratic variable.

We made a second attempt to measure policy actions favorable to Latino students. Bilingual education is a program that is strongly identified as linked to Latino students. A school board that holds positive attitudes about Latino student achievement is likely to respond by providing more adequate funding for such a program. To tap this attitude we regressed expenditures on bilingual education on the percentage of Latino students who were diagnosed as having "limited English" and the percentage who were foreign born. One would expect that most of the spending on bilingual education would be driven by the latter two variables for any given school district. Districts that spend more than would be expected by this calculation would then indicate governance systems in which there is a higher than typical level of advocacy for the needs and interests of Latinos. In a regression analysis, cases above the calculated line have what is termed a positive residual. Positive residuals in this equation, therefore, should indicate a preference for spending money to aid Latino students. This measure, when used in the equations of table 4.3, had no impact whatsoever on the results, as table 4.6 clearly demonstrates. In short, using ethnicity as our values surrogate for this set of analyses does not seem to have inadvertently omitted tapping similar values among others.

Do Political Appointees Matter?

A common conclusion of the political-control literature is that political appointees are a key way to control the bureaucracy. Wood and Waterman (1994) show that specific political appointees were associated with significant shifts in the rate of bureaucratic enforcement during the Reagan administration. Perhaps the key factor in control of school districts might be the appointees.

School boards generally have only a single political appointment, the superintendent. Despite the limited number of appointments, the superintendent is conceded

TABLE 4.5
Teacher Influence and Percentage of Latino Administrators

Dependent variable	Political Slope	Political t	Bureaucratic Slope	Bureaucratic t	Administrative Slope	Administrative t	Adjusted R^2	N
TAAS pass rate	.016	0.57	.120	2.38*	−.013	0.39	.30	935
Attendance	−.004	1.26	.024	6.81*	.018	1.23	.31	988
Dropouts	−.002	0.70	−.013	2.04*	.002	0.38	.23	929
Advanced classes	.003	0.12	.074	1.89*	.013	0.48	.34	851
Taking AP classes	.019	1.13	.000	0.01*	.039	1.64#	.44	682
Passing AP exams	−.088	0.94	.290	1.44#	−.195	1.24	.56	158
College test rate	.162	2.81*	.403	3.21*	−.083	0.92	.24	490
SAT scores	.168	0.69	.734	1.52#	−.242	0.65	.47	248
ACT scores	.003	0.63	.009	0.83	−.011	1.38	.42	284
Above 1,110	−.001	0.04	.126	1.75*	−.040	0.74	.32	360
Graduation rate	.021	0.73	−.015	0.24	.028	0.63	.79	538

Note: All equations control for Anglo performance on the same indicator, % state aid, teachers' salaries, % black students, % Latino students, class size, teacher experience, and % noncertified teachers.
   *$p < .05$ one-tailed test.
   #$p < .10$ one-tailed test.

TABLE 4.6
Representativeness of Teachers Controlling Bilingual Education Variable

Dependent variable	Political Slope	Political t	Bureaucratic Slope	Bureaucratic t	Bilingual Slope	Bilingual t	Adjusted R^2	N
TAAS pass rate	.019	0.70	.100	2.77*	−.418	2.85*	.31	935
Attendance	−.004	1.26	.024	6.81*	.018	1.23	.31	988
Dropouts	−.003	0.79	−.010	2.38*	.031	1.75*	.23	929
Advanced classes	.004	0.20	.084	3.04*	−.243	2.24*	.34	851
Taking AP classes	.018	1.09	.037	1.66*	−.142	1.57#	.44	682
Passing AP exams	−.091	0.98	.098	0.71	−.552	1.41#	.56	158
College test rate	.166	2.87*	.302	3.69*	−.506	1.60	.24	490
SAT scores	.174	0.71	.548	1.46#	−.760	0.67	.47	248
ACT scores	.003	0.58	−.002	0.36	.016	0.57	.42	284
Above 1,110	−.002	0.07	.086	1.86*	.059	0.33	.32	360
Graduation rate	.021	0.73	.016	0.40	.083	0.52	.79	538

Note: All equations control for Anglo performance on the same indicator, % state aid, teachers' salaries, % black students, % Latino students, class size, teacher experience, and % noncertified teachers.
   *$p < .05$ one-tailed test.
   #$p < .10$ one-tailed test.

to be a major influence on school district policies, procedures, and possibly outputs (Zeigler, Kehoe, and Reisman 1985). The relative power of the superintendent in Texas districts and in most others substantially exceeds that of most federal political appointees. Merit-system protections that make it difficult to move civil servants from policy-making positions are not in force for superintendents. Central office policy personnel and, in many districts, school principals can be replaced at will. The labor unions that some believe dominate school policy (Moe 2002; but see Hess 1999) are weak to nonexistent in Texas.

School superintendents also have greater advantages in overcoming the information asymmetries relative to the bureaucracy. Unlike most political appointees who have little experience managing complex bureaucracies (Durant 1993; Ingraham 1995) or modest substantive expertise, school superintendents are trained specialists who, in this sample, averaged twenty-four years of administrative experience in education and seven years in their current job (compared to the average tenure of eighteen months for federal political appointees). Superintendents, as a result, know a considerable amount about what goes on in schools and classrooms.

Given the relative advantages of school superintendents, therefore, we might expect Latino school superintendents to be the key missing link in the principal-agent puzzle. Of the districts in our study, sixty-six were led by Latino superintendents. A dummy variable (a variable that has only two possible values, yes or no) indicating the presence or absence of a Latino superintendent was added to the models in table 4.3 to provide a relative comparison of the influence of bureaucrats, political appointees, and politicians.

The results in table 4.7 provide little support for the idea that political appointees are a major factor in shaping bureaucratic actions.[20] Only in the symbolic realm of generating more Latino AP enrollments does the presence of a Latino superintendent matter, and that impact is relatively modest (the large coefficients reflect the dummy variable coding). In a second case, SAT scores, the regression coefficient is statistically significant and in the wrong direction. If anything, the influence of the superintendent on these variables appears to matter less than the influence of the school board. In both cases, influence can be characterized as modest at best.

Adding superintendents has little impact on the evidence regarding bureaucratic influence. All eight relationships remain significant, and the magnitudes of the coefficients in table 4.7 are similar to the respective coefficients in table 4.3. The inclu-

<hr />

20. The limited impact of superintendents in the representational function contrasts with their substantial impact in managerial roles (see Meier and O'Toole 2001, 2002; O'Toole and Meier 2003). The present test is restricted to assisting Latino students and doing so with controls for the impact on Anglo students. In a nonrepresentative role, superintendents are likely to increase the performance of both Latino and non-Latino students.

TABLE 4.7
Representativeness of Political Appointees and Bureaucratic Outputs

Dependent variable	Political		Bureaucratic		Appointee		Adjusted	
	Slope	t	Slope	t	Slope	t	R^2	N
TAAS pass rate	.015	0.55	.104	2.58*	.230	0.12	.29	935
Attendance	−.003	1.13	.026	6.55*	−.214	1.14	.30	988
Dropouts	−.002	0.67	−.011	2.13*	−.063	0.28	.22	929
Advanced classes	.002	0.11	.095	3.09*	−.732	0.53	.33	851
Taking AP classes	.032	1.45#	.082	2.34*	2.165	1.54#	.35	350
Passing AP exams	−.079	0.84	.146	1.01	−4.640	0.97	.52	158
College test rate	.158	2.71*	.298	3.28*	1.607	0.42	.22	490
SAT scores	.214	0.87	.736	1.87*	−20.861	1.54	.44	248
ACT scores	.003	0.67	.000	0.02	−.259	0.87	.40	284
Above 1,110	−.001	0.03	.090	1.77*	−.455	0.22	.30	360
Graduation rate	.020	0.72	.011	0.25	.362	0.20	.79	538

Note: All equations control for Anglo performance on the same indicator, % state aid, teachers' salaries, % black students, % Latino students, class size, teacher experience, and % noncertified teachers.
    *$p < .05$ one-tailed test.
    #$p < .10$ one-tailed test.

sion of political appointees in the model, therefore, does little to change our earlier findings that bureaucracy and bureaucratic values matter the most in the interaction between bureaucracy and political institutions.

CONCLUSION

If representativeness, in this case of Latinos, can be considered an appropriate values surrogate for both elected politicians and bureaucrats, the evidence presented here is unequivocal. The influence of the bureaucracy overwhelms that of elected political leaders on a wide range of performance measures. The large-N nature of the design, coupled with the use of appropriate controls and the array of dependent variables examined, provides presumptive evidence for the importance of bureaucracy in shaping outputs and outcomes.

The most obvious conclusion of this investigation is that it is critical to bring the bureaucracy back into the study of "bureaucratic control." The second, and ultimately more disquieting, conclusion is closely related to the first. If this study had been conducted in the pattern common in the literature on control, possible *spurious relationships* would have been mistaken for evidence of political impact. Tables 4.1 and 4.2 suggest as much, and the relative disappearance of "political control" in a more fully specified form of the equations in table 4.3 raises a concern about the validity of much of the received empirical wisdom accumulated during the last two decades. To the extent that scholars have left bureaucracy on the sidelines in their attempts to explain its actions, earlier findings and apparent theoretical and practical insights should be critically reexamined. The appropriate research designs for exploring this subject must account directly for bureaucratic values and bureaucratic influence.

The findings in this chapter should not be surprising. As we have indicated in explaining the results reported here, there are solid theoretical reasons to expect bureaucratic perspectives to exert a stronger influence on outputs and outcomes than political perspectives do. Analysts since Max Weber (1946) have noted the positional and technical advantages of expert bureaucrats vis-à-vis politicos, and it should come as no shock to see these reflected in shaping performance (see also Brehm and Gates 1997). In addition, several well-developed literatures have directed extensive attention to this theme and have indicated some of the subtle ways bureaucracy and its discretionary decision making can influence the results of public programs.

One should be careful to avoid caricaturing the general theory of political control. Other channels and modes of control are surely plausible. In the empirical portion of this analysis, we explored three and ultimately rejected each on the basis of the evidence. Latino public-education politicos in Texas do not exert representational *control* once removed, so to speak, by selecting or directing teacher-proxies as agents of school board advocacy. School systems without Latinos at the helm demonstrate just as much influence by the bureaucrats as does the full sample. Nor is a different sort of multilevel principal-agent chain at work: adding school-system superintendents to the picture does not reveal spurious or weakened relationships between bureaucratic values and performance. The evidence supports the claim of bureaucratic influence, even when assessed in light of these alternative causal possibilities. In terms of the model of governance and performance, as sketched in the appendix, the bureaucratic "values" slice of the organizational setting, considered as a measurable portion of the relatively stable setting, demonstrates an effect size substantially greater than the portion of the external-forces term (labeled the "X" term in the appendix), which is driven by and from political levels.

We have not eliminated all possible principal-agent explanations for the findings presented here, nor do we contend that political leaders are irrelevant. Politicians influence bureaucracy in a wide variety of instances. With more years of data to analyze, it is conceivable that the modest political relationships found here might build on themselves to become statistically significant. Control, however, is far too strong a term for the relationship of politicians to bureaucrats. Politicians influence bureaucracy, to be sure, but we are skeptical that they control it. A principal-agent interpretation for these results could be constructed, but it would have to be rather convoluted. We suggest that an explanation rooted in bureaucratic values and influence is more parsimonious, more plausible, and also comports with theory and empirical findings in several related fields. As such, it should be considered as one that future work on political control should confront. Studies built on the assumption of a passive and largely pliant bureaucracy should be treated with skepticism.

We should also note that the evidence presented in this chapter should not be taken to conclude that bureaucracies are out of control. Bureaucracies appear to respond to political actions (witness the correlations between school board membership and policy outcomes), however anemic those political actions. At the same time bureaucracies directly represent clientele. By relying on both political representation and bureaucratic representation, governance systems are more democratic than if they relied solely on top-down electoral influences.

CHAPTER FIVE

Inside the Bureaucracy

Principals, Agents, and Bureaucratic Strategy

Chapter 3 demonstrated that current structural arrangements in American governance make it difficult for electoral institutions to control administrative ones, because such arrangements blur lines of responsibility and also operate without the ability to compel action on the part of governing units. Chapter 4 focused on the kinds of cases that should be most amenable to political control and, in such settings, developed the argument that when bureaucratic variables are incorporated into an analysis, much of what looks like political control is actually spurious: Bureaucracy is acting consistently with its own values rather than being directed by electoral institutions. This chapter extends these arguments further. We do so by once more selecting a political-control scenario that is as close as possible to an ideal, or ideally "controllable," situation in the real world. Our case is again Texas education, but this time we focus on improving overall student performance rather than on selective benefits for one group of students.

Over the past twenty years, the state of Texas has engaged in ongoing efforts to improve public education by stressing performance standards for schools and providing resources in support of this goal. Political principals in this case (the legislature, the governor, the state agency, parents, etc.) are in almost universal agreement that the goal is to improve education and that the primary measure of that improvement is performance on standardized tests.[1] This chapter demonstrates that even in this ideal situation for political control, one sees substantial evidence that bureaucracy

This chapter was coauthored with John Bohte.

1. Smith (2003) documents this uniformity among policy makers despite the relatively vigorous debate among academics.

acts from its own perspective, and thereby shirks on merely implementing the principals' intent, by using its professional expertise to exempt students from taking the statewide exams. These bureaucratic actions are clearly linked to bureaucratic norms and values, which are understandable yet also readily open to critique (for coverage of the complex place of professionalism in public service, see Mosher 1982). Those values can sometimes support a representational function, as chapter 4 has shown, but they can also support actions that may have nothing to do with representation or responsiveness to key stakeholders. When this result occurs, the political-control approach does not succeed, and the bureaucratic-values approach becomes problematic in terms of any sensible version of democratic theory.

THE LITERATURE

We begin the analysis by placing the study within the theoretical literature on political control of the bureaucracy, primarily the principal-agent literature. As noted in chapter 2, using the concepts of information asymmetry and goal conflict, the principal-agent model has generated a wealth of research on political control over the bureaucracy (Calvert, McCubbins, and Weingast 1989; Carpenter 1996; McCubbins and Schwartz 1984; McCubbins, Noll, and Weingast 1989; Mitnick 1980; Moe 1982, 1985; Niskanen 1971; Potosky 1999; Weingast and Moran 1983; Weingast 1984; Wood 1988, 1990; Wood and Waterman 1991, 1993, 1994). Although critics of this literature can be found (Cook 1989; Worsham, Eisner, and Ringquist 1997), and some research goes so far as to challenge the basic concepts (Miller 2000; Meier, Wrinkle, and Polinard 1995; Waterman and Meier 1998), as shown earlier in this volume, the principal-agent model remains the predominant framework used in political science to study the interaction between bureaucracy and political institutions. A striking element of the empirical literature (as opposed to the theoretical work) is the contrast between the rich, varied *political* analysis and variables that are included and the paucity of *bureaucratic* analysis and associated variables. Political appointments, executive orders, budgets, legislative and executive ideologies, specific policy pronouncements, court decisions, interest-group pressures, and related policies are among the myriad factors measured for political institutions. Bureaucracy, in contrast, is typically treated as a soulless black box; it produces outputs (enforcements, decisions, etc.), but its internal processes, political skills, resources, cohesion, and other factors are generally ignored (but see Eisner and Meier 1990). The empirical portrait recently painted in political science is of multidimensional political principals taking strategic action in regard to a one-dimensional, naive bureaucracy that can respond to, but not shape, its environment (but see Krause 1996, 1999).

As we argue in chapter 2, the mysterious and empty portrayal of bureaucracy in the political science principal-agent literature contrasts vividly with studies in public administration and the formal theoretical literature. Public administration studies explore the impact of such variables as bureaucratic capacity (Barrilleaux, Feiock, and Crew 1992), agency mission or ideology (Meier 1988; Ringquist 1993), leadership (Kaufman 1981; Kettl 1986; McCraw 1984; Riccucci 1995; Wolf 1997), and strategy or goals (Bendor, Taylor, and Van Gaalen 1985; Brehm and Gates 1997; Eisner 1991; Niskanen 1971). To assume that bureaucracies—complex organizations that exercise discretion, have distinct policy preferences (Garand, Parkhurst, and Seoud 1991), and simultaneously possess the advantages of expertise and a longer, nonelectoral time frame—would not act strategically is a serious oversimplification and actually contradicts the basic premises of the principal-agent model. The core model is interesting and useful only because the agent (read *bureaucrat*) is strategic about his or her behavior. The *theoretical* work with the principal-agent model posits a dynamic interaction between a strategic principal and a strategic agent (see Bendor et al. 1985; Mitnick 1980; Perrow 1986). Without allowing for a strategic public organization, as the empirical literature does not, the principal-agent problem becomes trivial.

At one level, assuming a naive bureaucracy is a reasonable approach to simplifying the world so that empirical tests can be conducted. A number of insights have been gained in this process. At the same time we think that additional improvements are possible by reversing the assumptions and allowing for strategic bureaucrats facing relatively naive political actors. Such assumptions are generally consistent with the public administration literature.

This chapter explicitly incorporates additional bureaucratic factors into the study of administrative responses to political institutions by using the case of educational policy in Texas. Faced with the demand to produce higher student test scores, school systems have an incentive to shirk: Rather than increasing test-taking performance across the spectrum of students, they could manipulate district scores by not testing all students. This instance was selected because it exhibits characteristics that maximize the advantages of the political institutions to influence what public organizations do; the objectives of the policy are clear and measurable, and the political institutions are unified in their demands on bureaucracy. Principals—the school board, state political actors, and parents—all share the same goal, higher test scores, so little is lost by assuming that principals are unified (versus the situation framed in chapter 4, where differences in ethnicity generated differences in goals among the principals). Because principals directly control school budgets and other financial rewards, they should have sufficient incentives to minimize moral hazards in the bureaucracy.

Furthermore, the agents here are organizational, but they are not networked in the complicated manner of many program arrays, as chapter 3 has shown.

The analysis proceeds in six steps. First, we introduce organizational "cheating" as a shirking strategy within the principal-agent model.[2] Second, we sketch the theoretical logic for when cheating might occur. Third, we introduce the context of the study and precise measurements. Fourth, we sketch the empirical model used to test whether bureaucratic discretion is used to cheat on apparent organizational performance, as measured by a widely accepted performance criterion. Fifth, we test the model with a statistical technique called pooled regression, using school districts as the administrative units of analysis and including their results over a period of time. Finally, we discuss the implications of the findings for the study of public administration and democracy.

CHEATING AS A FORM OF SHIRKING

In any contractual arrangement between a principal and an agent, the latter must decide how to respond to the incentives and potential monitoring of the former. The common original dichotomy of responses, working versus shirking, has been replaced by a more varied set of options (Brehm and Gates 1997; Brehm, Gates, and Gomez 2003). When government bureaucracies are the agents in question, the response can become even more nuanced. We assume that government bureaucracies are generally responsive to environmental demands (i.e., they are open systems; see Thompson 1967) and have multiple goals (Downs 1967; Rainey 2003). With multiple goals a bureaucracy must consider how any response to a single principal will affect the agency's mission and its other goals. With the multiple principals faced by almost every government bureaucracy,[3] a decision must be made on how much to respond to the demands of any one principal and how that response affects the remaining web of principal-agent relationships.[4]

The range of bureaucratic options go from outright defiance to enthusiastic compliance and myriad steps in between (Golden 2000; O'Leary 1994). A bureaucracy facing resource constraints—that is, every one of them—is interested in responding enough to make the principal happy but not so much as to jeopardize other

2. We could easily frame this chapter within the bureaucratic politics literature. In fact, the reliance on bureaucratic values places this study in the center of that literature.

3. The multiple-principals feature is especially prominent in separation-of-powers systems, of course, but it is also present elsewhere.

4. The EPA had to decide how much to respond to the initiatives of the Reagan administration and at the same time keep relationships with Congress cooperative. Multiple principals require strategic choice on the part of agents.

agency activities. Using the doctor-patient relationship that was so instrumental in generating the principal-agent model to illustrate, we note that a doctor might be tempted to treat a patient's symptoms rather than the disease itself. Such a response is a subtle form of shirking akin to cheating, because the doctor would be using the patient's lack of technical understanding (in the language of principal-agent theory: information asymmetry) to the doctor's advantage by making the patient feel better in the short run. A bureaucracy could follow a similar strategy by determining what indicators political institutions use to judge bureaucratic behavior and focusing its efforts on those indicia to the exclusion of or underemphasis on others. If level of enforcement is a concern, for instance, regulatory agencies can enforce more cases by picking cases that are relatively easy to enforce.

Any attempt by an agent to shirk is made more difficult if the principal has a valid and objective performance measure (a policy outcome) to use as a bottom line in evaluating the agent. While such situations may not be common in public bureaucracies (see Downs 1967), bottom-line measures are available in several policy fields (Khademian 1995). In fact, the entire exercise of performance appraisal is predicated on the ability to generate objective criteria for evaluating performance (see also Wood and Waterman 1994). In virtually every situation, however, measured outcomes are determined only in part by agents' activities. Just as the health of a patient is affected by but clearly not totally determined by a physician's regimen of treatment, air quality is influenced by numerous factors other than the EPA's actions (Ringquist 1993). No indicator of performance is perfect. Given this measurement error, one interesting way of shirking is to focus on generating numbers for the performance measure rather than improving overall performance in the organization. Organizations are goal-based collectivities that respond to incentives (Downs 1967; Thompson 1967); if political principals reward an agency for scoring well on a given measure, a strategic organization is quite likely to generate "numbers" that make it look good (Behn 1997). Indeed, scoring by the "numbers" is a commonly discussed bureaucratic option within large organizations. A rational organization can do this in one of two ways: (1) Continue to operate as in the past but make an effort to improve overall levels of performance; (2) Strategically manipulate the output measure. This latter response is what we mean by *cheating*.[5]

If the choice is to shirk by manipulating the output measure strategically, the organization has three options: lying, cutting corners, and generating biased samples. Ly-

---

5. *Shirking* is the term used in the principal-agent literature and *cheating* is the term used in the compliance literature. Whether this behavior is actually cheating or not, in the common-language sense, is open to question. This designation should be taken as a term with a stipulative definition of bureaucrats seeking goals other than those sought by the principals.

ing is relatively simple—the organization merely reports numbers that make it look good, even if the numbers have no basis in fact (a prime example is the use of body counts during the U.S. war in Vietnam; more recent ones include tanks destroyed by the U.S. Air Force in Kosovo (Barry and Thomas 2000) and the Philadelphia Police Department reporting phony crime rates (Matza, McCoy, and Fazlollah 1999). In a comparative context, the Soviet bureaucracy long had a reputation for simply making up numbers to meet announced plans (Barry and Barner-Barry 1991; Conyngham 1982; for a Chinese case, see O'Brien and Li 1999). Lying, however, is an unattractive proposition if the principal has alternative sources of information about bureaucratic performance—not to mention if the agent has principles that preclude such overt misinformation.[6] Because virtually every bureaucracy is monitored by numerous politicians, interest groups, media, and academics, lying is a high-risk strategy with little chance of long-run positive results.[7] Being caught lying exposes a bureaucratic unit to increased controls from principals, more intrusive monitoring, and reduced discretion on decisions for which bureaucratic values have been influential.

A Texas school district example of lying is the recent Houston Independent School District (HISD) dropout scandal. HISD in 2003 was found guilty of turning in bogus statistics on high school dropouts.[8] Although dropout figures are notoriously unreliable, HISD actually reported that not a single student had dropped out of Sharpstown High School, an unlikely event given Sharpstown's disadvantaged student body. Because HISD was the home district of Secretary of Education Rod Paige, the district was used by the media as an example to challenge what has been termed the Texas Miracle. The result has been substantial negative press for the district, disciplinary action by the state of Texas, and proposals to change the way dropout numbers are calculated.[9] The moral of this story is that lying is a high-risk strategy and likely to be discovered.

6. Direct lying, that is making up facts, should be distinguished from interpretative lying or spin control. Spin control puts a positive gloss on an accepted set of facts. It is likely to be more common than interpretive lying (see Downs 1967), although it also entails some risks.

7. Many public agencies are in situations similar to Ostrom's (1990) successful common-pool resource organizations. A large number of monitors can provide independent feedback to the political principal (McCubbins and Schwartz 1984).

8. A second cheating scandal occurred in 2005 when the *Dallas Morning News* ran a story reporting on results from four hundred classrooms where changes in scores from one year to the next were dramatically large. Because the state of Texas has approximately two hundred thousand classrooms, four hundred discrepant test scores is not a large number. Subsequent investigations found only four cases of documented cheating (by individual teachers; see Spencer 2005). The "scandal" likely owes a great deal to what are fairly substantial teacher effects on students and the lack of understanding of statistical probability on the part of journalists.

9. The obvious solution to the dropout-data problem is to use a cohort measure through which ninth-grade students are tracked over the next four years. If they graduate with their class, they are then counted as graduates. This cohort measure is far superior to the current measures, which allow districts to code students who leave school in various categories and avoid terming them dropouts. Under the current measure, a school with 1,000 ninth grade students and 500 graduates four years later might report a dropout rate of 2.0% or less. Sharpstown High's strategic error was to report numbers that were simply too unrealistic to believe, even under the current questionable system.

Cutting corners is a second way to generate positive numbers. If the principal is interested in numbers, the rational agent could reduce the level of resources committed to each case and produce more outputs (although not of the same quality). A Federal Deposit Insurance Commission auditor or an Occupational Safety and Health Administration inspector might reduce the time spent on an individual site visit but make more site visits (Scholz and Wei 1986). A law enforcement agency might generate a series of arrests for trivial violations and ignore the more serious problems, or an Internal Revenue Service agent might focus audits on individuals who lack the resources to resist the agency (Scholz and Wood 1998).

Sampling bias is the conscious selection of cases that generate the most positive results. An employment agency might focus its efforts on individuals with the most job-ready skills, a process often referred to as "creaming" (Blau 1956); the Federal Bureau of Investigation has stressed high-visibility crimes with high clearance rates (bank robbery, kidnaping; see Poveda 1990); the Antitrust Division of the Justice Department prefers easy-to-win collusion cases to those of the more complex monopoly variety (Eisner 1991). Sampling bias is a relatively sophisticated way of cheating; the organization simultaneously works and shirks. The organization produces exactly what the political principal is demanding via the performance measure emphasized but does so by complying with the letter of the demand rather than the spirit—what Williamson (1990) refers to as perfunctory (as opposed to consummate) compliance.[10]

Not all methods of organizational cheating are equally likely in our specific case, school districts. The primary criterion used to evaluate schools in Texas has been performance on the Texas Assessment of Academic Skills, or TAAS, a state-wide mandatory exam.[11] Districts are explicitly rated and rewarded based on this performance measure, and political principals share a consensus that student performance on the TAAS is important. At the same time, school districts clearly recognize that education encompasses more than the ability to pass a standardized test of basic skills. The test taps only some skills that schools teach, and it does not fully measure the multiple goals that schools have in educating a diverse student body both as potential workers and as citizens.

---

10. One way to guard against this sort of cheating is for political principals or top managers to emphasize several performance measures, each tapping an aspect of performance, rather than one simple indicator. Doing so, however, requires more sophisticated monitoring systems, often demands considerable analytical capacity, and can impose substantial costs. Furthermore, political principals sometimes have a tendency to lock onto a particularly salient measure, even if it provides a distorted picture.

11. The TAAS exam was replaced by another standardized exam, the TAKS, in 2003. Although this is a different test, it is designed on the same basic principles as the TAAS and the results are highly correlated.

In this situation, lying is difficult because the test is scored and reported by the Texas Education Agency rather than the individual school districts.[12] Districts can cut corners somewhat by focusing more on the test and less on other aspects of their curriculum; in short, a district could cut corners by teaching the test. The most likely method of cheating, however, is biasing the sample. Within certain guidelines, school districts can influence which students take the test and thereby tilt the apparent aggregate results toward apparently higher performance. Among the districts the number of test exemptions averages 9.2 percent but ranges from 0.3 percent to 35.0 percent. While guidelines attempt to specify which students can be exempted (e.g., special education, see below), a great deal of discretion remains, so the possibility of exempting those students least likely to pass the test remains a real one.[13]

A MODEL OF ORGANIZATIONAL CHEATING

The decision to cheat rather than comply with the spirit of a principal's demand is no different from any other decision. An organization cheats because the perceived utility of cheating is greater than the perceived utility of not cheating.[14] In some cases this is a management decision and thus establishes a policy; in other cases individuals make these decisions based their own values or utility calculations. What factors affect the benefits and costs of cheating and thus might influence an organization to do so? From the literature on organization theory, we can identify six factors that either create the incentive to cheat or lower the costs of cheating within the organization: performance gaps, a history of cheating, scarce resources, difficult task demands, high transaction costs, and professional norms. For each factor, we identify specific indicators for use in this study.

12. The Austin Independent School District (ISD) was indicted in the mid-1990s for systematic cheating on the exam. The state uses sophisticated scanning equipment and statistical decision criteria to determine if exams are characterized by an excessive number of erasures that replace wrong answers with correct answers. Individual teachers have been caught in this process and disciplined (sometimes by dismissal).

13. Public concern over this issue was such that exemptions for any reason were prohibited starting with the 1999–2000 school year. Individual school districts, most notably Houston ISD in 1998, tried to prohibit exemptions but were unable to reduce the total number. Given a rise in the total number of exemptions in 1998–99, after the statewide prohibition was passed but before it was fully implemented, actual compliance with this policy is likely to be problematic. Data from the 2001–2 school year show that 11% of students were exempted from the exam. In 2005 the state of Texas was fined $440,000 by the federal government because the state was testing fewer students than required by the federal No Child Left Behind Act. The irony is, of course, that the state deliberately refused to test all students despite trying to force districts to do so earlier.

14. This formulation, like most principal-agent approaches, ignores the possibility that agents might respond in terms of their perceived obligations or commitments, rather than solely or primarily as consequentialist (e.g., utilitarian) actors. Presumably organizations (and managers) clearly committed to avoiding cheating even when it is likely to be advantageous for the organization will tend to resist the logic of this calculus. Still, if some portion of the decision makers act in accord with such an ends-oriented rationale, as there is good reason to expect, we should see across a large sample some evidence of the tendencies sketched here.

Performance Gaps

Downs (1967) argues that performance gaps, a disjuncture between an organization's expected and actual performance, will motivate an organization to reevaluate its activities and change behavior. Managers, in this case superintendents and school principals, are explicitly rewarded or punished based on district and school performance. A performance gap, however, is but a necessary condition for cheating. A performance gap might serve as a trigger for an organization to improve its performance rather than as a signal to cheat. Given the presence of a performance gap, whether the agency cheats or not depends on the benefits and costs of cheating per se when compared with other options. A performance gap might be measured in different ways. For public education organizations in settings like Texas, the most obvious is a low score on the standardized examination during the preceding cycle (the previous year), thus suggesting that different actions need to be taken—one of which might be to cheat. Organizations are inertial systems that prize stability, however, and a single year's score might be an aberration. A rational manager might rather look at the trend in scores over a two- or three-year period. Since we have no reason to think either length of time is preferred, we include both a two- and three-year trend as additional indicators of performance gaps.

Prior Efforts to Bias the Score

Organizations develop structures, cultures, and norms (Perrow 1986; Wilson 1989) that sanction certain types of behavior. If questionable activities are accepted by most individuals in the organization, then the cost of such behavior is likely to be low. In educational institutions, one common dysfunction created by performance indicators is that teachers will teach the test rather than their normal curriculum. For a fee, private organizations in Texas, for example, are willing to train teachers how to teach to the Texas exam.[15] While tests contain valuable information and teaching to them has some benefits, the perception is that this strategy can produce higher test scores without a corresponding improvement in educational quality.

The structure of the Texas examination process provides an unobtrusive measure of teaching to the test. Periodically the test undergoes a major revision. When this shift occurs, districts teaching to the test should be affected more and also affected more negatively than districts that teach their regular curriculum. Such a change occurred between the 1993 and 1994 versions of the exam. Subtracting the 1994

---

15. Confidential interview with a school official by the authors. The district in question hired the private firm for this reason.

exam score from the 1993 score creates our indicator of teaching to the test, and thus a measure of a structured prior effort to bias the score.

Resources

Any bureaucratic task is easier to achieve if the administrative organization has ample resources. Resources allow an organization to invest in more skilled human capital, add technology, or simply attempt to overwhelm problems with personnel.[16] Resource-rich organizations are less likely to cheat, simply because they have less need to do so. They have sufficient slack resources to adjust to principals' demands without compromising their defined mission.[17] Three measures of organizational resources are used: per-pupil instructional expenditures, class size (average number of students per teacher), and the proportion of the district's funds deriving from state aid. Because the test standards have been imposed on districts by the state, the last-mentioned indicator suggests the degree of leverage political principals have over these bureaucratic agents.

Task Demands

Government bureaucracies rarely have the kinds of uniform, patterned production processes that are common in manufacturing. While producing one Dodge Neon is no more difficult than producing any other Neon, public organizations often have high varying inputs. Some antitrust cases are more difficult to win than others; some regulatory problems are more tractable than others; and some welfare clients are easier to render ready for work (Mazmanian and Sabatier 1989). Students also vary in the challenge that they pose to the school system. In general, the more diverse a student body, the more difficulty a school will have in educating all its students (Chubb and Moe 1990). In particular, the needs of minority students and low-income students create greater demands on the school system. To create a measure of task demands or task difficulty, we simply standardize the percentage of black, Latino, and low-income students (defined as eligible for free or reduced-cost school lunch) and add them. As task demands become more difficult, the benefits of cheating should increase.

---

16. One district, for example, operates with an effective student to teacher ratio of ten to one at lower grades. These extremely small classes are then augmented by reading specialists. This level of resources, while effective, is well beyond that available to most school districts.

17. We call this the New York Yankees' approach to organizational performance. While few school districts can be characterized as resource rich in comparison to the New York Yankees, Texas districts have relatively large differences in taxable wealth, and these difference have not been completely overcome by differences in state aid.

The Costs of Coordination

Systematic shirking requires that an organization coordinate its efforts. Shirking by a few individuals will matter little and may even be more likely to be detected than will uniform shirking by the whole organization. Organizational shirking, therefore, is a collective action problem that management must solve. As Olson contends (1965), collective action (read shirking) is likely to be easier if there are fewer individuals to coordinate. Larger organizations, thus, have greater transaction costs for any type of action they take (Williamson 1990). To measure the organizational costs of shirking, we include a simple count of the number of full-time bureaucrats employed by the school district.[18]

Professional Norms

Professional norms can also lower the costs of what outsiders might think of as organizational cheating—at least in the field of education. One of the strongest, albeit still controversial, norms in the education profession is the idea that students should be assessed and grouped with similar students for instructional purposes (Heller, Holtzman, and Messick 1982; Meier and Stewart 1991; Oakes 1985). As professional education levels rise and thus acceptance of norms increases, we expect that school districts will engage in more efforts to sort and categorize students, including slotting students for special education and limited English proficiency (LEP) classes. Similar norms would discourage testing such students simply because these tests were designed primarily for students in regular classes. We assume that the willingness to exercise discretion in the examination process also increases as the general skill levels in the organization rise. Our measure of organizational skills and professionalism is a weighted average of the proportion of teachers with advanced degrees.[19] Higher levels of education should be positively associated with acceptance of the norm of sorting and grouping. Acceptance of the norm will result in using established *insti-*

18. We use bureaucrats (i.e., central office and campus administrators) rather than teachers because decisions to put a student into special education generally require administrative approval. Only administrators have the widespread contacts within the district to engage in systematic cheating. The correlation between total bureaucrats and total teachers was .99, so either could be used as an indicator of transaction costs. Because this variable was positively skewed, a logarithmic transformation of the variable was used so that the measure would fit the statistical assumptions that make regression analyses valid. The costs of coordination, and thus the collective-action challenge, is also a function of structural attributes of the organization. In this sample, however, school-district structures are similar enough to be ignored for purposes of this investigation.

19. Specifically, we weight PhD degrees as equivalent to two masters degrees and then simply take the sum of these two numbers and divide it by the total number of teachers. The education levels for teachers is positively skewed, so it has been subjected to a log transformation.

tutional procedures to classify more students as needing special education or having limited English. The result should be a larger pool of students who can then be exempted from the exam. A second, but less likely, explanation for a link between organizational skills and cheating is that organizations with higher skill levels are simply more adept at cheating. Those who can cheat with skill and finesse are less likely to be caught than those who make clumsy efforts at it. Education should be positively related to knowledge of the organization's rules and procedures and thus correlated with lower costs for cheating.

The professional-norms variable is in reality *a surrogate for bureaucratic values*, a variable we argue is the key to understanding the relationship between bureaucracy and political institutions. To the professional in the organization, these actions do not present themselves as cheating, but rather as the application of good educational practices. Unlike the ethnicity measure of values used in chapter 4, this measure of value does not correspond to the goals held by political elites (or some political elites). Political elites favor testing and universally seek higher test scores. In short, this is a situation with goal consensus on the part of the principals, a clear bottom line to assess performance, and some goal conflict between principals and agents.

DATA AND MEASURES

The universe for analysis includes all Texas school districts with more than 1,000 students during the time period 1996–99. The size criterion was used to avoid small school districts where a few students can have a significant impact on the results. While cheating might well be easier in these smaller districts (see below), the greater volatility of test scores in such districts is likely to mask the behavior.[20] Data on test exemptions, linked to our measure of cheating, are available for the years 1996–99. All data, 1,917 total cases, were obtained from the Texas Education Agency. These data were cleaned for obvious errors and used to construct a pooled data set by year within case.[21]

The first question that needs to be addressed is the extent of discretion exercised in exempting students from the exams. Students can be exempted for four reasons: an absence on the day of the examination, a situation involving transfer into the district after the beginning of the class year, participation in special education classes, or having lim-

---

20. The standard deviation of the percentage of students exempted from the exam was 9.56 for districts of 1,000 plus students whereas that for districts with fewer than 1,000 students was 11.14.

21. The TEA data are relatively clean, although on occasion they do include a misplaced decimal point or skip a value in a list of variables. We cleaned the data by examining the individual items in comparison with values for previous years and also by examining any data point in detail that regression diagnostics indicated might be problematic.

ited English proficiency. Of these, special education and limited English are the major rationales. The average district exempts 9.2 percent of the students: 6.3 percent for special education, 1.6 percent for limited English, 0.6 percent for absences, and 0.7 percent for mobility. Of these exemptions, absences and mobility appear to be essentially random from year to year and thus unlikely to reflect any systematic efforts at cheating.[22] The correlation between the same district measures for 1996 and 1997 is −0.07 for absences and 0.13 for mobility. Special education and limited English exemptions, however, are more strongly linked on an annual basis, with respective correlations of 0.74 and 0.77.

One way to illustrate the discretion involved in the exemption process is to compare the number of special education and limited-English students with the total number of exemptions. The average district has 8.3 percent LEP students and 12.9 percent special education students, yet exempts only 9.2 percent of its students.[23] The relatively low number of exemptions (on average, 46.0% of eligibles) indicates that cheating is not rampant. At the same time, the ratio of exemptions to eligibles ranges from 0.017 to 2.94 (i.e., one district exempts nearly three times the number of students that it has in LEP and special education classes), thus suggesting that districts vary a great deal in their implementation of the rules. Within this variation, we would expect to find what, if any, cheating occurs (see table 5.1 for descriptive statistics of the variables used in this chapter).

A second, more striking way to illustrate the disjuncture between rules and implementation is simply to regress the percentage of students in special education and classified as limited English on the percentage of students who are exempted from the exam.[24] Table 5.2 indicates that these legitimate reasons for exam exemptions account for *only 26 percent* of the variance in the percentage of exemptions issued.[25] Exempting students from the exam clearly involves the exercise of discre-

22. We replicated this analysis by including exemptions for absences and for mobility reasons. The results were identical. Absences had no predictive power; mobility did, but it did not affect the basic findings.

23. LEP students and special education students are almost mutually exclusive categories. Students with special education needs who lack English skills are generally classified as special education only.

24. To regress, in this context, means to seek to explain a variable statistically (here, the test exemption rate) as a linear additive function of other variables (here, the percentage of students in special education and classified as LEP). If test exemptions are mostly explained by the percentage of students classified in these two categories, such a finding would strongly suggest that discretion is not being used to manipulate the exemption rate—and thus the cohort of students taking the test, and thus the overall pass rate. As the text makes clear, however, this analytical step actually shows that the two classification rates do not explain most of the exemption rate. Discretionary decisions must be at work in the school districts. This line of analysis assumes that the original student designations are all proper and have not themselves been driven by some form of cheating at an earlier stage, perhaps even in response to incentives other than those we have sketched thus far. We ignore this issue here but explore it later in the chapter.

25. Adding mobility exemptions increases the explained variation by 10%, while absences have no impact on the predictive ability of the equation. Mobility exemptions are rigidly defined by when the student starts school in the district and thus are not discretionary. Mobility exemptions are not correlated with student pass rates, and absences are negatively, not positively, correlated with test scores.

TABLE 5.1
Descriptive Statistics

Variable	Mean	Standard deviation
Low-income students	45.4	20.3
Black students (%)	10.9	13.7
Latino students (%)	30.8	29.0
Class size	13.8	3.4
Salaries (000)	31.9	2.2
State aid (%)	50.2	21.0
Expenditures	2,888.0	348.0
Pass rate	78.2	12.3
Not tested (%)	9.2	4.9
LEP students	8.3	11.7
Special education students	12.9	3.2
Pass rate $(t-1)$	70.6	12.0
Two-year trend	4.3	4.0
Three-year trend	10.4	5.2
Teaching the test	4.2	5.9
Total bureaucrats	30.0	52.7
Teacher education	23.8	9.6

tion. The residuals from this equation, indicating departures from the exemption rates predicted by the formal designations of such students alone, can be viewed as the place where one might find efforts at shirking by biasing the sample.

Can one actually detect incentives to cheat, in terms of increased pass rates, that flow from exempting additional students from the test? Table 5.3 illustrates that such incentives do operate. The dependent variable in these regression analyses is the percentage of students who pass the exam; the equation is a common education production function (Hanushek 1996; see chap. 4) with performance a function of the types of students (% low income, black, and Latino) and resources (teachers' salaries, class size, and instructional spending). Model 2, displayed in the same table, adds the percentage of students exempted from the test. All other things being equal, a one percentage point increase in exemptions is associated with a 0.2 percentage point increase in the pass rate.[26] The difference between the extremes for this set of districts, from virtually all students taking the test to more than 35 percent exempted, translates into about seven-tenths of a standard deviation in the test pass rate, an incentive well worth seeking. A district that might be very active in using discretion in such a way to inflate apparent overall pass rates could move from scoring as a mediocre performer, in relative terms, to producing as an apparently much-better-than-expected one.

26. The size of this coefficient suggests that assignments of students have goals other than affecting test scores. In a world where all the students likely to fail or only students likely to fail were assigned exemptions, the coefficient would approach 1.0. That it does not implies that such actions might be aimed at attaining more than one value (possibly a blend of good educational practices and cheating).

TABLE 5.2
Exemptions and Reasons for Them

Independent variables	Dependent variable: Percentage of students exempted from exam	
	Coefficient	Standard error
LEP students	.2223	.0089
Special education students	.5118	.0323
R-squared	.26	
Adjusted R-squared	.26	
Standard error	4.22	
F	338.83	
N	1917	

Model 2 shows the incentive for the average district. For some districts, the incentives could well be higher. Model 3, for example, runs the model for those districts with the largest numbers of minority and low-income students.[27] In this model, the incentive to cheat is much larger; a one percentage point increase in exemptions is associated with a 0.34 percentage point increase in pass rates (potentially a full standard deviation over the range of the data). At the margins, therefore, the payoffs for more exemptions generate sufficient incentives for school districts to use the exemptions to select out students who are less likely to pass the exam. We know from the analysis in chapter 4 that bureaucratic discretion can be used in these governance systems on behalf of representing at least some interests of those served by the system (Latino students). This result can be seen as encouraging for those concerned with bureaucracy and democracy. But can bureaucratic discretion also be detected as working in support of values *not* so consistent with democratic governance? We are now in position to answer this question, in particular with regard to the matter of cheating.

FINDINGS

The strategy for determining the extent of organizational cheating is to use test exemptions as the dependent variable in a regression. The equation we use to try to explain the variation in exemptions across districts controls for both the percentage of students in special education and the percentage of students classified as limited English speaking, so as to account for legitimate exemptions. To this equation, we add the indicators drawn from the theoretical discussion earlier in the chapter—indicators, that is, of performance gaps, teaching the test, resources, task demands, coordination costs, and professional norms. Since the data set covers four years, dummy variables

27. This variable is the task diversity measure created above from summing standardized scores of the percentages of low-income, black, and Latino students. The regression includes all districts with scores greater than zero.

TABLE 5.3
Payoff for Test Exemptions

	Dependent variable: Percentage of students passing exam		
Independent variable	Model 1	Model 2	Model 3
Low-income students	−.2339	−.2649	−.2777
	(.0138)	(.0145)	(.0264)
Black students	−.1779	−.1869	−.2745
	(.0138)	(.0131)	(.0241)
Latino students	−.0719	−.0655	−.1159
	(.0102)	(.0102)	(.0190)
Class size	−.3799	−.3838	−.3782
	(.0422)	(.0418)	(.0638)
Teachers' salaries (000)	.4552	.4656	.6621
	(.0836)	(.0828)	(.1314)
Instructional spending	.0017	.0019	.0018
	(.0005)	(.0005)	(.0007)
Student exemptions	—	.2048	.3350
		(.0324)	(.0445)
R-squared	.69	.69	.63
Adjusted R-squared	.69	.69	.63
Standard error	5.82	5.76	6.36
F	465.72	431.69	153.53
N	1914	1914	902

Note: Coefficient for annual dummies not reported. Numbers in parentheses are standard errors. Model 3 contains districts with higher task demands.

for 1997, 1998, and 1999 were included to adjust for any serial correlation. A variety of regression diagnostics were examined to make sure that the regression did not suffer from problems of collinearity, extreme values, or unduly influential points.[28]

Table 5.4 estimates the coefficients for all variables and then provides a reduced model that retains only significant factors. What do the results show? The extent of organizational cheating is unrelated to performance gaps. None of the three performance measures was significantly linked to the number of test exemptions. This finding, along with the significant improvement in test scores from 1992 to 1999, suggests that cheating is probably not the first option considered by organizations facing a performance gap.

Past efforts to cheat, as indicated by our surrogate for teaching the test, are also not related to test exemptions. The absence of a relationship might well be the result of the oft-heard but never verified claim that virtually *all* districts teach the test.

28. Here are specifics of these diagnostics for those interested in the precise steps taken. Collinearity was assessed by examining the tolerances. We also examined the studentized residuals, the diagonal of the hat matrix, and the Cooks' D. The data were well behaved. Only twenty studentized residuals and fifty-four hat diagonals were significant, both well within the expected range of 5%. No large (greater than 1) Cooks' Ds were produced. Using the rule of thumb of 4/n, we deleted all cases with a Cooks' D greater than 0.003 and reran the analysis. That table, reproduced in table 5.A1, shows results that are consistent with those reported in table 5.6. In addition, table 5.A2 contains the results of a robust regression (eight iterations, using Andrews sine) and those results also compare favorably with table 5.6.

Alternatively, teaching the test is a behavior different in degree from attempting to manipulate the exam scores by exempting students. Tests, after all, contain valid information; and teaching toward such tests still imparts a level of skills to students. Excessive exemptions cannot claim this benefit.

Resources, or at least some resources, affect the propensity of an organization to cheat. As predicted, school districts with larger instructional budgets have lower levels of student exemptions, thus suggesting that some districts cheat because they lack the resources to improve scores by strengthening their curriculum and teaching.[29] State aid is insignificant, thereby implying that a large source of money from the state does not guarantee any more compliance with the spirit of testing. Such a finding makes sense because local pressures to produce high test scores are just as strong as the pressure from state government. Finally, class size is unrelated to cheating. While class size may be thought of as a resource, with smaller classes signifying greater teaching resources, some literature suggests that only major reductions in class size matter (Hanushek 1996; Hedges and Greenwald 1996; but see chap. 4). Ninety-five percent of these districts have student-teacher ratios of between twelve and eighteen, probably not sufficient variation to matter in terms of cheating.[30]

So then, what *does* influence cheating? The remaining three variables are related to test exemptions in the predicted direction. The difficulty of the organization's task, as measured by the percentages of students who are black, Latino, or poor, was positively related to test exemptions. The transaction costs of collective action, indicated by the number of bureaucrats, is negatively associated with organizational cheating. Other things being equal, larger organizations seem to encounter more difficulties in generating sufficient collusion to manipulate the exemption rate in response to the incentives. Most importantly for the themes of this book, the capacity and professionalization of the organization, measured by education levels, is *positively* related to the organization's propensity to cheat.

Overall, the findings present a relatively coherent view of organizational cheating. Public organizations disregard the intent of elected officials when they face severe problems (task demands), have few resources to invest in traditional methods of improvement (instructional spending), have low transaction costs to coordinate such efforts (bureaucratic size), and have the internal social capital and professional

29. One of the theoretical weaknesses of the principal-agent model is that it uses market-system logic, so the idea that a principal will pay less than necessary for an agent's actions is not considered. In a voluntary system with full information, or even with information asymmetry favoring the agent, this would not occur. In the public sector, the principal sets both the price and the output.

30. Class sizes will be larger than student-teacher ratios because not all teachers teach every hour of the day. Texas is among the leading states in emphasizing small class sizes, so these findings may not hold in other states.

TABLE 5.4
Determinants of Organizational Cheating

Independent variable	Dependent variable: Percentage of test exemptions	
	Model 1	Model 2
Legitimate exemptions		
Limited English	.1615	.1626
	(.0114)	(.0111)
Special education	.5168	.5211
	(.0324)	(.0314)
Performance gaps		
Last year	.0106	—
	(.0157)	
Two-year trend	.0050	—
	(.0366)	
Three-year trend	−.0142	—
	(.0268)	
Teaching the test	.0124	—
	(.0164)	
Resources		
Instructional spending	−.0023	−.0024
	(.0003)	(.0003)
State aid	.0011	—
	(.0052)	
Class size	.0493	—
	(.0283)	
Task demands	.9378	.9038
	(.0861)	(.0564)
Bureaucrats (logged)	−.5516	−.5364
	(.1167)	(.1129)
Teacher education (logged)	1.6467	1.6205
	(.2559)	(.2446)
R-squared	.39	.39
Adjusted R-squared	.38	.39
Standard error	3.85	3.84
F	80.73	135.50
N	1913	1917

Note: Standard errors in parentheses. Coefficient for years omitted.

norms to carry out their strategy (education levels). The last two reasons are especially important for the literature on political control of the bureaucracy, because they hold that bureaucrats resist political control when political goals conflict with their own goals and when resistance is relatively easy in terms of transaction costs.[31]

Table 5.4 considered all students classified as special education or limited English (LEP) as legitimate exemptions from the test. Assigning a student to either category, however, is a highly discretionary action, and some studies document abus-

---

31. The principal-agent model is silent on what occurs when the agent does not have the capacity to deliver what the principal wants. In the practical world of governance, this situation occurs frequently, as electoral institutions demand policy solutions to problems whose exact causes and solutions are not known.

es in these assignments (Heller, Holtzman, and Messick 1982; Meier and Stewart 1991). Such assignments can be used to create more homogeneous regular classes or to eliminate a problem student; both actions could make the teacher's task easier (Oakes 1985). One organizational strategy might be to institutionalize the cheating by imbedding it in the rules and procedures of the organization. In that way actions would seem to be the neutral application of decision rules, and individuals within the organization would have the support of their co-workers for decisions such as these (Meier and Stewart 1991).

An institutionalized way of cheating would be simply to have administrative and management policies that overassign students to special education or LEP classifications. This approach would provide more potential students who could be exempted from the exam without anyone having to make a special case. In both instances there are other incentives to overclassify students into these categories, since additional federal funds are allocated to districts based on the numbers. As noted above, some professional norms also support the grouping of students into homogeneous classes (Meier and Stewart 1991; Oakes 1985). Of the two classifications, designating a student as LEP is far easier than assigning a student to special education. In the special education situation, federal rules require that the decision be made in consultation with parents and that parents have the right to challenge such assignments.[32]

One way to provide some leverage on the notion of institutionalized cheating is to see how well assignments to these classes are determined by variables that should predict such classifications. For limited-English proficiency this approach is relatively straightforward; the largest group of students in this classification are Latinos; those who are recent immigrants and are also much more likely to be poor.[33] Districts that assign more students to LEP than would be expected given their number of Latino students and poor students, therefore, might well be engaged in institutionalized cheating. Assignment to special education has been modeled by Lankford and Wyckoff (1996) as a function of Latino students, poor students, black students, class size, LEP students, total enrollment, and special education funding. Districts that assign more students to special education than would be predicted by these factors, therefore, are also worth examining for potential cheating.

Table 5.5 presents the regression equations for LEP and special education students. The LEP equation explains 58 percent of the variation using only Latino students and poor students. The special education equation explains less variation (37%) but is

---

32. How effective these rights are has not been determined. The greater procedural protections as well as the trend in special education for more precise classifications should limit the excessive use of special education classifications. Whether they do or not remains to be proven.

33. LEP students in Texas are almost all Spanish speaking, except in Houston, and even in Houston the vast majority of LEP students speak Spanish.

highly consistent with past models. The residuals from these equations (designating the difference between "predicted" and actual rates of assignment) indicate variance distinct from accepted determinants of LEP and special education assignments *and* will be our measure of "institutionalized cheating." Large positive residuals indicate that a district assigns more students to the LEP (or special education) category than would be expected, given the types of students it has and other factors.

Adding the variable representing institutionalized cheating via LEP and special education assignments to the equation in table 5.4 produces some dramatic changes (see table 5.6). Rather than retaining the original measures of LEP and special education, we included the predicted values from the equations in table 5.5, thus dividing the students into predictable assignments (likely assignments based on criteria) and unpredictable assignments (overclassifications). The level of explained variation jumps a full five percentage points. Both measures of institutionalized cheating are strongly and positively related to test exemptions (one-fourth of an exemption for every student overclassified in LEP and nearly one-half of an exemption (0.44) for every student overassigned to special education). The original variable for students in LEP classifications drops to statistical insignificance; that is, only the LEP assignments not related to poverty and ethnicity generate additional test exemptions. These findings suggest that some of the organizational cheating is imbedded in the procedures used to classify students as having limited English skills and special education problems.[34]

The insignificance of legitimate LEP exemptions suggests that the relationships for some of the other variables might also reflect, not conscious decisions, but institutional processes that produce the same results. Task demands, which have been measured as student heterogeneity, are also likely to trigger greater use of the classification process. By fostering decision rules that institutionalize the sorting process (the equivalent of structure), school systems can generate better test scores without having to ask their teachers and administrators directly to engage in cheating. The organization's processes, therefore, both generate beneficial results and rationalize the exemptions to members of the organization.

Cheating behavior via the creation of a biased sample can therefore result from two processes. In one case the use of sampling bias may be the intent of bureaucrats in the organization as they respond to demands from a principal. In the second instance, the results may be unintended, with the sample-biasing procedures imbedded in the institutional framework of the organization (see Knight 1992 on

---

34. This finding is reinforced by the availability of a version of the exam in Spanish for children at lower grade levels. Students with limited English skills can be tested in either English or Spanish and be included in the test results.

TABLE 5.5
Determinants of Limited English and Special Education Classification

Independent variable	Dependent variable: Percentage of students in LEP classes	
	LEP classes	Special education
Latino students (%)	.2387	−.0478
	(.0094)	(.0046)
Low-income students (%)	.1183	.0895
	(.0134)	(.0059)
Black students (%)	n.a.	−.0547
		(.0058)
Class size	n.a.	−.0174ns*
		(.0174)
LEP students	n.a.	−.0969
		(.0081)
Enrollment total (000s)	n.a.	−.0164
		(.0040)
Special education funding	n.a.	.3178
		(.0167)
R-squared	.58	.37
Adjusted R-squared	.58	.37
Standard error	7.52	2.55
F	1343.74	161.57
N	1917	1917

Note: Standard errors in parentheses.
  *ns = not significant.

the general bias of institutions). As students of administration have long maintained, administrative agencies as institutions embed consequential values into their regular functioning (Selznick 1957). Indeed, layers of embedded values and processes accrete over time. While public administration scholars have often suggested that such institutionalization of values improves the prospect of democracy through bureaucratic organizations (Wamsley et al., 1990), an assessment of the consequences depends critically on which values are institutionalized and how these comport with public preferences. Professional and administrative procedures that might reinforce tendencies to cheat, of course, would not be defensible in terms of democratic theory. In addition, institutionalizing procedures that encourage biasing a student-testing sample also reduce the ability of political principals to exercise oversight. Even if such procedures are used intentionally to bias the sample, members of the organization with such an institutional framework can merely contend that they are following the rules of good educational practice. Such efforts to bias the sample will be more difficult to find and even more difficult for political actors to counter.

Although the analysis thus far has pointed to some behaviors that might be the result of cheating, it has not directly assessed the payoffs. Table 5.3, of course, demonstrates that exemptions are related to test scores. What remains to be seen is whether these institutionalized exemptions have a similar impact. To determine if that is the

TABLE 5.6
Institutionalized Organizational Cheating

Independent variable	Dependent variable: Percentage of test exemptions
Legitimate exemptions	
Limited English	.0042ns*
	(.0187)
Special education	.6659
	(.0574)
Resources	
Instructional spending	−.0018
	(.0003)
Task demands	1.4545
	(.0724)
Bureaucrats (logged)	−.5430
	(.1096)
Teacher education (logged)	1.0241
	(.2402)
Institutionalized cheating	
Limited English	.2580
	(.0136)
Special education	.4382
	(.0343)
R-squared	.44
Adjusted R-squared	.44
Standard error	3.69
F	135.47
N	1917

Notes: Standard errors in parentheses. Coefficient for years omitted.
   *ns = not significant.

case, we return to table 5.3 and add the two institutionalized exemptions to the model predicting test scores (we cannot add the predicted values to the model because LEP-predicted values are completely collinear with poor and Latino students). The findings, reported in table 5.7, are consistent with a conscious process. The impact of regular exemptions drops from 0.20 to 0.17. Although institutionalized LEP exemptions are related to higher test scores, their impact is smaller, about 0.13 (0.17 − 0.04 = 0. 13). The institutionalized special education exemptions, however, add approximately three times the impact of a regular exemption (0.54, or 0.17 + 0 .37). In short, a district that systematically overclassifies students into exempt categories, especially into special education classes, can have a significant impact on its overall test scores.

CONCLUSION

When political principals demand performance from bureaucratic agents, agents can choose from a wide repertoire of strategic actions available as potential responses. This chapter has examined one such possible action: cheating. Cheating allows the agent to provide the principal with exactly what had been requested while skirting the principal's actual intent.

Using data from school districts in Texas, we define cheating as exemptions from standardized tests that are not related to the permitted reasons for such exemptions. All other things being equal, districts with more exemptions have higher test scores; the incentive to cheat is clearly present. Overall, however, the level of cheating would have to be considered modest; organizations in general have taken far fewer exemptions than they have been entitled to take. This finding suggests that bureaucratic values have generally been benign in these instances.

Our model of cheating performs moderately well. While cheating is not related to performance gaps, it is related to a dearth of resources, more difficult task demands, fewer transaction costs, and higher levels of education (indicating professional norms in favor of classification). We further investigated the nature of the assignment process to determine if the "cheating" is institutionalized in the processes of the bureaucracy. Although this investigation cannot cover all methods of assignment, it does find evidence consistent with institutionalized processes. The implication of this finding is that such patterns, which often operate without conscious questioning by bureaucrats and the administrators who supervise their operations, can generate results that could be interpreted as cheating.

Second, to the extent that cheating is driven by factors inherent in the organization and its environment—difficult task demands, low levels of resources, professional norms—it will be extremely difficult for any political principal to counteract. The principal has to challenge the agent in realms where the agent has a substantial advantage because of information asymmetry (Moe 1982; Niskanen 1971). Professional norms also reflect what Sabatier and Jenkins-Smith (1993) refer to as deep core values, and as such they are highly resistant to change. This point suggests, in turn, that a residuum of bureaucratic independence, with associated bureaucratic values and experiences, must be kept squarely in the picture for any serious treatment of the bureaucracy-democracy question.

Third, the present study is situated in an environment that is close to optimal for political control over bureaucracy. This observation underlines the importance of the last point. The political principals in this investigation are united in their objectives for the agents; the goals are not incompatible with the professional values of the agents; and the political principals have a precise objective measure of performance. Even in this ideal situation, however, bureaucratic agents are able to influence agency outputs in ways unintended by the political principals. If bureaucratic deviance operates under ideal conditions such as these, then we can expect to find it in other instances where the model of political control does not have such

TABLE 5.7
The Benefits of Institutionalized Cheating

Independent variable	Dependent variable: Percentage of students passing exam
Low-income students	−.2530
	(.0145)
Black students	−.1872
	(.0129)
Latino students	−.0691
	(.0100)
Class size	−.3801
	(.0413)
Teachers' salaries (000)	.5700
	(.0832)
Instructional spending	.0010
	(.0005)
Student exemptions	.1662
	(.0348)
Institutionalized exemptions	
Special education	.3723
	(.0547)
Limited English	−.0382
	(.0184)
R-squared	.70
Adjusted R-squared	.70
Standard error	5.68
F	373.51
N	1914

Note: Coefficient for annual dummies not reported. Numbers in parentheses are standard errors.

overwhelming advantages—surely including networked contexts. We are not contending that bureaucracies are out of control, or that bureaucracies are unresponsive to political pressures. Bureaucracies are open systems and are responsive to a wide range of environmental pressures. Any external pressures from political institutions, however, must compete with other external pressures as well as internal bureaucratic values and procedures. Bureaucracies juggle many different forces and, therefore, respond to them strategically on the basis of the signals they receive and their own judgment of the situation (Carpenter 1996).

Fourth, any principal-agent study that relies on an assessment of organizational outcomes must go beyond the numbers produced by the organization and deal with the process by which the outcomes are generated. A strategic agent can provide ostensibly desired results by a wide variety of means, some acceptable and some not. Only by examining the bureaucracy's internal processes can the meaning of agency outcomes be determined. A principal who is satisfied with changes in the simple raw measures of outcomes risks being manipulated by a strategic agent, even if outcome figures are accurately reported. The principal-agent problem, we believe, is far more complex than is normally portrayed in the empirical literature based in political science. This complexity generated by a strategic agent, however, is what makes the principal-agent model theoretically interesting. A further implication here, then, is that those who care about democratic governance must begin to develop the portrayal of the public agency, its strategic perspective, its values, and its standard processes far beyond what has been done thus far in political science and even more fully than has been the standard fare in public administration.

Fifth, we have focused at length on the cheating question here, but it is prudent to keep in mind that the focus has actually been on only one form of cheating: generating biased samples. Other possibilities are often available to bureaucratic actors, as the discussion early in the chapter makes clear: lying and cutting corners. And even the biasing of samples can be a layered and intricate set of processes; we have sketched two aspects for one kind of public organization in this chapter alone. In short, the forms of bureaucratic discretion and influence are myriad; and it is unlikely that even the most intricate forms of oversight will be able to capture the on-the-ground realities of the impacts of these bureaucratic efforts.

Sixth, despite the many limitations of the principal-agent perspective, which have received special emphasis in this book, the results reported in this chapter imply that one should nonetheless be cautious in going too far in the direction away from political control, as have some of the more aggressive public administration scholars (see chap. 2). The present chapter has not determined whether the bureaucratic values evident in our sample of school systems actually produced better educational results for students. Exempted students might benefit from avoiding the stigma of failing a high-profile exam, but to the extent that students who are exempted would have benefited from assessment or consequent remedial actions, the quality of public education has been reduced by these bureaucratic decisions. The pros and cons of both special and bilingual education fill a massive literature. Whether students in districts that used a large number of exemptions are better off than students in other districts remains an empirical question and to some extent an issue about how different values should be weighed. What is unambiguous, however, is that such results do not score well on the criterion of top-down democratic governance. Subtle patterns of exempting students from test taking and improving districts' outcome reports are clearly not the intent of political principals, nor does any evidence remotely suggest that such results fit the preferences of students, their parents, or the communities in which these school systems operate. Patterns of outcomes driven by professional values, administrative routines, and the incentives operating in public bureaucracies—but not by discussion among stakeholders, decisions by locales or school boards, or open debate in community forums—hardly signal a close fit between bureaucracy and democracy.

This chapter's analysis illustrates the potential gains in theory from assuming a strategic agent, even if it also offers a potential complication in terms of the practical requisites for democratic governance. The chapter does not provide a crucial test between approaches that assume strategic politicians and those that assume strategic bureaucrats. Such a test would require precise and objectively verifiable definitions of goals and strategies for both principal and agent. In fact, political principals could be well aware that agents are manipulating numbers and acquiesce in such actions because their true goal might be higher numbers (regardless of the reasons for them).[35] High numbers help politicians solve their own problems with the electorate that employs them as agents. Such cooperative strategies between politicians and bureaucrats are always possible when an output measure is not perfect—in this case, when test scores are not the same as overall extent of quality education. So while the traditional view of strong principal control could technically be consistent with the results presented here, that explanation is more cumbersome and less parsimonious than simply returning to the more plausible assumption that agents are also strategic actors who seek to maximize bureaucratic values.

Note, finally, the disquieting consequence of such a theoretical improvement: a nontrivial challenge to democracy. The coverage in chapter 4 also shows clear evidence that bureaucratic discretion can shape agency outputs and outcomes, but there the context is more benign: agents improving performance for relatively disadvantaged clients. The function reported there is clearly representational. The present chapter does not show rogue agents out of control, but rather deliberate, and deliberative, professionalized educational decision makers apparently shaping results partially to score well on a metric with only tenuous links to any well-accepted mandated standard. Further, the results suggest that at least a portion of the discretion absorbed in the bureaucracy is not explicitly considered by thoughtful agents weighing the tradeoffs, but rather shaped implicitly by well-worn professional beliefs that may have little standing or even visibility in the broader community.

Before proceeding with an assessment of bureaucracy and democracy, it is useful to recapitulate the findings of our three empirical chapters. First, the structural relationship between politicians and bureaucrats is often not a simple one-to-one hierarchical relationship but rather a complex networked type of relationship that can frustrate efforts at top-down political control (chap. 3). Second, bureaucracies also

---

35. The efforts by principals to restrict cheating, including the ban of all test exemptions starting in 1999, suggest otherwise. Despite the ban on exemptions, recent reports suggest that 11 percent of students were exempted on the 2002 test, and the state was fined $440,000 by the U.S. Department of Education in 2005 for excessive exemptions.

perform representation functions. Many of the findings of political control could well involve bureaucrats maximizing their own values (chap. 4). Third, even in a structurally optimal case with unified political principals, bureaucracies can alter political programs to reflect bureaucratic values more closely (chap. 5).

Bureaucrats are strategic agents, but they are neither an inherently out-of-control antidemocratic force, as is sometimes claimed in the literature of political science, nor a natural and predictable ally of political principals or the citizenry, as students of public administration sometimes argue. Rather, they offer both possibilities, even within the same policy sphere, jurisdiction, and period of time. This Janus-faced feature of bureaucratic influence represents the complex reality. The implications of this finding for the broader questions under review are the subject of chapter 6.

Appendix

TABLE 5.A1
Regression Estimates without Influential Points

	Dependent variable: Percentage of test exemptions	
Independent variable	Coefficient	Standard error
Legitimate exemptions		
Limited English	.0188	.0176ns[*]
Special education	.6885	.0527
Resources		
Instructional spending	−.0019	.0002
Task demands	1.4778	.0659
Bureaucrats (logged)	−.6030	.0994
Teacher education (logged)	1.2960	.2229
Institutionalized cheating		
Limited English	.2862	.0140
Special education	.4276	.0318
R-squared	.49	
Adjusted R-squared	.49	
Standard error	3.23	
F	159.61	
N	1839	

Note: All points with Cooks' Ds over .3000 omitted.
[*]ns = not significant.

TABLE 5.A2
Robust Regression Estimates

Independent variable	Dependent variable: Percentage of test exemptions	
	Coefficient	Standard error
Legitimate exemptions		
Limited English	.0556	.0130
Special education	.6961	.0374
Resources		
Instructional spending	−.0018	.0002
Task demands	1.4134	.0472
Bureaucrats (logged)	−.5458	.0708
Teacher education (logged)	1.2574	.1599
Institutionalized cheating		
Limited English	.3229	.0104
Special education	.4024	.0229
R-squared	.65	
Adjusted R-squared	.65	
Standard error	2.01	
F	322.11	
N	1911	

Note: Estimated with Andrews Sine and eight iterations.

CHAPTER SIX

Democracy, Bureaucracy, and Modern Governance

How can the necessity of bureaucracy be reconciled with the values of democracy? The challenge remains a central issue in twenty-first century public life. As attention has been broadened to issues of governance rather than governments, administrative arrangements have come to take many forms but clearly have not withered away. Rather, they have become increasingly important as policy problems have become more difficult to solve, as electoral institutions have sought action but have become stymied about how to resolve contentious disputes, and as globalized pressures have subjected policies to forces beyond the control of national governance systems.

Although the initial chapter showed that specialists in many fields have analyzed the topic, this book has reexamined the bureaucracy-democracy question by concentrating on the two major streams of literature: the political control of the bureaucracy literature from political science and the normative bureaucratic values literature from public administration. While the political science literature offers an established body of systematic empirical work, the result exhibits several critical faults. The primary weakness has been the unwillingness of those conducting the empirical studies to take administrative institutions themselves seriously—to incorporate what administrative units are doing in the context of efforts by electoral institutions to influence them. For the political-control perspective to be persuasive, it would have to be grounded in evidence that electoral institutions somehow influence bureaucracy to act in a way that it would not have acted had there been no electoral-institution efforts. The easiest way to obtain such evidence would be to measure bureaucratic values as well as the preferences of the electoral institutions and then compare these values to actual policy actions over time (see chap. 1). If policies were to change to correspond with political values and away from bureaucratic ones, one could contend that political institutions had influenced the result. As chapter 2 shows, the studies in this genre have consistently fallen short of even such an elementary test of the core political-control hypothesis.

The bureaucratic-values literature within public administration, on the other hand, focuses most of its efforts on the question of the values held by the bureaucracy. This literature then quickly plunges into normative aspects, as various scholars have attempted to specify a set of values that administrative decision makers should hold. Missing in this literature is any systematic effort to document extant bureaucratic values, a crucial first step both in addressing the bureaucracy-democracy challenge and in taking practical action on the normative agenda espoused by many of these same scholars. Needless to say, the challenge cannot be met by invoking a circular logic: simply stipulating that whatever the bureaucratic values might happen to be will necessarily be appropriate or supportive of democratic governance. What little empirical literature can be found on bureaucratic values, as a result, has generally been limited to findings gleaned from surveys that were not designed to address questions of bureaucratic values or the relationship between bureaucrats and the broader polity.

Chapters 3 through 5 confronted these main approaches in the political science and public administration literatures with evidence on three key themes that bear on the bureaucracy-democracy question. Other questions deserve systematic treatment as well—later in this chapter we sketch additional issues that should be on the research agenda—but these three explorations were designed to move beyond merely analytical critiques and into the empirical settings where, we are convinced, the complex realities of and tensions between democracy and bureaucracy can best be discerned. Each of these chapters provides a key lesson. The first has to do with the structural realities of today's governing arrangements; the other two show the importance of administrative institutions in determining policy results, as well as how this considerable influence offers both support for democratic values and also a challenge to the democratic ideal.

Empirical Lesson 1: Bureaucracy in the strict sense does not accurately characterize many of the implementation settings of modern governance. The variety of administrative arrangements includes frequent use of networked forms, and these do not fit the assumptions of either the political science or public administration theoretical perspectives.

Not all public agencies are of a piece. They vary considerably in their schedules of values even within a single government, and structural differences can also be considerable. One important structural element in the bureaucracy-democracy linkage, the growth of networks as an implementation form, was examined in chapter 3. Numerous programs are designed as, or have evolved into, networked forms—collections of government agencies (often linked across different levels of government), private organizations, nonprofit providers, and others that are connected through a pattern in which no single actor has the power to compel compliance from the others. While networks are not a universal phenomenon, chapter 3 demonstrates their very frequent occurrence. By examining U.S. legislative and rule-making actions for two different time periods, we show that even by conservative measures, networked arrays are invoked in a high proportion of policy cases. Networks create serious problems for the notion of top-down democratic control simply because top-down control relies on a hierarchical chain of command, and such a chain does not exist in networks. Networks also raise challenges to the bureaucratic-values approach to the subject; when a dozen or more organizations of varying types, preferences, and recruitment patterns are networked on behalf of a public program, there may be little or no common, coherent base of values to serve as ballast across the multiple units. These complications pose serious difficulties for those who would advocate a simple, one-size-fits-all solution to the bureaucracy-democracy challenge; indeed, they call into question the conventional notion of "bureaucracy" itself. Although we shall employ this term through the remainder of this chapter, it should be understood as a shorthand encompassing the much broader array of institutional forms that have emerged in today's governance settings.

Empirical Lesson 2: Bureaucratic values are frequently more important than those of political overseers in driving policy results. This finding does not necessarily mean a weakening of democratic governance, since the bureaucracy can also perform representative functions.

Chapter 4 moved the analysis from the national to the local level, and also from the complicatedly networked settings that many programs now occupy to relatively simple and bureaucratic ones. Chapters 4 and 5 provide a pair of critical tests of whether electoral institutions can control bureaucratic action. Analysis at the local level offers the opportunity to compare performance rigorously across many distinct governing units, and studying the governance of school districts presents findings for the best—or optimal—case contexts for the exercise of political control. Using the case of Latino education policy, the theory of representative bureaucracy, and an improved research design for assessing political control, the chapter demonstrates that bureaucratic values are far more important than political ones in determining the final policy outcomes of the educational organizations examined. Latino teachers produce far more policy benefits for Latino students than Latino politicians do. This finding holds despite our best efforts to develop and test new variables crafted to tap other channels through which politicians might have been able to demonstrate some influence. The findings of chapter 4 not only challenge the overwhelming majority of political control findings, they also suggest that ways other than top-down political control can be found to reconcile bureaucracy with democracy. In this case, bureaucracy itself can perform representative functions and directly respond to at least some of the policy needs of the public.

Empirical Lesson 3: Even under almost optimal conditions for top-down political control of the bureaucracy, the bureaucracy can exert influence over policy outcomes in significant ways that are unintended by political leaders. And even in settings where the bureaucracy is capable of a representative function, it is also capable of acting on behalf of its own agenda and values rather than the preferences of political leaders or the broader public.

Chapter 5 continued the analysis at the local level by taking the investigation of the political control argument one step further. Many circumstances present less than optimal conditions for the exercise of top-down political control, so we sought out a situation in which political overseers could most clearly be expected to dominate the bureaucracy. Again the policy arena explored was education, but rather than focus on policy benefits for a subset of students, the emphasis was on compliance with political edicts. The chapter characterized a set of empirical circumstances that should maximize opportunities for political control: cases in which all political principals agree on a set of goals (higher standardized test scores), the process of monitoring bureaucratic action is both precise and widely publicized and thus of low cost to policy makers, and structural impediments (unmanageable spans of control, the presence of complex networked administrative forms, and such) do not play a factor. The empirical analysis showed, however, that even in this "ideal" situation, bureaucratic values are able to influence policy systematically in ways unintended by the electoral institutions. In this set of circumstances, the implementing apparatus used its expertise to exempt students from the mandated exam. Institutionalized processes of overclassifying students as either in need of special education or as having only limited English skills provide the bureaucracy with a large amount of discretion to determine which students take the exam, a decision that directly affects the overall score on standardized tests.

These empirical conclusions do not boil down to a simple nostrum or two; there are clearly no rabbit-from-the-hat solutions to the bureaucracy-democracy challenge. Rather, although political officials simply cannot exercise dominant control over the bureaucracy most, or all, of the time, that reality does not necessarily mean that administrative institutions consistently pose a clear threat to democratic governance. Sometimes they can act to further democratic values, sometimes otherwise. The first five chapters demonstrate not only how difficult it is for a system of governance to reconcile bureaucracy with democracy but also that the two are not necessarily at war. The subtleties matter, and these depend heavily on the particulars of the relevant empirical setting. At present, even a full specification of the range of issues and dimensions in play docs not seem feasible. Accordingly, because we have not solved all the problems associated with the dominant approaches to analysis means that we should resist the temptation to advocate a simple and compelling—but ultimately wrong—solution to what is a complex challenge. At the same time, we can say more than, in effect, "It all depends." We have learned a great deal about the issues, and we use the remainder of this chapter to cover a series of implications that flow from our prior analysis. These offer additional lessons and cautionary notes, and they also suggest directions for future studies of bureaucracy and democracy.

More specifically, we explore implications regarding institutional questions, the centrality of bureaucratic values, the need to look within the bureaucracy for hints and answers to questions about democracy, the relevance of public management to the bureaucracy-democracy challenge, and the dangers of wrongheadedly applying an exclusively incentives-driven logic to the public management function itself. These subjects also suggest research questions that need attention. Late in the chapter we unpack a sample of these to outline an agenda for making further progress.

TOWARD A PRAGMATIC INSTITUTIONALISM

Can the careful design of institutions, including those intended to implement policy, solve the bureaucracy-democracy problem? Even though institutional design shapes what happens to, and through, the bureaucracy, the analyses in the present volume show that the answer is no. Institutional details are clearly consequential, but to achieve effective democratic governance considerably more is needed than the up-front engineering of an implementation apparatus.

The creation, design, and operation of institutions are unquestionably important in the linkage between bureaucracy and democracy. Institutions, broadly construed, represent systematic efforts to shape the actions of individuals on an ongoing basis. As such, they create biases and influence outcomes. Notwithstanding this truism, the creed advocated by what we have called the "organizational creation-science" group (McCubbins, Noll, and Weingast 1987) clearly overstates the power of institutional control, especially in numerous governance systems in the United States. Institutions matter, but they are not determinative.

Consider the political-control perspective. The role of U.S. institutions is especially shaped by the national context, the separation of powers, and the federal system. For political control of bureaucracy to be a viable proposition, there must be some coherence in the actions of the political controllers as well as in the agents of political control. Unlike the unified political systems of the Westminster-style Anglo democracies (Australia, New Zealand, England) or the corporatist democracies of Europe (Austria, Sweden, the Netherlands), the United States is deliberately designed as a fragmented political system that operates to limit majoritarian impulses and thus policy coherence. The cross-national experience with "New Public Management" reforms, discussed more fully later in this chapter, clearly demonstrates that the extent of reform possible by means of political action is directly a function of the unity of political leadership in support of reform (Pollitt and Bouckaert 2000). Political control is subject to the same constraints.

As Norton Long (1952) perceptively noted many years ago, the failure of the U.S. political system to centralize political power is a key factor in encouraging bureaucracies to develop independent sources of support. The multiple and fragmented power bases just within the political branches of government mean that there are multiple views of what democracy means in practice—what the intentions of "the people" really are. Fragmentation of the political system, along with the independent power bases of the bureaucracy, makes the notion of top-down political *control* a virtually impossible goal to attain in the United States.

Many local governments in the United States, including the school districts examined in some of the empirical chapters earlier in this book, are formally unitary. Here too, however, as the results already reported make clear, even nearly ideal institutional design—from the perspective of political controllers—provides substantial independence of action for bureaucratic decision makers. Efforts from Washington to reshape educational outcomes encounter substantially longer odds, as they wend their way via indirect policy instruments through the federal system to independent local districts. Local districts then have many ways to comply with hierarchical edicts that may or may not be consistent with national reforms.

Although scholars of public administration have recognized the problems of political fragmentation, and some political scientists (Waterman, Rouse, and Wright 2004) are willing to consider what they term the "multiple principals problem," neither literature has incorporated a second important element of institutional design: the creation of networks for policy development and implementation. Examining the bewildering complexity of implementation networks in environmental policy, family planning, agricultural policy, economic development, and a variety of other fields, one might conclude that these institutional arrangements were designed intentionally to limit top-down political control. Furthermore, as indicated in chapter 3, networks have also been identified as a standard set of institutional relationships in numerous other countries, including many where separation-of-powers arrangements are not in place. Networks, whether in the United States or elsewhere, can incorporate nonprofit organizations with deeply held values, private sector organizations that theoretically are almost immune to political influences, and other units of government elected by different populations. Lines of command are severed or, at minimum, seriously weakened and stretched, with no single actor given the authority to compel action on the part of others.

One should be careful not to conclude that a networked form in the implementation apparatus drives policy results in some straightforward fashion. What can be concluded, however, is that the standard approaches must be called into question by the phenomenon. Neither the political science literature, which ignores the network implementation form (as well as most of the bureaucratic side of the equation), nor the public administration literature, which recognizes networks but does not systematically deal with the issues they raise, provides a democratic solution to this real-world situation. We have not resolved this conundrum, either. Our study does demonstrate, however, that top-down political control of such implementation webs is unlikely to work and that bottom-up grounding by an emerging multiorganizational institutional form is also likely to be rare. The actual creation of these networks offers fertile ground for organizational creation scientists to ply their trade, perhaps in ever-more-implausible ex post facto arguments that the complex and tangled patterns somehow engender the policy results that the political leaders actually wanted all along. Our assessment of the formation of networks, however, shows little evidence of systematic intelligent design (see chap. 3). In addition, our finding that even the relatively simple hierarchical forms found in public education are difficult to control politically implies that complex networks increase the difficulty many-fold.

We do not mean to imply that politicians are irrelevant. While they are less relevant in the United States than in many other countries, in some circumstances they can markedly influence the direction that administrative systems take. Politics is a key part of the bureaucratic environment, an aspect that is itself at times more or less organized. Our open-systems model of organizations, formalized in the appendix, takes as a given that bureaucracies will respond to environmental pressures, be they from political officials, the public, or other sources. Chapter 4, as an illustration, shows that the election of Latinos to school boards had implications that reverberated throughout the educational system. Meier, O'Toole, and Nicholson-Crotty (2004) use these same data to illustrate how school board representation is translated into bureaucratic representation, which in turn moves down through hierarchy to the street level (i.e., school boards influencing administrators who then hire teachers). With the politically informed change in personnel, and thus values, further ripples of influence can be discerned. Policy outputs and, more importantly, policy outcomes change in the intended direction. The process works across multiple levels of the governance system and does so in a manner that is as much indirect as direct. Bureaucrats are often able to achieve more than one might have expected on the basis of a small amount of political stimulus. Political influence is also implied by the wealth of studies on political control, as cited in chapter 2—although without a measure of bureaucratic values, it must remain open to question whether there has been any actual political influence (see also the case study literature summarized in Meier 2000). Political influence on U.S. bureaucratic entities is a reality; the notion of political *control*, however, is a brobdignagian exaggeration of the role politics plays in American governance.

Top-down control efforts, whether by bureaucratic leaders or by political officials,[1] have to confront the reality of discretion. So, too, do the predominantly institutionalist theories emphasized by some researchers in political science. Few policies are so simple in concept or application that they can be implemented without vesting discretion in the bureaucrats involved. Delegation is practiced by political branches out of necessity.[2] It provides to politicians the benefits of expertise, the policy distance they desire to avoid blame, a process of claiming credit, and the promise of administrative efficiencies. Administrative discretion in some cases can be displaced—that is, moved from one part of the administrative apparatus to another. It can be reduced somewhat if politicians are willing to make the tradeoffs between control and the quality and efficiency of the administrative process, but it cannot be eliminated.

The locus of discretion in an organization is important to how much top-down political influence is possible. Discretion vested in top-level administrators is more likely to be influenced by political actors, simply because it is more visible to them and because the actors are more accessible. Reaching great distances down the chain of command, however, is difficult. Spanning the policy spaces in a networked implementation system is even more difficult and might be done only on an occasional basis. Systematic control in such systems is not possible without taking on massive transactions costs. Relying on "fire-alarm" controls offers promise in theory, but given the number of policy networks and the number of actors and the multiple

1. For more careful coverage of this aspect of top-down influence, see the discussion of public management, below.

2. The real question is not the one currently occupying a portion of legislative scholars—whether or not to delegate control over a policy to the bureaucracy (Huber and Shippan 2002)—because legislative institutions have no possibility of implementing a policy on their own. The choice is between delegating power to bureaucracy or simply not adopting a policy at all. Given the decision to adopt a policy, the choice becomes how one might structure the implementing institution. The choice about delegation at that point is a foregone conclusion.

channels of political communication, such systems are easily overloaded; witness the repeated, confusing, and sometimes contradictory fire-alarm signals emanating in recent years from the homeland-security system. A fire alarm has value to the extent that it goes off only rarely; if it continually blares, it becomes background noise to be ignored.

We do not mean to imply that legislative design actions are irrelevant; they are not. By intelligent design, for instance, Congress can make its task of overseeing bureaucracies easier (or, lacking intelligent design, more difficult). To illustrate, we can point out that adopting a regulatory process that relies on cooperation between regulatory officials and the regulated in an effort to encourage voluntary compliance requires that street-level operatives be given real discretion. Only with discretion can officials overlook the minor violations or one-time major violations and develop the trust with the regulated needed to engender joint problem solving. The ability to control such a process politically from the top, as a result, becomes much more difficult.[3]

Similarly, the idea that political institutions can design accountability systems that operate to enforce their own goals is plausible in a purely theoretical sense, but not nearly as easy as it appears. Except with very simple bottom-line agencies—that is, units established to execute a policy or set of policies the results of which are fully transparent when reported via some simple output metrics (e.g., federal credit agencies; see Khademian 1995; Meier, Polinard, and Wrinkle 1999)[4]—the legislature has to create a second bureaucracy to monitor the first one. The No Child Left Behind Act in the United States, as an example, has generated a massive monitoring and verification process that has been imposed on state governments and local school districts. Political goal displacement occurs because a substantial portion of the money allocated for programs is devoted to auditing rather than policy implementation. Even in the presence of well-designed auditing and accountability systems, as is clear from the empirical analysis reported in chapter 5, bureaucratic cheating is quite possible. Accountability systems rely of necessity on data and are only effective if the data accurately represent what the organization actually does in all relevant respects. When a bureaucracy's function—say, education—diverges from the demands of an accountability system—say, standardized testing—incen-

---

3. Whether the amount of political influence from other sources is more or less is an open question. That is, individual legislators can try to intervene in individual cases to get the bureaucracy to act as the individual legislator desires (e.g., to benefit a constituent). Such efforts are not top-down political control and may take on aspects of political patronage. More generally, the inevitability and also advisability of administrative discretion is a theme, and a conclusion, developed at great length in the literature of public administration.

4. Even when intervention is needed, such policy areas tend to be highly complex, so Congress rarely intervenes unless absolutely necessary.

tives are thereby created to game the accountability system rather than focus on core functions.

Ignored in most of the institutional discussion is the role of management (for an important exception, see Miller 1992). While some attention in the political-control literature has been focused on political appointments, that emphasis has been on the appointments per se or, on rare occasions, the policy views of the appointee. The management skills of the appointee are rarely discussed. Our research on management and organizations (see the appendix) implies strongly that management plays a significant role in what organizations do. Our empirical studies validate the point (Meier and O'Toole 2001, 2002, 2003; O'Toole and Meier 2003, 2004), not merely from the perspective of political appointees but also from the standpoint of permanent cadres of managers.[5] The range of influences emanating from management includes matters of recruitment, motivation, communication, and many more key aspects (see Carpenter 2001; Rainey 2003). Accordingly, we single management out for additional attention below.

For now, we can conclude that institutions matter but do not fix the results. Formal institutions interact with the people who operate within them. Just as people are changed by the institution and its roles, so too are the institutions modified as people's values come into play in ways that may generate tension, creative or destructive, with the values regnant among the earlier designers of the institution. Were this not the case, the study of organizations would have ended with Max Weber.

Ironically for the attention to institutional themes among researchers in political science, the redesign of U.S. political institutions is treated for some reason as off limits in politics as well as academia—this despite the wealth of newly designed institutions of governance in other parts of the world. Even at the state level, where far more experimentation has occurred, large-scale constitutional changes (aside from symbolic alterations focused on such questions as the definition of marriage) appear to be a thing of the past. For the advocates of political control over bureaucracy, the current U.S. system provides only limited indications that structural changes are used to control bureaucracy.

A fundamental question remains. How much political control over bureaucracy is possible to achieve by the manipulation of political structures? While no definitive answer is possible, literally thousands of studies of public policy incorporate structural factors, from the form of government studies of U.S. local government

---

5. In a few agencies, such as the Civil Rights Division in the Department of Justice, there may be sufficient political appointees to control all the key managerial functions of the organization (see Golden 2000). Still, such organizations are relatively rare, and we have no systematic information on how they operate in the long run.

(Morgan and Pelissero 1982), to some efforts to estimate the impact of having initiative or referenda processes (Donovan and Bowler 1998; Gerber 1999), to the role of at-large elections versus single-member districts (Engstrom and McDonald 1981; Leal, Meier, and Martinez-Ebers 2004). Painting these studies with a broad brush, we conclude that structure frequently matters (although sometimes it does not), but it is rarely the most influential factor and is often a relatively minor one. One of the great myths of American politics is that we can solve long-lasting and deep-seated problems of governance by manipulating structures (Seidman 1970). The vast empirical evidence, in contrast, suggests that structures are only a small part of the answer. Another key component is the set of values held by discretionary decision makers.

THE CENTRALITY OF BUREAUCRATIC VALUES

Throughout this book, in a variety of ways, we stress the importance of values, particularly bureaucratic values. As indicated above, no one has discovered a way to eliminate discretion in any organization, so we must work from models that assume such discretion. Where discretion is present, the values of the individuals making the decision come into play.[6] Just as important as values in one institution is the difference in values between political and bureaucratic actors. To examine the dance of politicos and bureaucrats without knowing the values held by each is the equivalent of playing baseball without bats or balls. Nothing in the theory of principal-agent models suggests that principals and agents have conflicts on every value; to think that would be absurd. Both politicians and bureaucrats have zones of acceptance (Simon 1997) that overlap. By focusing on which values come into conflict, a far greater understanding of the interaction of agent and the principal is possible.

A general conclusion of this study is that, overall, *bureaucratic values trump political values in program implementation.* This conclusion should be a potent driver of research agendas, as we explain below. In chapter 4, as support for the proposition, we find that the influence of Latino teachers was far greater than the influence of Latino legislators; furthermore, Latino teachers' influence appears to be even greater when there are no Latino legislators in the district. In chapter 5 we show the subtle and intricate way that bureaucrats can get around political demands and implement policies that more closely match their own values. The requirement to subject all students to standardized testing was, and is, inconsistent with the professional values

6. Here, again, is an entree for the importance of recruitment, socialization, and other managerial lines of influence.

held by teachers. The logic of bureaucratic-values' dominance has been described by a variety of organizational scholars (e.g., Downs 1967). In this view, individuals at the top of an organization and political officials are at the top, have limited amounts of time, and lack detailed knowledge of the day-to-day functioning of the organization. Organizations, in fact, are designed this way so that top managers can focus on questions of leadership rather than the task of actually producing goods and services. Decisions at the apex of the organization are important and, as individual decisions go, might be the most important ones in the organization. Decisions taken at lower levels of the organization are not nearly as important, one by one, than those made near the top, but there are far more of them and they cumulate to a much larger total. In professionalized administrative settings with substantial devolution of decision making, these differences are even greater (see Mosher 1982).

Variations in Bureaucratic Values

Recognizing the discretion that must be retained at lower levels of an organization and the important role that values play in these lower-layered decisions, some of the best organization theorists have stressed that the function of organizational leadership is to try to shape these values (Barnard 1938; Simon 1947; see Kaufman 1960 for a public-organizational case involving this function). It is also important to consider the complexity of values that comes into play within the administrative apparatus. Bureaucratic values are shaped by professional training, socialization in the organization, the general forces of political socialization that operate with all citizens, and the vast array of factors that influences values in all individuals (race, gender, region, religion, salient events, etc.). Even in the most staid production process, bureaucrats offer an impressively broad and vivid palette of normative hues, not a monochromatic profile.

Chapters 4 and 5 demonstrate how values come into play in two different types of circumstances. In chapter 4, where the focus is on educational benefits for Latinos, political principals are not unified; that is, not all political principals feel that Latino education is the most important educational issue; African American board members could clearly offer alternative values. Differences among political elites quite logically provide space for bureaucratic values to operate, but the actual practice probably goes well beyond that point—as demonstrated by those districts that had no Latino politicians (or any other indicators of interest in better Latino education) to advocate such policies.

This values dimension, nonetheless, is not the only one observable in these cases. Chapter 5 goes on to demonstrate how complex these values can be, even in a single type of public organization. Texas schools operate in a unified political system, so there is but a single political principal: the school board. There are no separation-of-powers issues that inherently produce multiple principals. In the present case, involving standardized testing, valuing higher pass rates is a clear element of the preferences of members of the school board—and also of other political elites who have an interest in education: the governor, the state legislature, state education bureaucrats, federal education officials, etc. Even with these political principals unified on the importance of this value, bureaucrats have found space to inject their own perspectives. Whether the values of the bureaucrats merely involve efforts to cheat on the accountability system or whether they represent professional norms regarding the appropriateness of standardized testing for all students, the result is a set of behaviors at variance with the expressed goal of the politicos. It is useful to keep in mind, furthermore, that the situations analyzed are structured in ways to render bureaucratic independence unusually difficult. If even in such cases we see evidence of discretion and values in the administrative system shaping results, the modal case should offer considerably more opportunity for freedom of administrative action.

Bureaucracies can harbor an impressive array of values. That we were able to demonstrate empirical findings on both representative bureaucracy and organizational cheating with analyses involving the same set of organizations further underscores how varied and complex bureaucratic schedules of values are. No simple incentive systems or monitoring processes are likely to overcome these variegated patterns. At some point the transaction costs inherent in accountability systems can be expected to exceed the marginal benefit gained from them.

Representativeness in the Bureaucracy: Panacea or Chimera?

Some researchers, especially those approaching the bureaucracy-democracy challenge from the perspective of public administration, might find the notion of representative bureaucracies an attractive values-based option for reconciling the ideas of inevitable bureaucratic discretion and responsiveness to popular preferences. One argument treated seriously in chapter 4 is that bureaucrats might be able directly to represent the people (or some of the people) and press their interests within the bureaucracy. Although we favor more representative bureaucracies and despite the implications of these favorable findings, we urge caution on the part of those tempted to jump on the representative bureaucracy bandwagon, for four reasons.

First, although the concept of a representative bureaucracy is widely accepted by academics, it is highly unpopular with elected officials. Daley's (1984) survey of various methods of controlling the bureaucracy showed that legislators supported all the approaches mentioned, with the exception of representative bureaucracy, which they strongly opposed. Representative bureaucracy poses two challenges to political representatives. It rejects their prized role as the *exclusive* vehicle for representation, and it is inconsistent with the widely held, albeit incorrect, view among politicians that bureaucracy is not a political institution but operates merely to implement neutrally policies that are developed elsewhere.

Second, cases of active representation on the part of bureaucracy are exceptionally rare. Some values grounded in demographics do not become politicized, and thus bureaucrats have no way to express them. An example might be class issues in the United States. Other values might be relevant to policy or politics, but the bureaucrats involved might not have the discretion to act. The uniform application of the retirement program in the Social Security Administration is one example in which discretion is presently difficult to exercise (it has not always been so historically; see Lieberman 1998). Political systems are structured so as to emphasize some value conflicts and suppress others. The values likely to be encompassed by representative bureaucracy, therefore, vary by time and place (Keiser et al. 2002). Creating descriptively representative bureaucracies is also unlikely to be easy, as the relatively glacial pace of affirmative action in the federal government illustrates (Naff 2001). Given the need for discretion, the requirement for salient values, and the stipulation that bureaucracies be descriptively representative as preconditions, the number of cases of active bureaucratic representation is unlikely to be large.

Third, the values linked to representative bureaucracy are only one set of several that compete for the bureaucrats' attention. Equally, or perhaps more, important are the values socialized by the agency, the agency's mission, and the role the bureaucrat plays in attaining that mission. Similarly, professional values, particularly those tied to agency missions, are more likely to come into play than demographic origins.

Finally, representation may well conflict with other highly prized bureaucratic values—efficiency, effectiveness, impartiality (Kaufman 1956). Although one might look favorably on educational bureaucrats seeking to facilitate equal access to quality education for Latino students who have been denied it, a fully representative bureaucracy would be as contentious a setting as the political process often is now, since it would merely move the overt politics from the legislature to the administrative setting. While it is often viewed as perfectly acceptable for politicians to undercut public policy for political purposes, bureaucracies are not given the same leeway. Representative bureaucracy as an explicit model might also further the expectation that administrative institutions should provide preferential treatment rather than consider all citizens as equals.

To be sure, representative bureaucracy has been known to work on occasion, and in so doing generating what many would surely consider improved public policies (Keiser et al. 2002; Meier and Nicholson-Crotty 2005; Meier, Wrinkle, and Polinard 1999). Representative bureaucracy can be considered, therefore, as one tool in the governance process. More like a carpenter's level than a hammer or saw, it can be mobilized to add some adjustments to a process that is, in the main, fair and effective. As the predominant building block of bureaucracy and thus of a governance system, however, it is unlikely to forge a strong skeletal structure for governance.

Values and Distribution

An often-missed aspect of the values question in the bureaucracy is the issue of distribution — or redistribution. Politics is the determination of who gets what, when, and how (Lasswell 1936). Lost in the discussions of bureaucracy and democracy is this distributional dimension of the interactions among these institutions. The notion of goal conflict within the principal-agent model can be viewed as the contrast between the different values about public policy held by each set of institutions. Advocacy of principal-agent models and their top-down view of democracy means endorsing political values over bureaucratic ones regardless of the circumstances. Every political decision creates some winners and some losers. The same can be said for any bureaucratic policy decision. The locus of decision making, as a result, has distributional consequences.

In any dispute on values, however, rational individuals can prefer one set of values over another. Citizens could well prefer bureaucratic values over political ones;[7] if political values were always preferred, then the era of spoils system politics would never have ended. David Spence (2003) demonstrates formally that citizens in many cases would opt to take the "political" values out of a process to insure consistency over time, provide some emphasis on efficiency and fairness, or for a wide variety of other valued purposes. Bureaucrats may also value the preferences or interests of those under- or unrepresented in the short-term electoral cycles: immigrants, children, the impoverished, members of future generations. While democracy as expressed via electoral politics may treat such segments lightly, bureaucratic advocacy for them could arguably offer a leavening of the bias toward the immediate and short term, in favor of a longer-term view of the public interest.

Distributional consequences arise, in governance terms, because neither electoral nor administrative institutions are perfect translators of public values. Both sets

---

7. Or, bureaucratic values could emphasize responsiveness to public concerns more than do values of political overseers.

of institutions must rely on processes of aggregation that inevitably create biases. Political institutions rely on interest groups and political parties to accumulate preferences. We know from an extensive literature that such processes advantage the haves in society and disadvantage the have-nots. Similarly, bureaucratic institutions place a premium on the ability of members of the public to understand administrative processes and communicate the correct information to the bureaucracy. Such processes in theory also benefit the haves, although not necessarily the same haves advantaged by the political processes.

The distributional conflict between political institutions and bureaucracy is best illustrated by the urban services distribution literature. That set of studies has examined the services provided by municipal governments, in an effort to find those cases in which politics has been able to influence the allocation of basic urban services (Jones 1985; Lineberry 1977; Mladenka 1980). Research in the United States has found that political factors play a small role in the distribution of police, fire, recreation, and other services. In-depth analysis has revealed that services have been determined by bureaucratic decision rules that have eliminated much of the political favoritism that was expected to exist. Although the urban services literature has tended to focus on policies with little discretion (but see Meier, Stewart, and England 1991), the clear lesson is that political forces have desired one distribution of services (to reward political supporters) and bureaucratic forces have shaped a different distribution.

In this study we have not probed the distributional aspects of policy decisions in any depth, but we recognize that they are present and can be important. As an illustration, in chapter 3 we discussed the networked aspects of program implementation. One difference between using a relatively hierarchical process of policy implementation and relying on a network arrangement is that the latter brings more actors into the process—and, thereby, a different mix of values.[8] This distinction cannot but affect how discretionary decision making develops. To illustrate, in other research we examined the networking behavior of school superintendents (O'Toole and Meier 2004). We found consistent evidence that managers who operated more frequently in networked interactions with others outside the administrative setting produced organizational outputs and outcomes responsive to the interests of those actors in the network. In the cases investigated, networking has encouraged school districts to emphasize outcomes that benefit Anglo, college-bound students and de-emphasize outcomes that would have benefited disadvantaged students. Although

---

8. There may be other distinctions between these two types of arrangements, including different types and levels of capacity. One reason to opt for more networked forms may be to tap skills or abilities beyond those available in any single agency.

networks and networking have been a popular—and often encouraged—topic of general discussion recently in the public administration literature, these distributional issues have not been systematically explored.

Values in the Bureaucracy: Relevance for Democratic Governance

The general theme emphasized in this section—the importance of values for the bureaucracy-democracy challenge—points directly to a weakness of both the political science and public administration literatures. Political scientists are generally content to ignore bureaucratic values, despite the wealth of literature, both theoretical (principal-agent models, bureaucratic politics) and empirical, that shows that these matter (but see Carpenter 2001). Even the small band of representative-bureaucracy scholars is likelier to find a positive welcome in the public administration literature than among political science researchers.

The public administration literature has not been shy about discussing bureaucratic values; as noted in chapter 2, at least five sets of them have been presented as bases for normative roles for bureaucrats. Rohr (1986) advocates that bureaucrats adopt regime values and that these might be derived from considering the debates over constitutional issues. Wamsley (1990) proposes an agency perspective whereby bureaucrats become advocates of agency missions and, therefore, seek to participate fully in debates over policy questions. Frederickson's (1980) interpretation of the "New Public Administration" suggests that social equity is the primary value of bureaucracy. Terry (2003) advocates a more traditional set of norms, with an administrative conservator whose role is to protect the capacity of the bureaucracy to take future action. Finally, feminist theory (Stivers 2002) contends that bureaucracies need to adopt feminist values, implying that bureaucracies should be radically restructured in ways incorporating values that are currently missing. While each of these arguments is far more nuanced than these brief summaries indicate, for the most part they remain normative prescriptions at the theoretical level. None of the proposals has developed an empirical literature aimed at determining what values are actually held by bureaucrats and how those values might vary, given a wide range of bureaucratic factors (mission, level of government, extent of merit system, level of professionalization, demographic composition, and so forth).

The modest empirical literature on bureaucratic values within public administration generally shows that bureaucrats hold more public-regarding—and in that sense, relatively benign—political attitudes than the general population. They are more civic minded, more efficacious, and more willing to use the instruments of the positive state (Brewer 2001; Dolan 2000, 2002; Garand, Parkhurst, and Seoud 1991;

Lewis 1990). Yet even these findings are handicapped by the limitations of secondary analysis. Few of these studies use survey instruments specifically designed to capture bureaucratic values. They often involve reanalysis of public opinion poll data, thus essentially producing analyses of bureaucratic values measured primarily in terms of the values of postal workers and teachers, simply because the number of other public servants included in any poll remains relatively small. None of the studies has sufficient sample size to examine questions across organizations or time, although some rough approximations of the variation in agencies do appear to matter (Dolan 2000; Kelly and Newman 2001).

LOOKING INSIDE THE BUREAUCRACY

In this volume we consistently stress that to deal with the relationship between bureaucracy and democracy one must actually study administrative agencies and their denizens and not merely make assumptions about them from a distance. It is crucial to investigate the internal workings of administrative organizations (and, where relevant, clusters of organizations), to determine why they produce the observed results. To be sure, much can be learned about an institution by studying how it interacts with other known entities. Such a strategy could be quite useful under circumstances in which gaining access to the entity in question is difficult (e.g., studying the presidency or, in another realm entirely, remote star systems). But public organizations are generally not difficult institutions to access, and they are far more open to scholars than are most political institutions in the United States.

Bureaucracies are goal-oriented collectivities.[9] They seek objectives and do so with processes different from those used by ostensibly political institutions. Resolving the tension between bureaucracy and democracy requires knowledge of three sets of values: those held by the general public,[10] those held by electoral actors, and those held by the bureaucracy. Of these only the last is not well documented. If bureaucrats share values with electoral institutions, then the only principal-agent problem remaining is the requirement for a relatively modest monitoring scheme.[11]

9. We ignore here the extensive literature on organizational goals and effectiveness, which includes debates about many important details, as well as claims about the ambiguity of goals in public organizations (for interesting evidence on this point, see Chun and Rainey 2005). Our point is not that bureaucracies are *exclusively* directed at their goals, whether formal or operative, but that mission is clearly highly relevant in explaining bureaucratic behavior.

10. Of course, it can also be important to consider different slices of the public, some of whom can be more directly affected by and intensely interested in administrative decisions.

11. Since our focus is on bureaucracy and democracy, we ignore here the principal-agent challenge with respect to the public control of political actors. For a general use and treatment of some of the perspectives analyzed in this chapter, see Gormley and Balla (2003).

If they share values with the general public, then bureaucracy can be directly responsive to the people without any intervention at all by the electoral institutions.

How the bureaucracy translates its own values into concrete actions is important in the study of bureaucracy and democracy. Knowing the values held by individual bureaucrats is only the first step in this process; understanding the limits and restrictions on bureaucratic action is equally important. Bureaucrats typically operate within a set of established rules and procedures. Many of these are defined in the enabling statute and regulations; others involve the types of procedures discussed by the analysts who treat political-control mechanisms like "deck stacking" as the centerpiece. The discretion exercised by bureaucrats interacts with the values of the bureaucrat and a wide array of procedures, restrictions, structures, incentives, encouragements, and prohibitions. Only by examining this pattern of interaction can one tell why an administrative unit acted as it did; and, more importantly, whether the agency's actions have been supportive of democratic governance or contrary to it.

The empirical findings of this study illustrate that one cannot take bureaucratic outputs or outcomes at face value as regards evidence on the bureaucracy-democracy question. The outcomes might be exactly what the politicians have requested (higher test scores) but also have been produced by bureaucrats' manipulating processes (in this case, test exemptions) to achieve apparent compliance. Such actions do not necessarily mean that evil, or autocratic, bureaucrats are conspiring against the public interest as expressed by the politicians; they could also mean that bureaucrats are more sensitive to the values held by individuals who do not have a great deal of influence in the political system (or by some other subgroup of citizens). Whether or not such actions contribute to or detract from democratic governance depends on which operational notion of democracy one wishes to endorse; understanding how these processes work is an empirical question, one with major ramifications for how democracy and bureaucracy interact.

PUBLIC MANAGEMENT: A KEY PIECE OF THE PUZZLE

Even in the best of studies on bureaucracy and democratic governance, the crucial role of management tends to be ignored. Consider the many functions in any contemporary governance system that fall into the hands of public managers.

Some are heavily communicative, facilitative, and even political. Management has to interpret the administrative organization to its political masters as well as explain why certain policies are in place, why other policies might be feasible or infeasible, and how change might take place. Management exerts leverage both upward to the political appointees and downward to the production units of the system. Managerial influence might also reach across the agency to other administrative units, either because the organizations are linked in policy implementation networks or because they are inclined to reach out to potential allies or rivals; these lateral links may also include interest groups.

Many management functions are performed mostly or exclusively within the permanent civil service in most U.S. governance systems. Top- and mid-level managers in the civil service must take political directives and translate them into concrete patterns of action for the agency. In the process, managers will need to induce compliance from subordinates and take into consideration the values, interests, and objectives of those in the administrative institution. In structural situations that resemble more networked patterns, the demands on such managers are even greater (O'Toole and Meier 1999), because the institutional setting is more complex and more interests need to be balanced, but the managers generally lack the authority to compel the necessary action.[12]

Public management, in other words, is a key missing piece of the puzzle. It influences both institutions and values, as well as their progenitors, in the governance system. Sadly, this critical element is largely absent in the bureaucracy-democracy debate.

The literature of public administration could be expected to develop these themes of managerial influence with particular gusto, and a number of publications do suggest the myriad ways that public managers (albeit almost exclusively the permanent variety rather than political appointees) can plausibly shape what can happen during implementation (e.g., Ban 1995; Cohen and Eimicke 1995; Holzer and Callahan 1998; Riccucci 1995, 2005). Surprisingly, however, most analysts in this tradition have usually eschewed systematic empirical research. The literature of public administration validates few propositions about managerial influence on democratic performance (some of our own work, referenced earlier in this book, constitutes an exception in this regard). Further, although public administration researchers have treated structural themes as important (e.g., Seidman 1997; and see Kaufman 1956 for an influential exposition that links both institutional and values themes in a coherent logic), they have not emphasized the full institutional setting within which bureaucracies operate.

Neither major approach considers the essential role of management in linking bureaucracy to democracy. The political science literature reflects its discipline, which no longer considers management or for that matter the internal workings of the bureaucracy as a subject worth studying. The public administration literature

---

12. An irony here is that governments often opt for more networked forms, such as contracting out, because of a *deficit* in administrative capacity (O'Toole 1989).

clearly recognizes management; but other than idealized leadership in such roles as the so-called administrative conservator (Terry 2003) or Wamsley's agency perspective (1990), it also focuses little on the empirical role that management plays in reconciling bureaucracy with democracy. It seems clear that the importance of management to the bureaucracy-democracy challenge must itself be explored afresh.[13]

PRINCIPAL-AGENT MODELS AND THE NEW
PUBLIC MANAGEMENT

Given the importance of management in the bureaucracy-democracy challenge, it is worth considering a particular kind of institutional "solution," or at least agenda, that represents a connection between the management theme, generally speaking, and the cluster of ideas offered in principal-agent models. The latter, we have seen, are important in framing the intellectual roots, and missteps, associated with one prominent perspective on bureaucracy and democracy. The former theme, we argue, is a key but understudied aspect of governance. In recent years, a reformist approach to public management built partially on notions associated with a principal-agent logic has attracted considerable attention and support. While public management is unquestionably central to the bureaucracy-democracy challenge, we believe that wholesale implementation of these reformist ideas could easily do more harm than good.

The so-called New Public Management, which has influenced many governments in North America, Europe, and Oceania, builds on premises having to do with the prevalence of nonmarket failures in the public sector, the desirability of using financial and other policy instruments to apply marketlike forces to the operations of governance systems, the attractiveness of encouraging responsiveness to public service recipients, and often the desirability of shrinking the institutions of the public sector (see Pollitt and Bouckaert 2000). Although the NPM is, like most pragmatic reforms, composed of varying and in many cases contradictory elements, its general orientation fits within the principal-agent model. Despite this linkage, both the general model and this public-managerial manifestation of it represent overly simple solutions to complex problems; and both, we would argue, are dead ends in the quest for reconciling bureaucracy with democracy. While appearing superficially similar, these ideas—when subjected to a more detailed assessment—are connected to different conceptions of democracy; further, they become impaled on the horns of the same dilemma that is a central focus of this book.

13. For another critique of several normative arguments from public administration, with an emphasis on the key role of management, see Bertelli and Lynn (2006). They do not focus, however, primarily on the challenge posed by democratic theory.

In a way, this argument may seem ironic. Principal-agent models and also the NPM offer institutional approaches to considering the challenge of governance. We argue in this chapter that institutional perspectives are often oversold and cannot possibly fully meet the bureaucracy-democracy challenge. If implemented, however, they can influence the performance of government by administrative systems. That influence, to the extent that it is effective, can well be perverse. And some of what is influenced through the execution of these ideas over the longer term is the matrix of values that, we also argue, can be so consequential in shaping bureaucratic results.

The basic premise of principal-agent models is that relationships can be summarized, analyzed, and reformed by interpreting them as contracts between principals and agents. For politicians (principals) to get bureaucrats (agents) to act as politicians desire, politicians need to create incentives that encourage bureaucrats to act appropriately, along with some monitoring processes to check that results are acceptable. If the role of principal is restricted to the political actor, or if citizens are restricted to act as principals only with respect to politicians, we have the classic top-down view of bureaucracy and democracy.[14]

The New Public Management reform efforts can be divided into two parts: those targeted at consumer sovereignty and those designed to liberate management from overly restrictive bureaucratic constraints. The consumer-directed part of NPM involves treating citizens like customers and infusing private-sector practices of consumer service into government. (Barzelay 2001; Boston et al. 1996; Kettl 2000b). At one extreme, this responsiveness to citizens takes the part of downsizing government and letting citizens themselves determine what government services they want (public choice); somewhat less radical is heavy reliance on the private sector to deliver services via contracts. The private sector, the logic goes, flourishes because it can provide services more efficiently than government—because it is used to competing for survival. A whole range of other, market-sector-derived instruments can also be linked into the operations of administrative systems—for instance, myriad customer-service techniques derived from private organizations.

The liberation-management view of NPM involves eliminating the restrictions and red tape that keep public-sector managers from taking chances and being creative in delivering services. Managers are to be given greater discretion but held responsible for some bottom line, some measure of performance (National Performance Review 1993). This basic idea can be implemented through any number of

14. Note: this means that if one relaxes the principal-agent model and lets citizens be principals who act on both politicians and bureaucrats, the principal-agent model now echoes the same problem that is addressed in this book. The bureaucratic agent gets pressure from different directions based on whether democracy is a direct bottom-up process or an indirect top-down one mediated by politicians.

particulars, including performance contracts for public managers, various hybrid organizational forms, modified incentive systems, red-tape reduction programs, and many more.

The superficial similarity of principal-agent models and the NPM is their reliance on economic incentives. Both are greatly influenced by practices in the private sector–principal-agent models because contracts are the accepted way to order private-sector relationships, and NPM because it seeks to bring business practices and models to government. As governments decide to use the private sector to deliver services, principal-agent models become directly relevant to interpreting the relationship between government and its contractors, since the models are designed precisely to be concerned with contracts.

The NPM clearly encompasses considerably more than an embrace of contracting out for public programs. Pursuing this important variant, nonetheless, proves illuminating. The principal-agent model applied within the NPM becomes fairly complex. Rather than having a political principal interacting with a bureaucratic agent, one now has a political principal interacting with a bureaucratic agent, with the bureaucratic agent then becoming in turn a principal contracting with a private-sector agent.[15] The NPM approach thus involves adding additional principal-agent links to a chain of principal-agent relationships. In such cases, and even without considering the distinct values of the contractor,[16] efforts to increase control can be expected to encounter difficulty (Downs 1967). That is, by lengthening the chain of principal-agent relationships and attenuating the strength of the links in this way, the NPM makes it more difficult to establish top-down political control over the bureaucracy.[17]

This approach also involves, less directly, tensions with what is often a partially redistributive policy agenda on the part of democratic governments. The same point can be put differently: All institutional arrangements carry implications for the distribution of the costs and benefits of public action. Contracting out, operating in the midst of market forces, is more likely to run into conflict with redistribution downward than is direct production and provision (see O'Toole 1996). To the extent that this bias distorts the intentionally redistributive purpose of some policies, NPM can vitiate rather than energize democracy.

15. The contractor, in turn, often assumes a principal role with respect to subcontractors as agents.

16. The shift to contractors from government employees is likely to result in the incorporation of more starkly utilitarian values and the deemphasis of obligation and other nonutilitarian impulses. We are skeptical that this tradeoff will produce a more democratic polity.

17. Some ideas associated with the NPM do involve efforts to shorten the chain rather than lengthen it. Still, the regular endorsement of various public-private patterns over in-house production and provision is an important emphasis by NPM proponents. Such arrangements, we argue, necessarily involve challenges to top-down political control.

Proponents of the New Public Management often make several implicit but debatable assumptions with regard to the use of private-sector organizations via contracting. The most crucial premise is the existence of a competitive market, with firms competing to provide goods and services (see O'Toole 1991). A competitive market assumes not only a sufficiently large number of firms but also a relatively uniform product, so that it becomes irrelevant if the government contracts with A or with B to provide the good or service. Many government-provided services, although not all, are provided by government agencies partially because the market to provide them is not present. In situations with few producers and relatively rare products, competition is not automatic; and the process relies on the ability to write an acceptable contract that meets the needs of both government and the private contractor. In a relatively uncompetitive or thin market, changes in contractees will generate fairly large transactions costs as the new provider requires some assurance that investments in this contract will provide more than ephemeral returns. In an uncompetitive market, there is also the possibility that the government and the contractor will collude against the public either by not monitoring costs (the classic example is health care payments in the United States after the creation of Medicare and Medicaid) or by engaging in corruption.[18]

O'Toole's (1991) work on water pollution control shows that governments that contract out services can eventually lose the capacity to produce those services on their own. They sell or lease their capital base and hire contract managers rather than technical experts as employees. In the long run, this institutional shift creates a dependence on the contracting firms. Because the loss of capacity does not occur immediately, the New Public Management and its emphasis on contracting may well be the "mad cow disease" (or, for the purists, bovine spongiform encephalopathy) of public governance: a pathology with a long latency period, but one catalyzing the eventual sapping of governmental capacity to act independently.

Both principal-agent models and the NPM effectively advocate a narrowing of values by emphasizing the contract metaphor in theory and the use of contracts in practice. The array of incentives that we know can be found in administrative institutions (Etzioni 1964; Wilson 1989)—commitment to agency values, identification with programs, satisfaction of doing difficult jobs well, solidarity benefits of associating with like-minded others—are replaced by monetary ones. On the academic side, such a focus will result in the inability to predict bureaucratic actions (e.g., the budget-maximizing bureaucrat) because an incorrect set of values is specified. On the practical level, performance of government programs is likely to suffer in the

18. The further complications entailed by involving networks of public and private actors rather than relatively simple principal-agent chains should be obvious.

short run; and it is quite possible in the long run that only the types of persons who are attuned to monetary incentives will be attracted to public service.[19] Here, clearly, the link back to the critical nature of values is most direct and, we expect, eventually pernicious for democratic governance.

A more basic conflict between NPM and principal-agent models should also be noted. NPM is based on notions of consumer sovereignty. The core assumptions of welfare economics associated with this idea hold that individuals are the best judges of their own interest. Applied to the NPM, this assumption means that welfare improvements follow from citizens themselves, not government bureaucrats or government politicians, directly making the choices about services and service delivery. In short, the assumptions of the NPM are built upon a fully bottom-up view of democracy at the price of top-down political control.[20] Principal-agent models as applied in political science, in contrast, are strictly hierarchical and leave no direct role for the bottom-up pressures of citizens; citizens are to select political principals and leave it at that. In short, while the principal-agent model and the New Public Management share some common analytical tools, they seek radically different forms of democracy. Further, as this section demonstrates, each faces serious limitations.

The issue of how to frame the managerial function for creating an appropriate match between administrative systems and democratic governance, then, remains before us. Neither the New Public Management nor general principal-agent theory provides much leverage, and what it does provide us is contradictory. We return to this point again in our concluding suggestions about research that is worth pursuing.

FUTURE RESEARCH DIRECTIONS

Although the relationship between bureaucracy and democracy has occupied scholars for over a century, this book demonstrates several shortcomings that persist in efforts to address the challenge squarely. The limitations are partially theoretical, as we have explained in our coverage of the political science and public administration literatures. Still others have to do with a combination of empirical features and their theoretical implications. Numerous elements impinge on the bureaucracy-

---

19. The normative implications of recruiting public servants who are primarily interested in private gain should be obvious.

20. This is not a new argument or insight, even though it has been largely undiscussed by New Public Management advocates. Ostrom (1989) proposed a decentralized, consumer-choice approach to bureaucracy and democracy in the 1970s. This perspective draws from public choice economics, which has spawned some empirical literature as well as some challenges (Lyons, Lowery, and DeHoog 1992).

democracy relationship but remain poorly understood. Some aspects of the relationship have been studied a great deal (e.g., traditional principal-agent models) while many others have been virtually ignored (e.g., bureaucratic values). The empirical analyses presented in this volume have been crafted to shed light on some of the key questions, but they represent only a sampling of the questions that demand serious attention from researchers. Indeed, a key part of our argument is that one's understanding of the bureaucracy-democracy relationship must be grounded in the particulars of the context of interest. Institutional features, the values actuating the exercise of bureaucratic discretion in a particular time and place, and the management systems and people in situ must be examined systematically to come to grips with the ways in which bureaucracy and democracy might conflict with each other or reinforce each other's features. These factors are likely to vary over time within a governance system and vary dramatically across national boundaries. There is simply no one-size-fits-all resolution to the challenge—this despite the arguments of some formal theorists, the wishes of political control enthusiasts, or the hopes of some bureauphilic students of public administration. Plenty of serious research remains to be done to understand the dynamics, threats, and opportunities present in many key settings.

This section discusses some of the research subjects that could provide real leverage on the question of how to reconcile the needs of democracy with the imperatives of administrative organization. It is certainly not comprehensive. Still, building on the coverage in this book and especially the sketch of implications presented in this chapter, it indicates something of the range of salient matters that call for examination.

Bringing the Bureaucracy Back In

First, substantial benefits will accrue from efforts to bring the study of bureaucracy fully back into the study of political control. A recent collection of research essays chided political science for ignoring bureaucracy questions in general (Krause and Meier 2003); that bureaucracy would be ignored in political-control research—that is, research in which the administrative system is one of the two key institutions presumably under study—is even more surprising. "Bringing the bureaucracy back in" as an injunction for the research enterprise has a least four dimensions: assessing bureaucratic values, increasing the variety and number of administrative organizations studied, focusing on bureaucratic processes and how these respond to political processes and pressures, and specifying the representative function of bureaucracy. All have to do with the ways in which political and administrative systems interact and shape what happens; it is this interaction in the real world, not in some stylized principal-agent model or in some broad demonization of politicos' penchant for "interfering" with or "micromanaging" the experts, that must be understood.

Public organizations and bureaucrats exercise discretion; and where discretion exists, it can be expected to be used to further the values favored by the decision maker. The starting points for discussions of bureaucracy and democracy should be the questions: What would the bureaucracy do if left to its own devices? What types of decisions would it make? Are the decisions generally consistent with public preferences? If the answers are not too far from our conceptions of a responsive political institution, then the modest types of influences exercised by electoral institutions may be able to be tweaked to provide a satisfactory governance process. To the extent that bureaucratic values are grossly divergent from what would be needed for an administrative system to perform in accord with public preferences, then more radical reforms of such a system would have to be considered. We need to know how committed government bureaucrats are to democratic values, and if this commitment varies much across agencies (not to mention nations) and over time. Once we know the extent of the variance, then explaining that variance in terms of structures, agency missions, socialization experiences, and other factors becomes a feasible research agenda. It is startling to consider that more than fifty years after the behavioral revolution in the social sciences, we still do not know answers to these rather basic questions. We can glean hints, from studies designed for other purposes, that U.S. bureaucrats in general are fairly committed to democratic values, but we know little about how consistent this commitment is across agencies and over time. Likewise, some spotty evidence suggests that there is less to fear in this regard from bureaucrats in the United States than from counterparts in other putatively democratic systems, but the data are far from systematically comprehensive.

The importance of developing a better understanding of bureaucratic values holds not just for simple, hierarchical government bureaucracies but also for the other actors in networks that frequently deliver policy. Nonprofits play a major role in carrying out numerous policies; nonprofit bureaucrats are certainly likely to have different values than those held in government agencies, even in those agencies that eagerly collaborate with nonprofits. Many nonprofit organizations are single-issue entities and, as a result, attract highly committed individuals who place a high value on what the organization does. Consider as examples the nonprofit units devoted to public health, or even more specific public-health and advocacy causes, like combating AIDS or promoting women's health; protecting the environment (or the air or water, or radon free housing); or addressing the needs of the homeless. Such organizations rely heavily on recruiting true believers and thus are likely not to match up with general public values. The interweaving of numerous such organizations into the regular operations of public programs, not to mention the range of structural variation across network types, constitutes a set of phenomena we only dimly understand. The ways that values drive or complicate the execution of policies in such settings represent a virtual terra incognita.

Increasing the variance in the types of bureaucracies (and networks) studied could easily be incorporated into current research agendas. The political-control literature provides a wealth of information on its objects of study, but such analyses have for the most part only examined U.S. federal regulatory agencies. Theory suggests that such units differ from other types of agencies (Meier 2000), and the few studies that have been done on other types of organizations confirm this expectation (see chap. 2). This book relies heavily, though not exclusively, on evidence from local education agencies. The possible types of public organizations—and networks—are numerous, and organizational theory offers a wealth of suggestions about how responsive different types of administrative systems will be to political control. Even additional studies of federal regulatory agencies would be worthwhile, since much of our knowledge is based on activities during a very small chronological window: the 1980s during the Reagan administration. One might hypothesize that that phase of political leadership, with its revolutionary fervor about smaller government, its comprehensive personnel processes, and its perceived mandate, represents the high-water mark of the U.S. political control movement in practice.

We argue in several chapters that focusing on the processes and procedures used by administrative agencies to generate outputs and outcomes is crucial to understanding the linkage between democracy and bureaucracy. Chapter 5 demonstrates that public organizations can produce outcomes by administrative processes other than those expected or desired. Bureaucracies might deviate from political goals because they are responding directly to the public, because they are considering issues of efficiency and effectiveness, because professional values dictate another course, because the political goal is impossible to achieve, or because those executing policy reject the notion of political control. Similar deviations in networks can derive from these and even more sources. Implementing institutions are sophisticated; simple input-output assessments of their performance can be highly misleading.

Specifying the representative function of bureaucracy is important both for studying the linkage between bureaucracy and democracy and also for normative reasons. This book includes one case of bureaucracy directly representing a part of the public: the instance of Latino education. The now-extensive literature on representative bureaucracy includes a systematic effort to specify when and under what conditions bureaucracy can fulfill a representative function (see Keiser et al. 2002). Taking that effort seriously implies an extensive research agenda that could go a considerable distance toward determining when bureaucracy can be expected to respond directly to the public's preferences. A normative debate on the conditions under which a representative bureaucracy should be valued by proponents of democratic governance is also needed. While some might simply reject representation as an inappropriate administrative function, public organizations do sometimes represent; and the theoretical literature needs to grapple with the issue of when such representation enhances the goal of democratic governance and when it does not.

Treating Networks Seriously

Institutions are not everything, as we have tried to emphasize in this chapter. Still, the research agenda and theoretical literature linking aspects of structure to issues of democratic governance need to be greatly expanded. To be sure, a flourishing literature has grown out of the organizational creation-science movement (see Epstein and O'Halloran 1999; Huber and Shippan 2002), but those studies focus on selected aspects of structure and ignore other, equally or more important, structural considerations. One thus far ignored theme is that of implementation networks and their influence on the prospects for democracy.

In this volume, chapter 3 traces out the frequent use of networks rather than hierarchical forms of administrative organization to implement policy. The types of principal-agent relationships that drive the organizational creation-science literature are simply absent or seriously attenuated in many policy networks. We believe, however, that taking networks seriously (O'Toole 1997b) implies descriptive, theoretical, and empirical research agendas that should have significant impacts on the regnant ideas in both political science and public administration. Here we sketch some parts of these agendas as they relate to the subject of this book. We concentrate on three issues on which additional research is needed to clarify the relationship between "bureaucracy," broadly conceived, and democracy.

First, at present we are lacking even a catalogue of the basic organizational forms and their frequency. Chapter 3 demonstrates that networks have been a legislative and administrative tool for an extended period of time and that such arrays tend to become even more complex during implementation. Networks vary, of course, by the types of participants that are included and the types of relationships that are mandated, encouraged, or permitted (Cook and Whitmeyer 1992; Jordan and Schubert 1992; Knoke and Kuklinski 1982; Ostrom 1990; van Waarden 1992). There is no systematic classification of these networks in terms of their relative frequency.[21]

---

21. One problem with the network literature is that scholars tend to become fascinated by the unique aspects of the network(s) under investigation. In doing so, they limit themselves to a small number of networks and fail to generate any systematic generalizations (Bogason and Toonen 1998; for an analysis of the relative advantages and disadvantages of intensive vs. extensive network studies, see Meier and O'Toole 2005).

Such a classification would be a first step in examining the types of networks to see how they might be subject to democratic control either from the top down or from the bottom up. Nor has the extant networks literature really shown which network dimensions matter most in explaining behavior relevant to the bureaucracy-democracy question. This more ambitious challenge, both theoretical and empirical, must be addressed as well.

Second, theoretical studies are needed on what democratic accountability means in a network situation (see O'Toole 1997a). Clearly, the top-down principal-agent chains advocated by much of the political science literature do not operate in network settings. At the same time, legislatures persist in creating or encouraging these institutional forms, a result suggesting that they are either unaware of the problems of control or feel that the problems of control are compensated for by the benefits that networks provide. If legislatures think that other values are more important than control, specifying these other values becomes extremely important.

Third, networks can also introduce some bottom-up elements of democracy to the implementation process. Given the lack of empirical work on this question, however, and the presence of a large body of evidence regarding the elitist nature of participation in other settings, such claims at present are only hypothetical. There is no obvious reason why they should be treated as any more plausible than a counter-claim that, thanks to their lack of transparency, networks are likely to subvert the democratic process. Some network patterns, at a minimum, are likely to be subject to Michels' (1999) iron law of oligarchy, whereby institutions created with democratic intent evolve over time into arrangements controlled by an elite. Similarly, the participation of network actors in policy implementation mimics well-known patterns of administrative agencies interacting with, and being influenced by, interest groups. Since the classic study by Selznick (1949), we have known that co-optation can be expected in such situations.

In complicatedly networked arrays, with numerous diverse participants harboring somewhat distinct agendas, it is not at all clear whose issues are likely to get considered. Some analysts suggest fundamentally reformulating norms of governance in such circumstances (Behn 2001). Only empirical studies of who benefits from network actions and how public policy outputs change in the presence of networks, however, can help us make progress toward resolving this issue. In recent work, Weber (2003) offers some evidence that network patterns may sometimes be broadly responsive to a variegated set of stakeholders and may facilitate a farsighted and sustainable governance process. Other work, including some of our own (O'Toole and Meier 2004), points toward the danger that networks can produce benefits disproportionately for the advantaged. We need to know more, and more systematically, about the distributional consequences of these alternative governance forms.

Exploring the Importance of Management

The coverage earlier in this chapter points to the importance of public management to the bureaucracy-democracy challenge, the problematic aspects of some New Public Management notions about how management might best be structured, and also the relative lack of the right kind of empirical investigations on this subject. Several research questions relating management to the interplay of bureaucracy and democracy come to mind. Beyond modeling the hypothesized impacts of public managers on the performance of programs (see the appendix and the references therein), a number of matters are worth exploring.

First, are the values of managers different from those of the street-level bureaucrats? Ideally one might think that managers mix values, blending those held by street-level professionals and those held by elected officials and political appointees. Alternatively, one might even conceive of a unique set of managerial values that includes a recognition of the legitimate role of political appointees in setting policy direction. Still another cluster might involve the implicit elevation of a set of administrative and process features into normative primacy: "managerialism." Depending on the empirical evidence, very different implications for democratic governance might be discerned. At present, we know even less about these values-related questions than we do about public bureaucrats in general.

Second, the locus of discretion in an organization and its relative abundance or scarcity at the managerial level is a topic that is little studied but quite important to questions of bureaucracy and democracy. Two studies of representative bureaucracy and gender by the same research team illustrate the differences. A study of child support enforcement found that managers were the key decision makers (Wilkins and Keiser 2006), while another, which focused on girls' mathematics performance in public education, revealed street-level personnel as being more crucial (Keiser et al. 2002). As implied above, to the degree that discretion shifts to lower levels of the administrative system, overhead democratic controls are more difficult to operate effectively. In such situations, the importance of management increases, because only managers have frequent interaction with the street level, only managers can frame issues in a way that fits with the perceived norms of the organization, and in merit systems only managers can operate the human resources function on behalf of the organizational mission.

Third, a general weakness of the public management literature is that it has failed to identify when and where management can make a difference. The ability of managers to influence organizational actions has major implications at two levels for linkage between bureaucracy and democracy. Much has been made of the importance of political appointees in influencing bureaucracies, particularly via politicos selecting political appointees who share the same policy agenda as the elected chief executive. Equally important but usually neglected are the management skills of political appointees, since these individuals must translate political goals into operational imperatives and persuade the career civil servants to change how they do their jobs. Our knowledge of the management skills of political appointees is, at present, no better than journalistic. Systematic studies are needed of how political managers actually manage, and what difference these efforts make.[22] The second level of research concern is in the careerist strata. Directions by political appointees are mediated through mid- and upper-level career managers. Even if such managers enthusiastically adopt the new political priorities, they still need to be able to link these values to the structures, processes, and current programs of the bureaucracy. Much of our own recent work has been directed toward a systematic exploration of these questions by estimating impacts of various managerial behaviors, the contributions of personnel stability to program outcomes, and way that the strategic stance of management can mediate the impacts of a diverse workforce on the delivery of public services. These efforts constitute only a beginning, however, and a great deal of additional work is needed.

CONCLUSION

The bureaucracy-democracy challenge has occupied many thinkers for a considerable period. No one book can resolve all the issues, and this one surely has not. Even had we been able to answer the key questions definitively for governance in the United States, it is important to recall the comparative dimension and temper any overly broad generalizations with the limitations imposed by context. If bureaucracy in the United States consists of a set of institutions relatively (although clearly not universally) friendly toward democratic forms and functions, we might draw far different conclusions in other political systems, depending on a consideration of the institutional forms and values of the relevant administrative scheme, the operations of the broader political system, and the role and functions of public management as these operate in the setting in question.

We conclude that, in the United States, especially, neither the political-control approach nor the perspectives of public administration scholars can or should be

---

22. Of course, we believe the model presented in the appendix is an appropriate vehicle for exploring these questions. That model has generated a wealth of research findings by several different scholars (Donahue et al. 2004; Fernandez 2005; Goerdel 2004; Hicklin 2004; Juenke 2005a; Pitts 2005). Logic suggests that political appointees need to deal with many of the same aspects of internal and external management that nonpolitical appointees do.

accepted; both need to be thoroughly challenged. Perhaps this book's clearest contribution is its emphasis on this critical kind of analysis.

We would be remiss, however, if we did not end by noting that the literatures of political science and public administration do contain important elements of wisdom as well as distortion. Political science has largely ignored public administration and actual functioning bureaucracies for decades, and public administration has likewise marginalized the broader political system in considering the appropriate role for administrative systems in democratic regimes. But public administration has correctly pointed to the inevitability of the exercise of bureaucratic discretion, the key role of values in the bureaucracy, the potential for democratic impulses to shape the operations of governance through channels other than the electoral, and the inability of political controllers to solve the democracy puzzle through organizational creation science or some autopilot mechanism embedded in a monitoring device. Students of political control, meanwhile, have appropriately emphasized the theme of accountability, the legitimacy of democratically elected political leaders, the need for effective forms of oversight, and the potential for rogue administrative systems to make a mockery of supposedly popular government.

Reframing the point in terms of a classic debate on this crucial issue, we note that the accumulated wisdom in and on public administration demonstrates the validity of Carl Friedrich's famously clear sketch (1940) of the central role of public administration in democratic governance. Likewise, the wisdom that can be distilled from the literature on political control of the bureaucracy appropriately validates the skepticism of Herman Finer (1941), that any bureaucracy, no matter how benign its values or how farsighted its administrative leadership, can substitute for appropriately broad and general direction from political levels. How much of which kernel of wisdom to focus on, or critique, must depend on the dynamic balance in a system of governance and the nature of the challenges faced. The question must be joined, and rejoined, seriously and on a regular basis, far into the future.

Appendix

A Specific Model of Governance

Our research agenda operated from a specific model of governance. Although we do not explicitly use this model in the discussion throughout this volume, the model fits the analysis presented here and ties our arguments into this broader research agenda. The model was developed in earlier work (O'Toole and Meier 1999) and parts were tested in the kinds of settings that are under investigation in several chapters of this book (Meier and O'Toole 2001; 2002; 2003; O'Toole and Meier 2003). The model was developed out of a particular interest in examining the influence of public managers on public program performance, and it also incorporates stability-inducing features of governmental bureaucratic settings as variables. Although the approach is not framed explicitly as a general model of governance (see O'Toole and Meier 2000), we believe it could be generalized beyond bureaucratic performance to other governance institutions. Further, the model does incorporate consideration of the influence of political forces, including political leadership, on the operations of bureaucratic systems. We believe this model can be used as an aid in analyzing the bureaucracy-democracy question—to be precise, in organizing the coverage, assisting in analysis, and avoiding any tendency subtly to shift the formulation of the issues at different points in the treatment.

Consider the operations of some institutionalized, semipermanent part of a governance system (called, for the moment, the "bureaucracy") authorized by political decision makers to carry out some authorized public purpose on a regular basis (a "program"). We can consider the performance or outcome of such efforts as largely shaped by the institutional arrangements that contribute to what programs can accomplish, the forces from outside the program that can shape or reshape how it operates, and the administrative or managerial influences that are aimed at making the program work effectively.

How can the joint impact of these sets of influences be understood? The model we employ offers a specific form for understanding the functioning of this class of governance systems:

$$O_t = \beta_1(S+M_1)O_{t-1} + \beta_2(X_t/S)(M_3/M_4) + \varepsilon_t$$

where

O is some measure of outcome,

S is a measure of stability,

M denotes management, which can be divided into three parts

    M_1 management's contribution to organizational stability through additions to hierarchy/structure as well as regular operations,

M_3 management's efforts to exploit the environment,

M_4 management's effort to buffer environmental shocks,[1]

X is a vector of environmental forces,

ε is an error term,

the other subscripts denote time periods, and

β_1 and β_2 are estimable parameters.

Note that the model is autoregressive, nonlinear, and contingent. The actual performance of public programs managed through the bureaucracy at any given time is likely to be heavily explained by performance in the recent past. The first term of the right-hand side of the model captures this inertial-system aspect of how an implementing apparatus operates. It suggests not only that program operations tend toward stability but also that a number of features of the program's institutional setting can bolster the stability of the system (thus, the set of factors summarized by the shorthand S in the first term reinforce the status quo). In addition, a component of managerial efforts—the energy and talent of public administrators—is also focused on maintaining operations.

The second term of the model can be thought of as the "environmental" component. Whereas the operations of bureaucracy tend toward stability, a wide array of forces outside the operating unit can encourage or even dictate change. The vector of X influences represent these: economic, political, and social forces. These include top-down or bottom-up democratic components. Clearly, the efforts of political leaders to shape bureaucratic action are a part of these influences; similarly, the attempts by interest groups and others to mold what and how the bureaucracy works can be included as well. To the extent that a set of stabilizing influences are at work, these can be thought of as limiting the impact of perturbations from the environment—thus the S term appears in the denominator at this point in the model. The efforts of administrators or managers, on the other hand, could work in one or both of two directions: capturing and exploiting environmental opportunities, resources, allies, and other potentially useful X elements—the M_3 component of management—or buffering, insulating, or protecting the program's operations from potentially threatening or negatively destabilizing forces in the environment—the M_4 portion of public management.

The emphasis on management means that we do not view bureaucracies as passive and swept along by their environments. Managers exercise discretion both inside and outside the organization. These managerial choices interact with democratic pressures to determine the extent of tension between bureaucracy and democracy.

As explained in the first chapter of this book, we treat the institutional component of regular program operations as the "bureaucracy." The actual institutional arrangements operating in any given governance setting, however, can vary considerably. The model as sketched above emphasizes the stability-inducing or -reducing features of institutional forms. A key aspect is the extent to which, at one extreme, public programs are carried out through a classic and stable hierarchy, on the one hand, or by a set of actors tied together in a less hierarchical and less stable fashion—a "network"—on the other.

---

1. In our formulation, managing the environment in general is M_2, and $M_2 = M_3/M_4$.

As has often been argued in studies of public management (e.g., Provan and Milward 1995) and as is demonstrated in this book, public programs established by governments in recent times may be placed in the hands of single bureaucratic units or, alternatively, networks of organizations. The networks can be relatively simple—two administrative agencies sharing responsibility for achieving a public goals—or bewilderingly complex—for instance, the dozens of U.S. agencies tasked with cooperating to combat international terrorism in the wake of the September 11, 2001 attacks. These less institutionally firm patterns can include units of the same or of different governments (the latter represented, e.g., by intergovernmental grant programs). They can involve for-profit or nonprofit organizations, and they might also comprise a mix of all these kinds of entities.

This point about the involvement of multiple parties in the joint production of public programs is an important part of what has been emphasized in recent years in the developing literature on "governance." Carrying out public responsibilities can require reliance on "governance, not governments." The emphasis is on developing cooperative and sometimes coordinated efforts across institutions, with the purpose of concerting action for effective policy response. If political decision makers sometimes choose, and perhaps must choose, to link bureaucracies to produce policy results, these possibilities must be incorporated into the model. They must also be taken into account in a treatment of the democracy-bureaucracy problem. Accordingly, the issue of networks and hierarchies receives some attention in the model (the S term) and in the analysis of this book.

The model's form might lead some to consider, as a shorthand, that the second (environmental) term effectively provides the "democracy" portion of the picture, since the model specifies that here political influences have the potential to direct or perturb the ongoing efforts of those executing policy decisions. In contrast, the first (stability) term might be thought of as the "bureaucracy" slice, since it emphasizes the inertial character by which bureaucracy is so often known. Such shorthands involve significant distortions. Career administrators can show their influence in both portions of the model, as can bureaucratic structure. More fundamentally, as suggested earlier, one should avoid thinking of democracy in simplistic terms such as immediate responsiveness to public opinion. The operations of bureaucracy itself, as embedded in legitimate public programs, can reflect political decisions to undertake certain key tasks on a stable and long-term basis. The bureaucracy may sometimes be partially protected from political demands in its environment, but such protection can often buy not only more efficiency and effectiveness but also stable functioning of a governance system that is highly valued by the polity (e.g., central bank autonomy). In short, both portions of the model refer to issues important in the bureaucracy-democracy challenge. The solution, even from the perspective of an ardent democrat or a zealous bureauphile, is not simply to maximize one term at the expense of the other.

References

Aberbach, Joel D. 1990. *Keeping a Watchful Eye: The Politics of Congressional Oversight.* Washington, DC: Brookings Institution Press.

Agranoff, Robert, and Michael McGuire. 2003. *Collaborative Public Management: New Strategies for Local Governments.* Washington, DC: Georgetown University Press.

Appleby, Paul H. 1949. *Policy and Administration.* Tuscaloosa: University of Alabama Press.

Appleby, Paul H. 1952. *Morality and Administration in Democratic Government.* Baton Rouge: Louisiana State University Press.

Balla, Steven J. 1998. "Administrative Procedures and Political Control of the Bureaucracy." *American Political Science Review* 92 (3): 663–74.

Balla, Steven J., and John R. Wright. 2001. "Interest Groups, Advisory Committees and Congressional Control of the Bureaucracy." *American Journal of Political Science* 45 (4): 799–813.

Ban, Carolyn. 1995. *How Do Public Managers Manage?* San Francisco: Jossey-Bass.

Banks, Jeffrey S., and Barry R. Weingast. 1992. "The Political Control of Bureaucracies under Asymmetric Information." *American Journal of Political Science* 36 (2): 509–24.

Bardach, Eugene. 1998. *Getting Agencies to Work Together: The Practice and Theory of Managerial Craftsmanship.* Washington, DC: Brookings Institution Press.

Barnard, Chester. 1938. *The Functions of the Executive.* Cambridge, MA: Harvard University Press, Belknap Press.

Barrilleaux, Charles, Richard Feiock, and R. Crew. 1992. "Measuring and Comparing American States' Administrative Characteristics." *State and Local Government Review* 24 (1): 12–19.

Barry, Donald D., and Carol Barner-Barry. 1991. *Contemporary Soviet Politics.* Englewood Cliffs, NJ: Prentice Hall.

Barry, John, and Evan Thomas. 2000. "The Kosovo Cover-Up." *Newsweek*, May 15, 23–26.

Barzelay, Michael. 2001. *The New Public Management: Improving Research and Policy Dialogue.* Berkeley: University of California Press.

Bawn, Kathleen. 1995. "Political Control versus Expertise: Congressional Choices about Administrative Procedures." *American Political Science Review* 89 (1): 62–73.

Becker, Gary S. 1993. *Human Capital.* 3rd ed. Chicago: University of Chicago Press.

Behn, Robert D. 1997. "Linking Measurement to Motivation." *Advances in Educational Administration* 5: 15–50.

Behn, Robert D. 2001. *Rethinking Democratic Accountability.* Washington, DC: Brookings Institution Press.

Bendor, Jonathan. 1988. "Review Article: Formal Models of Bureaucracy." *British Journal of Political Science* 18 (3): 353–95.

Bendor, Jonathan, Serge Taylor, and Roland Van Gaalen. 1985. "Bureaucratic Expertise versus Legislative Authority." *American Political Science Review* 79 (4): 1041–60.

Bendor, Jonathan, Serge Taylor, and Roland Van Gaalen. 1987. "Politicians, Bureaucrats, and Asymmetric Information." *American Journal of Political Science* 31 (4): 796–828.

Bennett, C., and E. Ferlie. 1996. "Contracting in Theory and in Practice: Some Evidence from the NHS." *Public Administration* 74: 49–66.

Bertelli, Anthony Michael, and Laurence E. Lynn Jr. Forthcoming. *Madison's Managers: Public Administration and the Constitution.* Baltimore: Johns Hopkins University Press.

Blais, Andre, and Stephane Dion. 1991. *The Budget-Maximizing Bureaucrat: Appraisals and Evidence.* Pittsburgh: University of Pittsburgh Press.

Blau, Peter M. 1956. *Bureaucracy and Modern Society.* New York: Random House.

Bogason, Peter, and Theo Toonen. 1998. "Comparing Networks." *Public Administration* 76 (2): 205–407.

Bohte, John, and Kenneth J. Meier. 2000. "Goal Displacement: Assessing the Motivation for Organizational Cheating." *Public Administration Review* 60 (2): 173–82.

Boston, Jonathan, John Martin, June Pallot, and Pat Walsh. 1996. *Public Management: The New Zealand Model.* Oxford: Oxford University Press.

Brehm, John, and Scott Gates. 1997. *Working, Shirking and Sabotage: Bureaucratic Response to a Democratic Public.* Ann Arbor: University of Michigan Press.

Brehm, John, Scott Gates, and Brad Gomez. 2003. "Donut Shops, Speed Traps, and Paper Work: Supervision and the Allocation of Time to Bureaucratic Tasks." In *Politics, Policy, and Organizations: Frontiers in the Scientific Study of Bureaucracy,* edited by George A. Krause and Kenneth J. Meier, 133–59. Ann Arbor: University of Michigan Press.

Brewer, Gene A. 2001. "A Portrait of Public Servants: Empirical Evidence from Comparisons with Other Citizens." PhD diss., Department of Public Administration and Policy, University of Georgia.

Brewer, Gene A., and Sally Coleman Selden. 1998. "Whistleblowers in the Federal Civil Service: New Evidence of the Public Service Ethic." *Journal of Public Administration Research and Theory* 8 (3): 413–39.

Burtless, Gary D. 1996. *Does Money Matter? The Effect of School Resources on Student Achievement and Adult Success.* Washington, DC: Brookings Institution Press.

Calvert, Randall L, Mathew D. McCubbins, and Barry Weingast. 1989. "A Theory of Political Control and Agency Discretion." *American Journal of Political Science* 33 (3): 588–611.

Canes-Wrone, Brandice. 2003. "Bureaucratic Decisions and the Composition of the Lower Courts." *American Journal of Political Science* 47 (2): 205–14.

Carpenter, Daniel P. 1996. "Adaptive Signal Processing, Hierarchy, and Budgetary Control in Federal Regulation." *American Political Science Review* 90 (2): 283–302.

Carpenter, Daniel P. 2001. *The Forging of Bureaucratic Autonomy.* Princeton, NJ: Princeton University Press.

Chaney, Carole Kennedy, and Grace Hall Saltzstein. 1998. "Democratic Control and Bureaucratic Responsiveness: The Police and Domestic Violence." *American Journal of Political Science* 42 (3): 745–68.

Chubb, John E. 1985. "The Political Economy of Federalism." *American Political Science Review* 79 (4): 994–1015.

Chubb, John E., and Terry M. Moe. 1990. *Politics, Markets, and America's Schools.* Washington, DC: Brookings Institution Press.

Chun, Young Han, and Hal G. Rainey. 2005. "Goal Ambiguity and Organizational Performance in U.S. Federal Agencies." *Journal of Public Administration Research and Theory* 15 (4): 529–57.

Cohen, Steven, and William Eimicke. 1995. *The New Effective Public Manager.* San Francisco: Jossey-Bass.

Cole, Richard L., and David A. Caputo. 1979. "Presidential Control of the Senior Civil Service: Assessing the Strategies of the Nixon Years." *American Political Science Review* 73 (2): 399–413.

Conyngham, William J. 1982. *The Modernization of Soviet Industrial Management.* Cambridge: Cambridge University Press.

Cook, Brian. 1989. "Principal-Agent Models of Political Control of the Bureaucracy." *American Political Science Review* 83 (3): 965–78.

Cook, Karen S., and J. M. Whitmeyer. 1992. "Two Approaches to Social Structure: Exchange Theory and Network Analysis." *Annual Review of Sociology* 18: 109–29.

Cooper, Philip. 1990. "Comments." In *Refounding Public Administration,* edited by Wamsley et al., 311–13. Newbury Park, CA: Sage.

Corder, J. Kevin. 1998. "Political Control of Federal Credit Subsidy: Small Business Administration 7(a) Loan Guarantees." *American Review of Public Administration* 28 (3): 166–87.

Corder, J. Kevin. 1999. "Structural Choice, Reorganization, and Control of Bureaucracy." Paper presented at the Fifth National Public Management Research Conference, College Station, TX, December.

Crewdson, John. 2002. *Science Fictions: A Scientific Mystery, a Massive Cover-up, and the Dark Legacy of Robert Gallo.* Boston: Little, Brown.

Crewson, Philip E. 1997. "Public-Service Motivation: Building Empirical Evidence of Incidence and Effect." *Journal of Public Administration Research and Theory* 7 (4): 499–518.

Dahl, Robert. 1947. "The Science of Public Administration: Three Problems." *Public Administration Review* 7 (1): 1–11.

Dahl, Robert. 1970. *Preface to Democratic Theory.* Chicago: University of Chicago Press.

Daley, Dennis. 1984. "Controlling the Bureaucracy among the States." *Administration and Society* 15 (4): 475–88.

Denhardt, Robert. 1993. *The Pursuit of Significance: Strategies for Managerial Success in Public Organizations.* Belmont, CA: Wadsworth.

Derthick, Martha. 1970. *The Influence of Federal Grants.* Cambridge, MA: Harvard University Press.

Dodd, Lawrence C., and Richard L. Schott. 1979. *Congress and the Administrative State.* New York: Wiley.

Dolan, Julie. 2000. "The Senior Executive Service: Gender Attitudes and Representative Bureaucracy." *Journal of Public Administration Research and Theory* 10 (3): 513–29.

Dolan, Julie. 2002. "The Budget-Minimizing Bureaucrat? Empirical Evidence from the Senior Executive Service." *Public Administration Review* 62 (1): 42–50.

Donahue, Amy K., Willow S. Jacobson, Mark D. Robbins, Ellen V. Rubin, and Sally C. Selden. 2004. "Management and Performance Outcomes in State Government." In *The*

Art of Governance: Analyzing Management and Administration, edited by Patricia W. Ingraham and Laurence E. Lynn Jr., 125–51. Washington, DC: Georgetown University Press.

Donovan, Todd, and Shaun Bowler. 1998. "Direct Democracy and Minority Rights: An Extension." *American Journal of Political Science* 42 (3): 1020–24.

Downs, Anthony. 1967. *Inside Bureaucracy*. Boston: Little, Brown.

Durant, Robert. 1993. *The Administrative Presidency Revisited*. Albany: State University of New York Press.

Eisinger, Peter K. 1982. "Black Employment in Municipal Jobs." *American Political Science Review* 76 (2): 380–92.

Eisner, Marc Allen. 1991. *Antitrust and the Triumph of Economics*. Chapel Hill: University of North Carolina Press.

Eisner, Marc Allen, and Kenneth J. Meier. 1990. "Presidential Control Versus Bureaucratic Power: Explaining the Reagan Revolution in Antitrust." *American Journal of Political Science* 34 (1): 269–87.

Engstrom, Richard, and Michael McDonald. 1981. "The Election of Blacks to City Councils: Clarifying the Impact of Electoral Arrangements on the Seats/Population Relationship." *American Political Science Review* 75 (2): 344–54.

Epstein, David, and Sharyn O'Halloran. 1999. *Delegating Powers: A Transactions Cost Politics Approach to Policy Making under Separate Powers*. New York: Cambridge University Press.

Erikson, Robert, Michael MacKuen, and James Stimson. 2002. *The Macro Polity*. New York: Cambridge University Press.

Espino, Rudolfo. 2003. "Electoral Influences on Latino Representation in Congress: Responsiveness to Populations or Electorates." Paper presented at the National Meeting of the Midwest Political Science Association, April 3, Chicago.

Etzioni, Amitai. 1964. *Modern Organizations*. Englewood Cliffs, NJ: Prentice Hall.

European Commission. 2001. *European Governance: A White Paper*. Brussels: European Commission. See europa.eu.int/eur-lex/en/com/cnc/2001/com2001_0428en01.pdf.

Evans, Peter B., Dietrich Rueschemeyer, and Theda Skocpol, eds. 1985. *Bringing the State Back In*. Cambridge: Cambridge University Press.

Evans, Robert G. 1980. "Professionals and the Production Function." In *Occupational Licensing and Regulation*, edited by Simon Rottenberg, 225–64. Washington, DC: American Enterprise Institute.

Ferguson, Kathy E. 1984. *The Feminist Case against Bureaucracy*. Philadelphia: Temple University Press.

Fernandez, Sergio. 2004. "Explaining Contracting Effectiveness: An Empirical Analysis of Contracting for Services among Local Governments." PhD diss., University of Georgia.

Fernandez, Sergio. 2005. "Developing and Testing an Integrative Framework of Public Sector Leadership: Evidence from the Public Education Arena." *Journal of Public Administration Research and Theory* 15 (2): 197–218.

Finer, Herman. 1941. "Administrative Responsibility in Democratic Government." *Public Administration Review* 1 (4): 335–50.

Follett, Mary Parker. 1987. *Freedom and Coordination*. New York: Garland.

Frederickson, H. George. 1980. *New Public Administration*. Tuscaloosa: University of Alabama Press.

Frederickson, H. George. 1996. *The Spirit of Public Administration*. San Francisco: Jossey-Bass.

Friedrich, Carl J. 1940. "Public Policy and the Nature of Administrative Responsibility." *Public Policy* 1: 3–24.

Garand, James C., Catherine T. Parkhurst, and Rusanne Jourdan Seoud. 1991. "Bureaucrats, Policy Attitudes, and Political Behavior: Extensions of the Bureau Voting Model of Government Growth." *Journal of Public Administration Research and Theory* 1 (2): 177–212.

General Accounting Office. 1996. *Executive Guide: Effectively Implementing the Government Performance and Results Act*. Washington, DC: GPO.

General Accounting Office. 1997. *The Government Performance and Results Act: 1997 Governmentwide Implementation will be Uneven*. Washington, DC: GPO.

General Accounting Office. 1999a. *Managing for Results: Opportunities for Continued improvements in Agencies' Performance Plans*. Washington, DC: GPO.

General Accounting Office. 1999b. *Performance Budgeting: Initial Experiences Under the Results Act in Linking Plans with Budgets*. Washington, DC: GPO.

General Accounting Office. 2000a. *Management Reform: Continuing Attention is Needed to Improve Government Performance*. Washington, DC: GPO.

General Accounting Office. 2000b. *Managing for Results: Using GPRA to Help Congressional Decisionmaking and Strengthen Oversight*. Washington, DC: GPO.

Gerber, Elisabeth R. 1999. *Populist Paradox: Interest Influence and the Promise of Direct Legislation*. Princeton, NJ: Princeton University Press.

Goerdel, Holly. 2004. "Taking Initiative: Proactive Management and Organizational Performance in Networked Environments." Manuscript, Texas A&M University.

Golden, Marissa Martino. 2000. *What Motivates Bureaucrats*. New York: Columbia University Press.

Golembiewski, Robert T. 1995. *Practical Public Management*. New York: Marcel Dekker.

Goodnow, Frank J. 1900. *Politics and Administration: A Study in Government*. New York: Russell & Russell.

Goodsell, Charles. 2004. *The Case for Bureaucracy*. 4th ed. Washington, DC: Congressional Quarterly Press.

Gormley, William T., Jr., and Steven J. Balla. 2003. *Bureaucracy and Democracy: Accountability and Performance*. Washington, DC: Congressional Quarterly Press.

Gormley, William, John Hoadley, and Charles Williams. 1983. "Potential Responsiveness in the Bureaucracy: Views of Public Utility Regulation." *American Political Science Review* 77 (3): 704–71.

Hall, Thad E. 2002. "Live Bureaucrats and Dead Public Servants: How People in Government are Discussed on the Floor of the House." *Public Administration Review* 62 (2): 242–51.

Hall, Thad E., and Laurence J. O'Toole Jr. 2000. "Structures for Policy Implementation: An Analysis of National Legislation, 1965–1966 and 1993–1994." *Administration and Society* 31 (6): 667–86.

Hall, Thad E., and Laurence J. O'Toole Jr. 2004. "Shaping Formal Networks through the Regulatory Process." *Administration and Society* 36 (2): 1–22.

Hamilton, James. 1996. "Going by the (Informal) Book: The EPA's Use of Informal Rules in Enforcing Hazardous Waste Laws." In *Reinventing Government and The Problem of Bureaucracy*, edited by Gary Libecap, 109–55. Greenwich, CT: JAI Press.

Hamilton, James, and Christopher H. Schroeder. 1994. "Strategic Regulators and the Choice of Rulemaking Procedures: The Selection of Formal and Informal Rules in Regulating Hazardous Waste." *Law and Contemporary Problems* 57: 111–60.

Hammond, Thomas H. 1986. "Agenda Control, Organizational Structure, and Bureaucratic Politics." *American Journal of Political Science* 30 (2): 379–420.

Hammond, Thomas H., and Jack H. Knott. 1996. "Who Controls the Bureaucracy? Presidential Power, Congressional Dominance, Legal Constraints, and Bureaucratic Autonomy in a Model of Multi-institutional Policy-making." *Journal of Law, Economics, and Organization* 12 (1): 119–66.

Hanushek, Erik. 1996. "School Resources and Student Performance." In *Does Money Matter?*, edited by Gary Burtless, 43–73. Washington, DC: Brookings Institution Press.

Hedge, David, and Michael Scicchitano. 1994. "Regulating in Space and Time: The Case of Regulatory Federalism." *Journal of Politics* 56 (1): 134–53.

Hedges, Larry V., and Rob Greenwald. 1996. "Have Times Changed? The Relation between School Resources and Student Performance." In *Does Money Matter?*, edited by Gary Burtless, 74–92. Washington, DC: Brookings Institution Press.

Heinrich, Carolyn, and Laurence E. Lynn, Jr., eds. 2000. *Governance and Performance: New Perspectives*. Washington, DC: Georgetown University Press.

Heller, Kirby A., Wayne H. Holtzman, and Samuel Messick. 1982. *Placing Children in Special Education*. Washington, DC: National Academy Press.

Hero Rodney E., and Carolyn J. Tolbert. 1995. "Latinos and Substantive Representation in the U.S. House of Representatives." *American Journal of Political Science* 39 (3): 640–52.

Herring, H. Pendleton. 1936. *Public Administration and the Public Interest*. New York: McGraw-Hill.

Hess, Frederick M. 1999. *Spinning Wheels: The Politics of Urban School Reform*. Washington, DC: Brookings Institution Press.

Hicklin, Alisa. 2004. "Network Stability: Opportunity or Obstacle?" *Public Organization Review* 4: 121–33.

Hindera, John J. 1993. "Representative Bureaucracy: Further Evidence of Active Representation in the EEOC District Offices." *Journal of Public Administration Research and Theory* 3 (4): 415–30.

Hjern, Benny, and David O. Porter. 1981. "Implementation Structures: A New Unit of Administrative Analysis." *Organization Studies* 2 (3): 211–37.

Holzer, Mark, and Kathe Callahan. 1998. *Government at Work: Best Practices and Model Programs*. Thousand Oaks, CA: Sage.

Hood, Christopher. 2002. "Control, Bargains, and Cheating: The Politics of Public Service Reform." *Journal of Public Administration Research and Theory* 12 (3): 309–32.

Hopenhayn, Hugo A., and Susanne Lohmann. 1996. "Fire-Alarm Signals and the Political Control of Regulatory Agencies." *Journal of Law, Economics, and Organization* 12 (1): 199–216.

Huber, John D., and Charles R. Shippan. 2002. *Deliberate Discretion: The Institutional Foundations of Bureaucratic Autonomy*. New York: Cambridge University Press, 2002.

Hyneman, Charles. 1950. *Bureaucracy in a Democracy*. New York: Harper & Bros.

Inglehart, Ronald. 1997. "Postmaterialist Values and the Erosion of Institutional Authority." In *Why People Don't Trust Government*, edited by Nye, Zelikow, and King, 217–36.

Ingraham, Patricia W. 1995. *The Foundation of Merit: Public Service in American Democracy.* Baltimore: Johns Hopkins University Press.

Jencks, Christopher, and Meredith Phillips. 1998. *The Black-White Test Score Gap.* Washington, DC: Brookings Institution Press.

Jensen, Michael, and William Meckling. 1976. "Theory of the Firm: Managerial Behavior, Agency Costs, and Capital Structure." *Journal of Financial Economics* 3 (4): 305–60.

Jones, Bryan D. 1985. *Governing Buildings and Building Government.* Tuscaloosa: University of Alabama Press.

Jordan, Grant, and Klaus Schubert. 1992. "A Preliminary Ordering of Policy Network Labels." *European Journal of Political Research* 21 (1–2): 7–27.

Juenke, Eric Gonzalez. 2005a. "Management Tenure and Network Time: How Experience Affects Bureaucratic Dynamics." *Journal of Public Administration Research and Theory.* 15 (1): 113–31.

Juenke, Eric Gonzalez. 2005b. "Minority Influence on Public Organization Change: Latinos and Local Education Politics." PhD diss., Department of Political Science, Texas A&M University.

Kaufman, Herbert. 1956. "Emerging Conflicts in the Doctrines of Public Administration." *American Political Science Review* 50 (4): 1057–73.

Kaufman, Herbert. 1960. *The Forest Ranger: A Study in Administrative Behavior.* Baltimore: Johns Hopkins University Press.

Kaufman, Herbert. 1981. *The Administrative Behavior of Federal Bureau Chiefs.* Washington, DC: Brookings Institution Press.

Kaufman, Herbert. 1985. *Time, Chance, and Organizations: Natural Selection in a Perilous Environment.* Chatham, NJ: Chatham House.

Kaufman, Herbert. 1990. "Comments." In *Refounding Public Administration*, edited by Wamsley et al., 313–15. Newbury Park, CA: Sage.

Keiser, Lael R., Vicky M. Wilkins, Kenneth J. Meier, and Catherine Holland. 2002. "Lipstick or Logarithms: Gender, Identity, Institutions, and Representative Bureaucracy." *American Political Science Review* 96 (3): 553–64.

Kelly, Rita Mae, and Meredith Newman. 2001. "The Gendered Bureaucracy: Agency Mission, Equality of Opportunity, and Representative Bureaucracies." *Women and Politics* 22 (3): 1–33.

Kerr, Brinck, and Will Miller. 1997. "Latino Representation: It's Direct and Indirect." *American Journal of Political Science* 41 (3): 1066–71.

Kerwin, Cornelius M. 2003. *Rulemaking: How Government Agencies Write Law and Make Policy.* Washington, DC: Congressional Quarterly Press.

Kettl, Donald F. 1986. *Leadership at the Fed.* New Haven, CT: Yale University Press.

Kettl, Donald F. 1993. "Searching for Clues about Public Management: Slicing the Onion Different Ways." In *Public Management: The State of the Art,* edited by Barry Bozeman, 55–68. San Francisco: Jossey-Bass.

Kettl, Donald F. 2000a. "The Transformation of Governance: Globalization, Devolution, and the Role of Government." *Public Administration Review* 60 (6): 488–97.

Kettl, Donald F. 2000b. *The Global Public Management Revolution.* Washington, DC: Brookings Institution Press.

Kettl, Donald F. 2002. *The Transformation of Governance: Public Administration for Twenty-first Century America.* Baltimore: Johns Hopkins University Press.

Kettner, P. M., and L. L. Martin. 1990. "Purchase of Service Contracting: Two Models." *Administration in Social Work* 14 (1): 15–31.

Khademian, Anne M. 1995. "Reinventing a Government Corporation: Professional Priorities and a Clear Bottom Line." *Public Administration Review* 55 (1): 17–28.

Kickert, Walter J. M., Erik-Hans Klijn, and Joop F. M. Koppenjan, eds. 1997. *Managing Complex Networks: Strategies for the Public Sector.* London: Sage.

Klijn, Erik-Hans. 1996. "Analyzing and Managing Policy Processes in Complex Networks: A Theoretical Examination of the Concept Policy Network and Its Problems." *Administration and Society* 28 (1): 90–119.

Knight, Jack. 1992. *Institutions and Social Conflict.* New York: Cambridge University Press.

Knoke, David, and James H. Kuklinski. 1982. *Network Analysis.* Newbury Park, CA: Sage.

Kooiman, Jan. 2003. *Governing as Governance.* London: Sage.

Krause, George A. 1996. "The Institutional Dynamics of Policy Administration: Bureaucratic Influence Over Securities Regulation." *American Journal of Political Science* 40 (4): 1083–1121.

Krause, George A. 1999. *A Two-Way Street: The Institutional Dynamics of the Modern Administrative State.* Pittsburgh: University of Pittsburgh Press.

Krause, George A., and Kenneth J. Meier. 2003. *Politics, Policy, and Organizations.* Ann Arbor: University of Michigan Press.

Kronenberg, Philip S. 1990. "Public Administration and the Defense Department: Examination of a Prototype." In *Refounding Public Administration*, edited by Wamsley et al., 274–306. Newbury Park, CA: Sage.

Lankford, Hamilton, and James Wyckoff. 1996. "The Allocation of Resources to Special Education and Regular Instruction." In *Holding Schools Accountable*, edited by Helen F. Ladd, 221–57. Washington, DC: Brookings Institution Press.

Lasswell, Harold. 1936. *Politics: Who Gets What When How.* New York: McGraw-Hill.

Leal, David, Kenneth J. Meier, and Val Martinez-Ebers. 2004. "The Politics of Latino Education: The Biases of At-large Elections." *Journal of Politics* 66 (4): 1224–44.

Lewis, Gregory B. 1990. "In Search of the Machiavellian Milquetoasts: Comparing Attitudes of Bureaucrats and Ordinary People." *Public Administration Review* 50 (2): 220–27.

Lieberman, Robert C. 1998. *Shifting the Color Line: Race and the American Welfare State.* Cambridge, MA: Harvard University Press.

Light, Paul. 1999a. *The New Public Service.* Washington, DC: Brookings Institution Press.

Light, Paul. 1999b. *The True Size of Government.* Washington, DC: Brookings Institution Press.

Lilienthal, David. 1944. *TVA: Democracy on the March.* New York: Harper & Bros.

Lineberry, Robert. 1977. *Equality and Urban Policy.* Beverley Hills, CA: Sage.

Long, Norton E. 1949. "Power and Administration." *Public Administration Review* 9 (4): 257–64.

Long, Norton E. 1952. "Bureaucracy and Constitutionalism." *American Political Science Review* 46 (3): 808–18.

Lowery, David. 2000. "The Presidency, Reinvention, and Bureaucracy: A Gentle Plea for Chaos." *Presidential Studies Quarterly* 30 (1): 79–108.

Lowi, Theodore J. 1969. *The End of Liberalism.* New York: Norton.

Lubell, Mark. 2004. "Collaborative Watershed Management: A View from the Grassroots." *Policy Studies Journal* 32 (3): 341–61.

Lubell, Mark, Mark Schneider, John T. Scholz, and Mihriye Mete. 2002. "Watershed Partnerships and the Emergence of Collective Action Institutions." *American Journal of Political Science* 46 (1): 148–63.

Lupia, Arthur, and Mathew McCubbins. 1994. "Learning From Oversight: Police Patrols and Fire Alarms Reconsidered." *Journal of Law, Economics, and Organization* 10 (1): 96–125.

Lynn, Laurence E., Carolyn J. Heinrich, and Carolyn J. Hill. 2001. *Improving Governance: A New Logic for Empirical Research*. Washington, DC: Georgetown University Press.

Lyons, William E., David Lowery, and Ruth Hoagland DeHoog. 1992. *The Politics of Dissatisfaction: Citizens, Services and Institutions*. Armonk, NY: M. E. Sharpe.

Macey, Jonathan R. 1992. "Organizational Design and the Political Control of Administrative Agencies." *Journal of Law, Economics, and Organization* 8 (1): 93–109.

Mandell, Myrna, ed. 2001. *Getting Results through Collaboration: Networks and Network Structures for Public Policy and Management*. Westport, CT: Quorum Books.

Marini, Frank, ed. 1971. *Toward a New Public Administration: The Minnowbrook Perspective*. San Francisco, CA: Chandler.

Matza, Michael, Craig R. McCoy, and Mark Fazlollah. 1999. "Major Crimes Climb in Philadelphia." *Philadelphia Inquirer*, Jan. 17, 1.

Maynard-Moody, Steven, and Michael Musheno. 2003. *Cops, Teachers, Counselors: Stories from the Front Lines of Public Service*. Ann Arbor: University of Michigan Press.

Mazmanian, Daniel A., and Paul A. Sabatier. 1989. *Implementation and Public Policy*. Rev. ed. Washington, DC: University Press of America.

McCraw, Thomas K. 1984. *Prophets of Regulation*. Cambridge, MA.: Harvard University Press.

McCubbins, Mathew D. 1985. "The Legislative Design of Regulatory Structure." *American Journal of Political Science* 29 (4): 721–48.

McCubbins, Mathew D., Roger G. Noll, and Barry Weingast. 1987. "Administrative Procedures as Instruments of Popular Control." *Journal of Law, Economics, and Organization* 3 (2): 243–77.

McCubbins, Mathew D., Roger G. Noll, and Barry Weingast. 1989. "Structure and Process as Solutions to the Politician's Principal Agency Problem?" *Virginia Law Review* 74 (2): 431–82.

McCubbins, Mathew D., and Talbot Page. 1987. "A Theory of Congressional Delegation." In *Congress: Structure and Policy*, edited by Mathew D. McCubbins and Terry Sullivan, 409–25. New York: Cambridge University Press.

McCubbins, Mathew D., and Thomas Schwartz. 1984. "Congressional Oversight Overlooked: Police Patrols versus Fire Alarms." *American Journal of Political Science* 28 (1): 165–79.

McFarlane, Deborah R., and Kenneth J. Meier. 2001. *The Politics of Fertility Control: Family Planning and Abortion Policies in the American States*. New York: Chatham House.

McGuire, Michael. 2002. "Managing Networks: Propositions on What Managers Do and Why They Do It." *Public Administration Review* 62 (5): 599–609.

Meier, Kenneth J. 1988. *The Political Economy of Regulation: The Case of Insurance*. Albany: State University of New York Press.

Meier, Kenneth J. 1993. "Latinos and Representative Bureaucracy: Testing the Thompson and Henderson Hypotheses." *Journal of Public Administration Research and Theory* 3 (4): 393–415.

Meier, Kenneth J. 1997. "Bureaucracy and Democracy: The Case for More Bureaucracy and Less Democracy." *Public Administration Review* 57 (3): 193–99.

Meier, Kenneth J. 2000. *Politics and the Bureaucracy: Policymaking in the Fourth Branch of Government.* 4th ed. Fort Worth, TX: Harcourt Brace.

Meier, Kenneth J., and Jill Nicholson-Crotty. Forthcoming. "Gender, Representative Bureaucracy, and Law Enforcement: The Case of Sexual Assault." *Public Administration Review.*

Meier, Kenneth J., and Laurence J. O'Toole, Jr. 2001. "Managerial Strategies and Behavior in Networks: A Model with Evidence from U.S. Public Education." *Journal of Public Administration Research and Theory* 11 (3): 271–95.

Meier, Kenneth J., and Laurence J. O'Toole Jr. 2002. "Public Management and Organizational Performance: The Impact of Managerial Quality," *Journal of Policy Analysis and Management* 21 (4): 629–43.

Meier, Kenneth J., and Laurence J. O'Toole Jr. 2003. "Public Management and Educational Performance: The Impact of Managerial Networking." *Public Administration Review* 63 (6): 689–99.

Meier, Kenneth J., and Laurence J. O'Toole Jr. 2005. "Managerial Networking: Issues of Measurement and Research Design." *Administration and Society* 37 (5): 523–41.

Meier, Kenneth J., and Laurence J. O'Toole Jr. 2006. "Political Control versus Bureaucratic Values: Reframing the Debate." *Public Administration Review* 66 (2).

Meier, Kenneth J., Laurence J. O'Toole Jr., and Sean Nicholson-Crotty. 2004. "Multilevel Governance and Organizational Performance: Investigating the Political-Bureaucratic Labyrinth." *Journal of Policy Analysis and Management* 23 (1): 31–48.

Meier, Kenneth J., J. L. Polinard, and Robert Wrinkle. 1999. "Politics, Bureaucracy, and Farm Credit." *Public Administration Review* 59 (4): 293–302.

Meier, Kenneth J., and Kevin B. Smith. 1994. "Representative Democracy and Representative Bureaucracy: Examining the Top-Down and the Bottom-Up Linkages." *Social Science Quarterly* 75 (4): 790–803.

Meier, Kenneth J., and Joseph Stewart Jr. 1991. *The Politics of Hispanic Education.* Albany: State University of New York Press.

Meier, Kenneth J., Joseph Stewart Jr., and Robert E. England. 1991. "The Politics of Bureaucratic Discretion: Educational Access as an Urban Service." *American Journal of Political Science* 35 (1): 155–77.

Meier, Kenneth J., Robert Wrinkle, and J. L. Polinard. 1995. "Politics, Bureaucracy, and Agricultural Policy: An Alternative View of Political Control." *American Politics Quarterly* 23 (4): 427–60.

Meier, Kenneth J., Robert D. Wrinkle, and J. L. Polinard. 1999. "Representative Bureaucracy and Distributional Equity: Addressing the Hard Question." *Journal of Politics* 61 (4): 1025–39.

Mete, Mihriye. 2002. "Bureaucratic Behavior in Strategic Environments: Politicians, Taxpayers, and the IRS." *Journal of Politics* 64 (2): 384–407.

Michels, Robert. 1999. *Political Parties: A Sociological Study of the Oligarchical Tendencies of Modern Democracy.* Introduction by Seymour Martin Lipset; translated by Eden and Cedar Paul. New Brunswick, NJ: Transaction.

Miller, Gary J. 1992. *Managerial Dilemmas: The Political Economy of Hierarchy.* New York: Cambridge University Press.

Miller, Gary. 2000. "Above Politics: Credible Commitment and Efficiency in the Design of Public Agencies." *Journal of Public Administration Research and Theory* 10 (2): 289–327.

Milward, H. Brinton. 2001. "Theoretical Perspectives on Public-Private Partnerships." Plenary address, Fifth International Research Symposium on Public Management, Barcelona, Spain, April 10.

Mitnick, Barry M. 1980. *The Political Economy of Regulation: Creating, Designing, and Removing Regulatory Forms.* New York: Columbia University Press.

Mladenka, Kenneth R. 1980. "The Urban Bureaucracy and the Chicago Political Machine." *American Political Science Review* 74 (4): 991–98.

Mladenka, Kenneth R. 1989. "Blacks and Hispanics in Urban Politics." *American Political Science Review* 83 (1): 165–91.

Moe, Terry M. 1982. "Regulatory Performance and Presidential Administration." *American Journal of Political Science* 26 (4): 197–224.

Moe, Terry M. 1984. "The New Economics of Organization." *American Journal of Political Science* 28 (4): 739–77.

Moe, Terry M. 1985. "Control and Feedback in Economic Regulation: The Case of the NLRB." *American Political Science Review* 79 (4): 1094–1116.

Moe, Terry M. 1987. "An Assessment of the Positive Theory of 'Congressional Dominance.'" *Legislative Studies Quarterly* 12 (1): 475–520.

Moe, Terry M. 1990. "Politics and the Theory of Organization." *Journal of Law, Economics, and Organization* 7 (1): 106–29.

Moe, Terry M. 1993. "Presidents, Institutions, and Theory." In *Researching the Presidency: Vital Questions, New Approaches,* edited by George C. Edwards III, John Kessel, and Bert A. Rockman, 337–86. Pittsburgh: University of Pittsburgh Press.

Moe, Terry M. 1998. "The Presidency and the Bureaucracy: The Presidential Advantage." In *The Presidency and the Presidential System.* 5th ed., edited by Michael Nelson, 437–68. Washington, DC: Congressional Quarterly Press.

Moe, Terry M. 2002. "Teachers Unions and School Board Elections." In *Besieged: School Boards and the Future of Education Politics,* edited by William G. Howell, 254–87. Washington, DC: Brookings Institution Press.

Moe, Terry M., and William Howell. 1999a. "Unilateral Action and Presidential Power: A Theory." *Presidential Studies Quarterly* 29 (4): 850–72.

Moe, Terry M., and William Howell. 1999b. "The Presidential Power of Unilateral Action." *Journal of Law, Economics, and Organization* 15 (1): 132–79.

Morgan, David R., and John P. Pelissero. 1982. "Urban Policy: Does Political Structure Matter." *American Political Science Review* 74 (4): 999–1006.

Mosher, Frederick C. 1982. *Democracy and the Public Service.* New York: Oxford University Press.

Mosher, Frederick C. 1992. "Public Administration Old and New: A Letter from Frederick C. Mosher." *Journal of Public Administration Research and Theory* 2 (2): 199–202.

Naff, Katherine C. 2001. *To Look Like America.* Boulder, CO: Westview Press.

Nalbandian, John, and J. Terry Edwards. 1983. "The Values of Public Administrators." *Review of Public Personnel Administration,* Fall, 114–27.

National Performance Review. 1993. *From Red Tape to Results: Creating a Government That Works Better and Costs Less.* Washington, DC: GPO.

Niskanen, William A. 1971. *Bureaucracy and Representative Government.* Chicago: Aldine, Atherton.

Nye, Joseph S., Jr., Philip D. Zelikow, and David C. King, eds. 1997. *Why People Don't Trust Government.* Cambridge, MA: Harvard University Press.

Oakes, Jeannie. 1985. *Keeping Track: How Schools Structure Inequality.* New Haven, CT: Yale University Press.

O'Brien, Kevin J., and Lianjiang Li. 1999. "Selective Policy Implementation in Rural China." *Comparative Politics* 31 (2): 167–86.

Ogul, Morris S. 1976. *Congress Oversees the Bureaucracy: Studies in Legislative Supervision.* Pittsburgh: University of Pittsburgh Press.

Ogul, Morris S., and Bert A. Rockman. 1990. "Overseeing Oversight: New Departures and Old Problems." *Legislative Studies Quarterly* 15 (1): 5–24.

O'Leary, Rosemary. 1994. "The Bureaucratic Politics Paradox: The Case of Wetlands Legislation in Nevada." *Journal of Public Administration Research and Theory* 4 (4): 443–68.

Olson, Mancur. 1965. *The Logic of Collective Action.* Cambridge, MA: Harvard University Press.

Orren, Gary. 1997. "Fall from Grace: The Public's Loss of Faith in Government." In *Why People Don't Trust Government,* edited by Nye, Zelikow, and King, 77–107.

Ostrom, Elinor. 1990. *Governing the Commons: The Evolution of Institutions for Collective Action.* New York: Cambridge University Press.

Ostrom, Vincent. 1989. *The Intellectual Crisis in American Public Administration.* Rev. ed. Tuscaloosa: University of Alabama Press.

O'Toole, Laurence J., Jr. 1977. "Lineage, Continuity, Frederickson, and the 'New Public Administration.'" *Administration and Society* 9 (2): 233–52.

O'Toole, Laurence J., Jr. 1989. "Alternative Mechanisms for Multiorganizational Implementation: The Case of Wastewater Management." *Administration and Society* 21 (3): 313–39.

O'Toole, Laurence J., Jr. 1991. "Public and Private Management of Wastewater Treatment: A Comparative Study." In *Evaluation and Privatization,* edited by John Heilman, 13–32. San Francisco: Jossey-Bass.

O'Toole, Laurence J., Jr. 1996. "Hollowing the Infrastructure: Revolving Loan Programs and Network Dynamics in the American States." *Journal of Public Administration Research and Theory* 6 (2): 225–42.

O'Toole, Laurence J., Jr. 1997a "Implications for Democracy of a Networked Bureaucratic World." *Journal of Public Administration Research and Theory* 7 (3): 443–59.

O'Toole, Laurence J., Jr. 1997b. "Treating Networks Seriously: Practical and Research-based Agendas in Public Administration." *Public Administration Review* 57 (1): 45–52.

O'Toole, Laurence J., Jr. 1998. *Institutions, Policy, and Outputs for Acidification: The Case of Hungary.* Aldershot, UK: Ashgate.

O'Toole, Laurence J., Jr., ed. 2000a. *American Intergovernmental Relations: Foundations, Perspectives, and Issues.* 3d ed. Washington, DC: Congressional Quarterly Press.

O'Toole, Laurence J., Jr. 2000b. "Research on Policy Implementation: Assessment and Prospect." *Journal of Public Administration Research and Theory* 10 (2): 263–88.

O'Toole, Laurence J., Jr. 2000c. "Different Public Managements? Implications of Structural Context in Hierarchies and Networks." In *Advancing Public Management*, edited by Jeffrey Brudney, O'Toole, and Hal G. Rainey, 1–12. Washington, DC: Georgetown University Press.

O'Toole, Laurence J., Jr. 2006. "Governing Outputs and Outcomes of Governance Networks." In *Theories of Democratic Network Governance*, edited by Eva Sørensen and Jacob Torfing. Hampshire, UK: Palgrave Macmillan.

O'Toole, Laurence J., Jr., and Kenneth J. Meier. 1999. "Modeling the Impact of Public Management: The Implications of Structural Context." *Journal of Public Administration Research and Theory* 9 (4): 505–26.

O'Toole, Laurence J., Jr., and Kenneth J. Meier. 2000. "Networks, Hierarchies, and Public Management: Modeling the Nonlinearities," in Heinrich and Lynn, eds., *Governance and Performance*, 263–91.

O'Toole, Laurence J., Jr., and Kenneth J. Meier. 2003. "*Plus ça Change*: Public Management, Personnel Stability, and Organizational Performance." *Journal of Public Administration Research and Theory* 13 (1): 43–64.

O'Toole, Laurence J., Jr., and Kenneth J. Meier. 2004. "Desperately Seeking Selznick: Cooptation and the Dark Side of Public Management in Networks." *Public Administration Review* 64 (6): 681–93.

Perrow, Charles. 1972. *Complex Organizations: A Critical Essay.* Glenview, IL: Scott Foresman.

Perrow, Charles. 1986. *Complex Organizations: A Critical Essay.* 3rd ed. New York: McGraw-Hill.

Perry, James L. 1996. "Measuring Public Service Motivation: An Assessment of Construct Reliability and Validity." *Journal of Public Administration Research and Theory* 6 (1): 5–22.

Perry, James L. 2000. "Bringing Society Back In: Toward a Theory of Public-Service Motivation." *Journal of Public Administration Research and Theory* 10 (2): 471–88.

Perry, James L., and Lois Recascino Wise. 1990. "The Motivation Bases of Public Service." *Public Administration Review* 50 (3): 367–73.

Pfeffer, Jeffrey, and Gerald R. Salancik. 1978. *The External Control of Organizations: A Resource Dependence Perspective.* New York: Harper & Row.

Pierre, Jon, and B. Guy Peters. 2000. *Governance, Politics, and the State.* London: Macmillan.

Pitkin, Hanna F. 1967. *The Concept of Representation.* Berkeley: University of California Press.

Pitts, David W. 2005. "Diversity, Representation, and Performance: Evidence about Race and Ethnicity in Public Organizations." *Journal of Public Administration Research and Theory* 15 (4): 615–31.

Pollitt, Christopher, and Geert Bouckaert. 2000. *Public Management Reform: A Comparative Analysis.* London: Oxford University Press.

Potosky, Matthew. 1999. "Managing Uncertainty through Bureaucratic Design: Administrative Procedures and State Air Pollution Control Agencies." *Journal of Public Administration Research and Theory* 9 (4): 623–39.

Poveda, Tony. 1990. *The FBI in Transition: Lawlessness and Reform*. Pacific Grove, CA: Brooks/Cole.

Pressman, Jeffrey, and Aaron Wildavsky. 1984. *Implementation*. 3rd ed. Berkeley: University of California Press.

Provan, Keith G., and H. Brinton Milward. 1991. "Institutional-Level Norms and Organizational Involvement in a Service-Implementation Network." *Journal of Public Administration Research and Theory* 1 (4): 391–417.

Provan, Keith G., and H. Brinton Milward. 1995. "A Preliminary Theory of Interorganizational Network Effectiveness: A Comparative Study of Four Community Mental Health Systems." *Administrative Science Quarterly* 40 (1): 1–33.

Rainey, Hal G. 1982. "Reward Preferences among Public and Private Managers: In Search of the Service Ethic." *American Review of Public Administration* 16 (4): 288–302.

Rainey, Hal G. 2003. *Understanding and Managing Public Organizations*. 3rd ed. San Francisco: Jossey-Bass.

Redford, Emmette S. 1969. *Democracy in the Administrative State*. New York: Oxford University Press.

Rhodes, R. A. W. 1997. *Understanding Governance: Policy Networks, Reflexivity, and Accountability*. Buckingham, UK: Open University Press.

Riccucci, Norma M. 1995. *Unsung Heroes: Federal Execucrats Making a Difference*. Washington, DC: Georgetown University Press.

Riccucci, Norma M. 2005. *How Management Matters: Street-level Bureaucrats and Welfare Reform*. Washington, DC: Georgetown University Press.

Ringquist, Evan. 1993. "Does Regulation Matter? Evaluating the Effects of State Air Pollution Control Programs." *Journal of Politics* 55 (4): 1022–45.

Ringquist, Evan J. 1995. "Political Control and Policy Impact in EPA's Office of Water Quality." *American Journal of Political Science* 39 (2): 336–63.

Rockman, Bert A. 1984. "Legislative-Executive Relations and Legislative Oversight." *Legislative Studies Quarterly* 9 (3): 387–440.

Rohr, John A. 1986. *To Run a Constitution: The Legitimacy of the Administrative State*. Lawrence: University Press of Kansas.

Rohr, John A. 1990. "The Constitutional Case for Public Administration." In *Refounding Public Administration*, edited by Wamsley et al., 52–95. Newbury Park, CA: Sage.

Rohr, John A. 2002. *Civil Servants and Their Constitutions*. Lawrence: University of Kansas Press.

Rosenbloom, David. 2000. *Building a Legislative-Centered Public Administration: Congress and the Administrative State, 1946–1999*. Tuscaloosa: University of Alabama Press.

Ross, Stephen A. 1973. "The Economic Theory of Agency: The Principal's Problem." *American Economic Review: Papers and Proceedings from the American Economic Association* 63 (2): 134–39.

Rourke, Francis. 1969. *Bureaucracy, Politics, and Public Policy*. Boston: Little, Brown.

Rubin, Irene S. 1985. *Shrinking the Federal Government*. New York: Longman.

Sabatier, Paul A., and Hank Jenkins-Smith. 1993. *Policy Change and Learning: An Advocacy Coalition Approach*. Boulder, CO: Westview Press.

Sabatier, Paul A., John Loomis, and Catherine McCarthy. 1995. "Hierarchical Controls, Professional Norms, Local Constituencies, and Budget Maximization: An Analysis of U.S. Forest Service Planning Decisions." *American Journal of Political Science* 39 (1): 204–42.

Schattschneider, E. E 1960. *The Semi-Sovereign People: A Realist's View of Democracy in America.* New York: Holt, Rinehart & Winston.

Scher, Seymour. 1963. "Conditions for Legislative Control." *Journal of Politics* 25 (3): 526–51.

Schneider, Mark, John T. Scholz, Mark Lubell, Denisa Mindruta, and Matt Edwardsen. 2003. "Building Consensual Institutions: Networks and the National Estuary Program." *American Journal of Political Science* 47 (1): 143–58.

Scholz, John T., Jim Twombly, and Barbara Headrick. 1991. "Street-Level Political Controls over Federal Bureaucracy." *American Political Science Review* 85 (3): 829–50.

Scholz, John T., and Feng Heng Wei. 1986. "Regulatory Enforcement in a Federalist System." *American Political Science Review* 80 (4): 1249–70.

Scholz, John T., and B. Dan Wood. 1998. "Controlling the IRS: Principals, Principles, and Public Administration." *American Journal of Political Science* 42 (1): 141–62.

Scholz, John T., and B. Dan Wood. 1999. "Efficiency, Equity, and Politics: Democratic Controls over the Tax Collector." *American Journal of Political Science* 43 (4): 1166–88.

Schumpeter, Joseph A. 1950. *Capitalism, Socialism, and Democracy.* 3d ed. New York: Harper.

Sclar, E. D. 2000. *You Don't Always Get What You Pay For: The Economics of Privatization.* Ithaca, NY: Cornell University Press.

Seidman, Harold. 1970. *Politics, Position, and Power: The Dynamics of Federal Organization.* New York: Oxford University Press.

Seidman, Harold. 1997. *Politics, Position, and Power: The Dynamics of Federal Organization.* 5th ed. New York: Oxford University Press.

Selden, Sally C. 1997. *The Promise of Representative Bureaucracy.* New York: M. E. Sharpe.

Selznick, Philip. 1949. *TVA and the Grass Roots.* Berkeley: University of California Press.

Selznick, Philip. 1957. *Leadership in Administration.* New York: Harper & Row.

Simon, Herbert A. 1947. *Administrative Behavior.* New York: Free Press.

Simon, Herbert A. 1997. *Administrative Behavior.* 4th ed. New York: Free Press.

Smith, Kevin B. 2003. *The Ideology of Education: The Commonwealth, the Market, and America's Schools.* Albany: State University of New York Press.

Smith, S. R. 1996. "Transforming Public Services: Contracting for Social and Health Services in the US." *Public Administration* 74 (1): 113–27.

Snow, C. P. 1961. *Science and Government.* Cambridge, MA: Harvard University Press.

Spence, David B. 1999. "Agency Discretion and the Dynamics of Procedural Reform." *Public Administration Review* 59 (5): 425–42.

Spence, David B. 2003. "The Benefits of Agency Policy-making: Perspectives from Positive Theory." In *Politics, Policy, and Organizations,* edited by George A. Krause and Kenneth J. Meier, 104–31. Ann Arbor: University of Michigan Press.

Spencer, Jason. 2005. "Probe Finds 4 Schools Cheated on TAKS Test." *Houston Chronicle,* May 5, A1, A6.

Spulber, Daniel F., and David Besanko. 1992. "Delegation, Commitment, and the Regulatory Mandate." *Journal of Law, Economics, and Organization* 8 (1): 126–54.

Stillman, Richard J. II. 1991. *Preface to Public Administration.* New York: St. Martin's.

Stivers, Camilla. 2002. *Gender Issues in Public Administration.* Thousand Oaks, CA: Sage.

Suleiman, Erza. 2003. *Dismantling Democratic States.* Princeton, NJ: Princeton University Press.

Terry, Larry D. 1990. "Leadership in the Administrative State: The Concept of Administrative Conservatorship." *Administration and Society* 21 (4): 395–413.

Terry, Larry D. 2003. *Leadership of Public Bureaucracies: The Administrator as Conservator.* Armonk, NY: M. E. Sharpe.

Thompson, James D. 1967. *Organizations in Action.* New York: McGraw-Hill.

Thompson, Victor. 1975. *Without Sympathy or Enthusiasm: The Problem of Administrative Compassion.* Tuscaloosa: University of Alabama Press.

Tiebout, Charles M. 1956. "A Pure Theory of Local Expenditures." *Journal of Political Economy* 64 (2): 416–24.

van Waarden, Frans. 1992. "Dimensions and Types of Policy Networks." *European Journal of Political Research* 21 (1–2): 29–52.

Vigil, Maurilio E. 1997. "Hispanics in the 103rd Congress." In *Pursuing Power: Latinos in the Political System,* edited by F. Chris Garcia, 234–64. Notre Dame, IN: University of Notre Dame Press.

Waldo, Dwight. 1948. *The Administrative State.* New York: Ronald Press.

Waldo, Dwight. 1952. "The Development of a Theory of Democratic Administration." *American Political Science Review* 46 (1): 81–103.

Waldo, Dwight, ed. 1971. *Public Administration in a Time of Turbulence.* Scranton, PA: Chandler.

Wamsley, Gary L. 1990. "The Agency Perspective: Public Administrators as Agential Leaders." In *Refounding Public Administration,* edited by Wamsley et al., 114–62. Newbury Park, CA: Sage.

Wamsley, Gary L., Robert N. Bacher, Charles T. Goodsell, Philip S. Kronenberg, John A. Rohr, Camilla M. Stivers, Orion F. White, and James F. Wolf, eds. 1990. *Refounding Public Administration.* Newbury Park, CA: Sage.

Wamsley, Gary L., Charles T. Goodsell, John A. Rohr, Camilla M. Stivers, Orion F. White, and James F. Wolf. 1987. "The Public Administration and the Governance Process: Refocusing the American Dialogue." In *A Centennial History of the American Administrative State,* edited by Ralph Clark Chandler, 291–317. New York: Free Press.

Wamsley, Gary L., and James F. Wolf, eds. 1996. *Refounding Democratic Public Administration: Modern Paradoxes, Postmodern Challenges.* Thousand Oaks, CA: Sage.

Waterman, Richard, and Kenneth J. Meier. 1998. "Principal-Agent Models: An Expansion?" *Journal of Public Administration Research and Theory* 8 (2): 173–202.

Waterman, Richard W., Amelia A. Rouse, and Robert L. Wright. 2004. *Bureaucrats, Politics, and the Environment.* Pittsburgh: University of Pittsburgh Press.

Weber, Edward P. 2003. *Bringing Society Back In: Grassroots Ecosystem Management, Accountability, and Sustainable Communities.* Cambridge, MA: MIT Press.

Weber, Max. 1946. *From Max Weber: Essays in Sociology.* Translated and edited by H. H. Gerth and C. Wright Mills. Oxford: Oxford University Press.

Weiher, Gregory. 2000. "Minority Student Achievement: Passive Representation and Social Context in Schools." *Journal of Politics* 62 (3): 886–95.

Weingast, Barry. 1984. "The Congressional-Bureaucratic System: A Principal-Agent Perspective with Applications to the SEC." *Public Choice* 44 (2): 147–91.

Weingast, Barry, and Mark Moran. 1983. "Bureaucratic Discretion or Congressional Control? Regulatory Policymaking by the Federal Trade Commission." *Journal of Political Economy* 91 (5): 756–800.

West, William F. 1995. *Controlling the Bureaucracy: Institutional Constraints in Theory and Practice.* Armonk, NY: M. E. Sharpe.

Whitford, Andrew B. 2002. "Bureaucratic Discretion, Agency Structure, and Democratic Responsiveness: The Case of the United States Attorneys." *Journal of Public Administration Research and Theory* 12 (1): 3–27.

Wilkins, Vicky M., and Lael R. Keiser. 2006. "Linking Passive and Active Representation by Gender: The Case of Child Support Agencies." *Journal of Public Administration Research and Theory.* 16 (1): 87–102.

Williamson, Oliver E. 1985. *The Economic Institutions of Capitalism.* New York: Free Press.

Williamson, Oliver E. 1990. *Organization Theory: From Chester Barnard to the Present and Beyond.* New York: Oxford University Press.

Williamson, Oliver E. 1996. *The Mechanisms of Governance.* New York: Oxford University Press.

Wilson, James Q. 1989. *Bureaucracy: What Government Agencies Do and Why They Do It.* New York: Basic Books.

Wilson, Woodrow. 1887. "The Study of Administration." *Political Science Quarterly* 2 (2): 197–222.

Wolf, Patrick J. 1997. "Why Must We Reinvent the Federal Government." *Journal of Public Administration Research and Theory* 7 (3): 353–88.

Wood, B. Dan. 1988. "Principals, Bureaucrats, and Responsiveness in Clean Air Enforcements." *American Political Science Review* 82 (1): 213–34.

Wood, B. Dan. 1990. "Does Politics Make a Difference at the EEOC?" *American Journal of Political Science* 34 (2): 503–30.

Wood, B. Dan. 1992. "Modeling Federal Implementation as a System." *American Journal of Political Science* 36 (1): 40–67.

Wood, B. Dan, and James E. Anderson. 1993. "The Politics of U.S. Antitrust Regulation." *American Journal of Political Science* 37 (1): 1–39.

Wood, B. Dan, and Richard Waterman. 1991. "The Dynamics of Political Control of the Bureaucracy." *American Political Science Review* 85 (3): 801–28.

Wood, B. Dan, and Richard Waterman. 1993. "The Dynamics of Political-Bureaucratic Adaptation." *American Journal of Political Science* 37 (2): 497–528.

Wood, B. Dan, and Richard W. Waterman. 1994. *Bureaucratic Dynamics: The Role of Bureaucracy in a Democracy.* Boulder, CO: Westview Press.

Woolley, John T. 1993. "Conflict among Regulators and the Hypothesis of Congressional Dominance." *Journal of Politics* 55 (1): 92–114.

Worsham, Jeff, Marc Allen Eisner, and Evan J. Ringquist. 1997. "Assessing the Assumptions: A Critical Analysis of the Positive Theory of Political Control." *Administration and Society* 28 (4): 419–40.

Zeigler, L. Harmon, Ellen Kehoe, and Jane Reisman. 1985. *City Managers and School Superintendents.* New York: Praeger.

Index